The Rebel

An Essay on Man in Revolt

Albert Camus

The Rebel

An Essay on Man in Revolt

With a Foreword by Sir Herbert Read

A revised and complete translation
of L'HOMME RÉVOLTÉ
by Anthony Bower

 New York Vintage Books

A DIVISION OF RANDOM HOUSE

✳

Foreword

✷

With the publication of this book a cloud that has oppressed the European mind for more than a century begins to lift. After an age of anxiety, despair, and nihilism, it seems possible once more *to hope*—to have confidence again in man and in the future. M. Camus has not delivered us by rhetoric, or by any of the arts of persuasion, but by the clarity of his intelligence. His book is a work of logic. Just as an earlier work of his (*Le Mythe de Sisyphe*) began with a meditation on living or not living—on the implications of the act of suicide—so this work begins with a meditation on enduring or not enduring—on the implications of the act of rebellion. If we decide to live, it must be because we have decided that our personal existence has some positive value; if we decide to rebel, it must be because we have decided that a human society has some positive value. But in each case the values are not "given" —that is the illusionist trick played by religion or by philosophy. They have to be deduced from the conditions of living, and are to be accepted along with the suffering entailed by the limits of the possible. Social values are rules of conduct implicit in a tragic fate; and they offer a hope of creation.

The Rebel, that is to say, offers us a philosophy of politics. It is a kind of book that appears only in France, devoted, in a passionate intellectual sense, to the examination of such concepts as liberty and terror. Not that it is a theoretical work—on the contrary, it is an examination of the actual situation of Europe today, informed by a precise historical knowledge of the past two centuries of its social development. It is "an attempt to understand the times."

Camus believes that revolt is one of the "essential dimensions" of mankind. It is useless to deny its historical reality—rather we must seek in it a principle of existence. But the nature of revolt has changed radically in our times. It is no longer the revolt of the slave against the master, nor even the revolt of the poor against the rich; it is a metaphysical revolt, the revolt of man against the conditions of life, against creation itself. At the same time, it is an aspiration toward clarity and unity of thought—even, paradoxically, toward order. That, at least, is what it becomes under the intellectual guidance of Camus.

He reviews the history of this metaphysical revolt, beginning with the absolute negation of Sade, glancing at Baudelaire and the "dandies," passing on to Stirner, Nietzsche, Lautréamont, and the surrealists. His attitude to these prophetic figures is not unsympathetic, and once more it is interesting to observe the influence of André Breton on the contemporary mind. Camus then turns to the history of revolt in the political sense, his main object being to draw a clear distinction between rebellion and revolution. Here, and not for the first time, Camus's ideas come close to anarchism, for he recognizes that revolution always implies the establishment of a new government, whereas rebellion is action without planned issue—it is spontaneous protestation. Camus reviews the history of the French Revolution, of the regicides and deicides, and shows how inevitably, from Rousseau to Stalin, the course of revolution leads to authoritarian dictatorship. Saint-Just is the precursor of Lenin. Even Bakunin, to whom Camus devotes some extremely interesting pages (pointing out, for example, that he alone of his time, with exceptional profundity, declared war against the idolatry of science)—even Bakunin, if we examine the statutes of the Fraternité Internationale (1864–7) which he drew up, is found insisting on the absolute subordination of the individual to a central committee of action.

All revolutions in modern times, Camus points out, have led to a reinforcement of the power of the State. "The strange and terrifying growth of the modern State can be considered as the logical conclusion of inordinate technical and philosophical ambitions, foreign to the true spirit of rebellion, but which nevertheless gave birth to the revolutionary spirit of our time. The prophetic dream of Marx and the over-inspired predictions of Hegel or of Nietzsche ended by conjuring up, after the city of God had been razed to the ground, a rational or irrational State, which in both cases, however, was founded on terror." The counterrevolutions of fascism only serve to reinforce the general argument.

Camus shows the real quality of his thought in his final pages. It would have been easy, on the facts marshaled in this book, to have retreated into despair or inaction. Camus substitutes the idea of "limits." "We now know, at the end of this long inquiry into rebellion and nihilism, that rebellion with no other limits but historical expediency signifies unlimited slavery. To escape this fate, the revolutionary mind, if it wants to remain alive, must therefore return again to the sources of rebellion and draw its inspiration from the only system of thought which is faithful to its origins: thought that recognizes limits." To illustrate his meaning Camus refers to syndicalism, that movement in politics which is based on the organic unity of the cell, and which is the negation of abstract and bureaucratic centralism. He quotes Tolain: "*Les êtres humains ne s'émancipent qu'au sein des groupes naturels*"—human beings emancipate themselves only on the basis of natural groups. "The commune against the State . . . deliberate freedom against rational tyranny, finally altruistic individualism against the colonization of the masses, are, then, the contradictions that express once again the endless opposition of moderation to excess which has animated the history of the Occident since the time of the ancient world." This tradition of "*mesure*" belongs to the Mediterranean world, and has been destroyed by the excesses of German ideology and of Christian otherworldliness—by the denial of nature.

Restraint is not the contrary of revolt. Revolt carries with it the very idea of restraint, and "moderation, born of rebellion, can only live by rebellion. It is a perpetual conflict, continually created and mastered by the intelligence. . . . Whatever we may do, excess will always keep its place in the heart of man, in the place where solitude is found. We all carry within us our places of exile, our crimes and our ravages. But our task is not to unleash them on the world; it is to fight them in ourselves and in others. Rebellion, the secular will not to surrender of which Barres speaks, is still today at the basis of the struggle. Origin of form, source of real life, it keeps us always erect in the savage, formless movement of history."

In his last pages Camus rises to heights of eloquence which are exhilarating. It is an inspiring book. It is particularly a book that should be read by all those who wish to see the inborn impulse of revolt inspired by a new spirit of action—by those who understand "that rebellion cannot exist without a strange form of love." Not to calculate, to give everything for the sake of life and of living men—in that way we can show that "real generosity toward the future lies in giving all to the present."

Herbert Read

Contents

＊

The Rebel

An Essay on Man in Revolt

✳

For Jean Grenier

And openly I pledged my heart to the grave and suffering land, and often in the consecrated night, I promised to love her faithfully until death, unafraid, with her heavy burden of fatality, and never to despise a single one of her enigmas. Thus did I join myself to her with a mortal cord.

HÖLDERLIN:
The Death of Empedocles

Introduction

∗

There are crimes of passion and crimes of logic. The boundary between them is not clearly defined. But the Penal Code makes the convenient distinction of premeditation. We are living in the era of premeditation and the perfect crime. Our criminals are no longer helpless children who could plead love as their excuse. On the contrary, they are adults and they have a perfect alibi: philosophy, which can be used for any purpose—even for transforming murderers into judges.

Heathcliff, in *Wuthering Heights*, would kill everybody on earth in order to possess Cathy, but it would never occur to him to say that murder is reasonable or theoretically defensible. He would commit it, and there his convictions end. This implies the power of love, and also strength of character. Since intense love is rare, murder remains an exception and preserves its aspect of infraction. But as soon as a man, through lack of character, takes refuge in doctrine, as soon as crime reasons about itself, it multiplies like reason itself and assumes all the aspects of the syllogism. Once crime was as solitary as a cry of protest; now it is as universal as science. Yesterday it was put on trial; today it determines the law.

This is not the place for indignation. The purpose of this essay is once again to face the reality of the present, which is logical crime, and to examine meticulously the arguments by which it is justified; it is an attempt to understand the times in which we live. One might think that a period which, in a space of fifty years, uproots, enslaves, or kills seventy million human beings should be condemned out of hand. But its culpability must still be understood. In more ingenuous times, when the tyrant razed cities for his own greater glory, when the slave chained to the conqueror's chariot was dragged through the rejoicing streets, when enemies were thrown to the wild beasts in front of the assembled people, the mind did not reel before such unabashed crimes, and judgment remained unclouded. But slave camps under the flag of freedom, massacres justified by philanthropy or by a taste for the superhuman, in one sense cripple judgment. On the day when crime dons the apparel of innocence— through a curious transposition peculiar to our times—it is innocence that is called upon to justify itself. The ambition of this essay is to accept and examine this strange challenge.

Our purpose is to find out whether innocence, the moment it becomes involved in action, can avoid committing murder. We can act only in terms of our own time, among the people who surround us. We shall know nothing until we know whether we have the right to kill our fellow men, or the right to let them be killed. In that every action today leads to murder, direct or indirect, we cannot act until we know whether or why we have the right to kill.

The important thing, therefore, is not, as yet, to go to the root of things, but, the world being what it is, to know how to live in it. In the age of negation, it was of some avail to examine one's position concerning suicide. In the age of ideologies, we must examine our position in relation to murder. If murder has rational foundations, then our period and we ourselves are rationally consequent. If it has no rational foundations, then we are insane and there is no alternative but to find some justification or to avert our faces. It is incumbent upon us, at all events, to give a definite answer to the question implicit in the blood and strife of this century. For we are being put to the rack. Thirty years ago, before reaching a decision to kill, people denied many things, to the point of denying themselves by suicide. God is deceitful; the whole world (myself included) is deceitful; therefore I choose to die: suicide was the problem then. Ideology today is concerned only with the denial of other human beings, who alone bear the responsibility of deceit. It is then that we kill.

Each day at dawn, assassins in judges' obes slip into some cell: murder is the problem today.

The two arguments are inextricably bound together. Or rather they bind us, and so firmly that we can no longer choose our own problems. They choose us, one after another, and we have no alternative but to accept their choice. This essay proposes, in the face of murder and rebellion, to pursue a train of thought which began with suicide and the idea of the absurd.

But, for the moment, this train of thought yields only one concept: that of the absurd. And the concept of the absurd leads only to a contradiction as far as the problem of murder is concerned. Awareness of the absurd, when we first claim to deduce a rule of behavior from it, makes murder seem a matter of indifference, to say the least, and hence possible. If we believe in nothing, if nothing has any meaning and if we can affirm no values whatsoever, then everything is possible and nothing has any importance. There is no pro or con: the murderer is neither right nor wrong. We are free to stoke the crematory fires or to devote ourselves to the care of lepers. Evil and virtue are mere chance or caprice.

We shall then decide not to act at all, which amounts to at least accepting the murder of others, with perhaps certain mild reservations about the imperfection of the human race. Again we may decide to substitute tragic dilettantism for action, and in this case human lives become counters in a game. Finally, we may propose to embark on some course of action which is not entirely gratuitous. In the latter case, in that we have no higher values to guide our behavior, our aim will be immediate efficacy. Since nothing is either true or false, good or bad, our guiding principle will be to demonstrate that we are the most efficient—in other words, the strongest. Then the world will no longer be divided into the just and the unjust, but into masters and slaves. Thus, whichever way we turn, in our abyss of negation and nihilism, murder has its privileged position.

Hence, if we claim to adopt the absurdist attitude, we must prepare ourselves to commit murder, thus admitting that logic is more important than scruples that we consider illusory. Of course, we must have some predisposition to murder. But, on the whole, less than might be supposed, to judge from experience. Moreover, it is always possible, as we can so often observe, to delegate murder. Everything would then be made to conform to logic—if logic could really be satisfied in this way.

But logic cannot be satisfied by an attitude which first demonstrates that murder is possible and then that it is impossible. For after having proved that the act of murder is at least a matter of indifference, absurdist analysis, in its most important deduction, finally condemns murder. The final conclusion of absurdist reasoning is, in fact, the repudiation of suicide and the acceptance of the desperate encounter between human inquiry and the silence of the universe. Suicide would mean the end of this encounter, and absurdist reasoning considers that it could not consent to this without negating its own premises. According to absurdist reasoning, such a solution would be the equivalent of flight or deliverance. But it is obvious that absurdism hereby admits that human life is the only necessary good since it is precisely life that makes this encounter possible and since, without life, the absurdist wager would have no basis. To say that life is absurd, the conscience must be alive. How is it possible, without making remarkable concessions to one's desire for comfort, to preserve exclusively for oneself the benefits of such a process of reasoning? From the moment that life is recognized as good, it becomes good for all men. Murder cannot be made coherent when suicide is not considered coherent. A mind imbued with the idea of the absurd will undoubtedly accept fatalistic murder; but it would never accept calculated murder. In terms of the encounter between human inquiry and the silence of the universe, murder and suicide are one and the same thing, and must be accepted or rejected together.

Equally, absolute nihilism, which accepts suicide as legitimate, leads, even more easily, to logical murder. If our age admits, with equanimity, that murder has its justifications, it is because of this indifference to life which is the mark of nihilism. Of course there have been periods of history in which the passion for life was so strong that it burst forth in criminal excesses. But these excesses were like the searing flame of a terrible delight. They were not this monotonous order of things established by an impoverished logic in whose eyes everything is equal. This logic has carried the values of suicide, on which our age has been nurtured, to their extreme logical consequence, which is legalized murder. It culminates, at the same time, in mass suicide. The most striking demonstration of this was provided by the Hitlerian apocalypse of 1945. Self-destruction meant nothing to those madmen, in their bomb-shelters, who were preparing for their own death and apotheosis. All that mattered was not to destroy oneself alone and to drag a whole world with one. In a way, the man who kills himself in solitude still preserves certain values since he, apparently, claims no rights over the lives of others. The proof of this is that he never makes use, in order to dominate others, of the enormous power and freedom of action which his decision to die gives him. Every solitary suicide, when it is not an act of resentment, is, in some way, either generous or contemptuous. But one feels contemptuous in the name of something. If the world is a matter of indifference to the man who commits suicide, it is because he has an idea of something that is not or could not be indifferent to him. He believes that he is destroying everything or taking everything with him; but from this act of self-destruction itself a value arises which, perhaps, might have made it worth while to live. Absolute negation is therefore not consummated by suicide. It can only be consummated by absolute destruction, of oneself and of others. Or, at least, it can only be lived by striving toward that delectable end. Here suicide and murder are two aspects of a single system, the system of a misguided intelligence that prefers, to the suffering imposed by a limited situation, the dark victory in which heaven and earth are annihilated.

By the same token, if we deny that there are reasons for suicide, we cannot claim that there are grounds for murder. There are no half-measures about nihilism. Absurdist reasoning cannot defend the continued existence of its spokesman and, simultaneously, accept the sacrifice of others' lives. The moment that we recognize the impossibility of absolute negation—and merely to be alive is to recognize this—the very first thing that cannot be denied is the right of others to live. Thus the same idea which allowed us to believe that murder was a matter of indifference now proceeds to deprive it of any justification; and we return to the untenable position from which we were trying to escape. In actual fact, this form of reasoning assures us at the same time that we can kill and that we cannot kill. It abandons us in this contradiction with no grounds either for preventing or for justifying murder, menacing and menaced, swept along with a whole generation intoxicated by nihilism, and yet lost in loneliness, with weapons in our hands and a lump in our throats.

This basic contradiction, however, cannot fail to be accompanied by a host of others from the moment that we claim to remain firmly in the absurdist position and ignore the real nature of the absurd, which is that it is an experience to be lived through, a point of departure, the equivalent, in existence, of Descartes's methodical doubt. The absurd is, in itself, contradiction.

It is contradictory in its content because, in wanting to uphold life, it excludes all value judgments, when to live is, in itself, a value judgment. To breathe is to judge. Perhaps it is untrue to say that life is a perpetual choice. But it is true that it is impossible to imagine a life deprived of all choice. From this simplified point of view, the absurdist position, translated into action, is inconceivable. It is equally inconceivable when translated into expression. Simply by being expressed, it gives a minimum of coherence to incoherence, and introduces consequence where, according to its own tenets, there is none. Speaking itself is restorative. The only coherent attitude based on non-signification would be silence—if silence, in its turn, were not significant. The absurd, in its purest form, attempts to remain dumb. If it finds its voice, it is because it has become complacent or, as we shall see, because it considers itself provisional. This complacency is an excellent indication of the profound ambiguity of the absurdist position. In a certain way, the absurd, which claims to express man in his solitude, really makes him live in front of a mirror. And then the initial anguish runs the risk of turning to comfort. The wound that is scratched with such solicitude ends by giving pleasure.

Great explorers in the realm of absurdity have not been lacking. But, in the last analysis, their greatness is measured by the extent to which they have rejected the complacencies of absurdism in order to accept its exigencies. They destroy as much, not as little, as they can. "My enemies," says Nietzsche, "are those who want to destroy without creating their own selves." He himself destroys, but in order to try to create. He extols integrity and castigates the "hog-faced" pleasure-seekers. To escape complacency, absurdist reasoning then discovers renunciation. It refuses to be sidetracked and emerges into a position of arbitrary barrenness—a determination to be silent—which is expressed in the strange asceticism of rebellion. Rimbaud, who extols "crime puling prettily in the mud of the streets," runs away to Harrar only to complain about having to live there without his family. Life for him was "a farce for the whole world to perform." But on the day of his death, he cries out to his sister: "I shall lie beneath the ground but you, you will walk in sun!"

The absurd, considered as a rule of life, is therefore contradictory. What is astonishing about the fact that it does not provide us with values which will enable us to decide whether murder is legitimate or not? Moreover, it is obviously impossible to formulate an attitude on the basis of a specially selected emotion. The perception of the absurd is one perception among many. That it has colored so many thoughts and actions between the two wars only proves its power and its validity. But the intensity of a perception does not necessarily mean that it is universal. The error of a whole period of history has been to enunciate—or to suppose already enunciated—general rules of action founded on emotions of despair whose inevitable course, in that they are emotions, is continually to exceed themselves. Great suffering and great happiness may be found at the beginning of any process of reasoning. They are intermediaries. But it is impossible to rediscover or sustain them throughout the entire process. Therefore, if it was legitimate to take absurdist sensibility into account, to make a diagnosis of a malady to be found in ourselves and in others, it is nevertheless impossible to see in this sensibility, and in the nihilism it presupposes, anything but a point of departure, a criticism brought to life—the equivalent, in the plane of existence, of systematic doubt. After this, the mirror, with its fixed stare, must be broken and we are, perforce, caught up in the irresistible movement by which the absurd exceeds itself.

Once the mirror is broken, nothing remains which can help us to answer the questions of our time. Absurdism, like methodical doubt, has wiped the slate clean. It leaves us in a blind alley. But, like methodical doubt, it can, by returning upon itself, open up a new field of investigation, and the process of reasoning then pursues the same course. I proclaim that I believe in nothing and that everything is absurd, but I cannot doubt the validity of my proclamation and I must at least believe in my protest. The first and only evidence that is supplied me, within the terms of the absurdist experience, is rebellion. Deprived of all knowledge, incited to murder or to consent to murder, all I have at my disposal is this single piece of evidence, which is only reaffirmed by the anguish I suffer. Rebellion is born of the spectacle of irrationality, confronted with an unjust and incomprehensible condition. But its blind impulse is to demand order in the midst of chaos, and unity in the very heart of the ephemeral. It protests, it demands, it insists that the outrage be brought to an end, and that what has up to now been built upon shifting sands should henceforth be founded on rock. Its preoccupation is to transform. But to transform is to act, and to act will be, tomorrow, to kill, and it still does not know whether murder is legitimate. Rebellion engenders exactly the actions it is asked to legitimate. Therefore it is absolutely necessary that rebellion find its reasons within itself, since it cannot find them elsewhere. It must consent to examine itself in order to learn how to act.

Two centuries of rebellion, either metaphysical or historical, present themselves for our consideration. Only a historian could undertake to set forth in detail the doctrines and movements that have followed one another during this period. But at least it should be possible to find a guiding principle. The pages that follow only attempt to present certain historical data and a working hypothesis. This hypothesis is not the only one possible; moreover, it is far from explaining everything. But it partly explains the direction in which our times are heading and almost entirely explains the excesses of the age. The astonishing history evoked here is the history of European pride.

In any event, the reasons for rebellion cannot be explained except in terms of an inquiry into its attitudes, pretensions, and conquests. Perhaps we may discover in its achievements the rule of action that the absurd has not been able to give us; an indication, at least, about the right or the duty to kill and, finally, hope for a new creation. Man is the only creature who refuses to be what he is. The problem is to know whether this refusal can only lead to the destruction of himself and of others, whether all rebellion must end in the justification of universal murder, or whether, on the contrary, without laying claim to an innocence that is impossible, it can discover the principle of reasonable culpability.

Part One

The Rebel

*

What is a rebel? A man who says no, but whose refusal does not imply a renunciation. He is also a man who says yes, from the moment he makes his first gesture of rebellion. A slave who has taken orders all his life suddenly decides that he cannot obey some new command. What does he mean by saying "no"?

He means, for example, that "this has been going on too long," "up to this point yes, beyond it no," "you are going too far," or, again, "there is a limit beyond which you shall not go." In other words, his no affirms the existence of a borderline. The same concept is to be found in the rebel's feeling that the other person "is exaggerating," that he is exerting his authority beyond a limit where he begins to infringe on the rights of others. Thus the movement of rebellion is founded simultaneously on the categorical rejection of an intrusion that is considered intolerable and on the confused conviction of an absolute right which, in the rebel's mind, is more precisely the impression that he "has the right to . . ." Rebellion cannot exist without the feeling that, somewhere and somehow, one is right. It is in this way that the rebel slave says yes and no simultaneously. He affirms that there are limits and also that he suspects—and wishes to preserve—the existence of certain things on this side of the borderline. He demonstrates, with obstinacy, that there is something in him which "is worth while . . ." and which must be taken into consideration. In a certain way, he confronts an order of things which oppresses him with the insistence on a kind of right not to be oppressed beyond the limit that he can tolerate.

In every act of rebellion, the rebel simultaneously ex-

periences a feeling of revulsion at the infringment of his
rights and a complete and spontaneous loyalty to certain
aspects of himself. Thus he implicitly brings into play a
standard of values so far from being gratuitous that he is
prepared to support it no matter what the risks. Up to this
point he has at least remained silent and has abandoned
himself to the form of despair in which a condition is accepted even though it is considered unjust. To remain
silent is to give the impression that one has no opinions,
that one wants nothing, and in certain cases it really
amounts to wanting nothing. Despair, like the absurd, has
opinions and desires about everything in general and nothing in particular. Silence expresses this attitude very well.
But from the moment that the rebel finds his voice—even
though he says nothing but "no"—he begins to desire and
to judge. The rebel, in the etymological sense, does a complete turnabout. He acted under the lash of his master's
whip. Suddenly he turns and faces him. He opposes what
is preferable to what is not. Not every value entails rebellion, but every act of rebellion tacitly invokes a value.
Or is it really a question of values?

Awareness, no matter how confused it may be, develops from every act of rebellion: the sudden, dazzling
perception that there is something in man with which he
can identify himself, even if only for a moment. Up to
now this identification was never really experienced. Before he rebelled, the slave accepted all the demands made
upon him. Very often he even took orders, without re-
acting against them, which were far more conducive to
insurrection than the one at which he balks. He accepted
them patiently, though he may have protested inwardly,
but in that he remained silent he was more concerned with
his own immediate interests than as yet aware of his own
rights. But with loss of patience—with impatience—a reaction begins which can extend to everything that he
previously accepted, and which is almost always retro-
active. The very moment the slave refuses to obey the
humiliating orders of his master, he simultaneously rejects
the condition of slavery. The act of rebellion carries him
far beyond the point he had reached by simply refusing.
He exceeds the bounds that he fixed for his antagonist, and
now demands to be treated as an equal. What was at first

the man's obstinate resistance now becomes the whole man, who is identified with and summed up in this resistance. The part of himself that he wanted to be respected he proceeds to place above everything else and proclaims it preferable to everything, even to life itself. It becomes for him the supreme good. Having up to now been willing to compromise, the slave suddenly adopts ("because this is how it must be . . .") an attitude of All or Nothing. With rebellion, awareness is born.

But we can see that the knowledge gained is, at the same time, of an "all" that is still rather obscure and of a "nothing" that proclaims the possibility of sacrificing the rebel to this "All." The rebel himself wants to be "all"— to identify himself completely with this good of which he has suddenly become aware and by which he wants to be personally recognized and acknowledged—or "nothing"; in other words, to be completely destroyed by the force that dominates him. As a last resort, he is willing to accept the final defeat, which is death, rather than be deprived of the personal sacrament that he would call, for example, freedom. Better to die on one's feet than to live on one's knees.

Values, according to good authorities, "most often represent a transition from facts to rights, from what is desired to what is desirable (usually through the intermediary of what is generally considered desirable)." [1] The transition from facts to rights is manifest, as we have seen, in rebellion. So is the transition from "this must be" to "this is how I should like things to be," and even more so, perhaps, the idea of the sublimation of the individual in a henceforth universal good. The sudden appearance of the concept of "All or Nothing" demonstrates that rebellion, contrary to current opinion, and though it springs from everything that is most strictly individualistic in man, questions the very idea of the individual. If the individual, in fact, accepts death and happens to die as a consequence of his act of rebellion, he demonstrates by doing so that he is willing to sacrifice himself for the sake of a common good which he considers more important than his own destiny. If he prefers the risk of death to the negation of the rights that he defends, it is because he considers these

[1] Lalande: *Vocabulaire philosophique.*

rights more important than himself. Therefore he is acting in the name of certain values which are still indeterminate but which he feels are common to himself and to
all men. We see that the affirmation implicit in every
act of rebellion is extended to something that transcends
the individual in so far as it withdraws him from his supposed solitude and provides him with a reason to act. But
it is already worth noting that this concept of values as
pre-existant to any kind of action contradicts the purely
historical philosophies, in which values are acquired (if
they are ever acquired) after the action has been completed. Analysis of rebellion leads at least to the suspicion
that, contrary to the postulates of contemporary thought,
a human nature does exist, as the Greeks believed. Why
rebel if there is nothing permanent in oneself worth pre-
serving? It is for the sake of everyone in the world that the
slave asserts himself when he comes to the conclusion that
a command has infringed on something in him which
does not belong to him alone, but which is common
ground where all men—even the man who insults and
oppresses him—have a natural community.[2]

Two observations will support this argument. First,
we can see that an act of rebellion is not, essentially, an
egoistic act. Of course, it can have egoistic motives. But
one can rebel equally well against lies as against oppression. Moreover, the rebel—once he has accepted the motives and at the moment of his greatest impetus—preserves
nothing in that he risks everything. He demands respect
for himself, of course, but only in so far as he identifies
himself with a natural community.

Then we note that rebellion does not arise only, and
necessarily, among the oppressed, but that it can also be
caused by the mere spectacle of oppression of which someone else is the victim. In such cases there is a feeling of
identification with another individual. And it must be
pointed out that this is not a question of psychological
identification—a mere subterfuge by which the individual
imagines that it is he himself who has been offended. On
the contrary, it can often happen that we cannot bear to

[2] The community of victims is the same as that which
unites victim and executioner. But the executioner does not
know this.

see offenses done to others which we ourselves have accepted without rebelling. The suicides of the Russian terrorists in Siberia as a protest against their comrades' being whipped is a case in point. Nor is it a question of the feeling of a community of interests. Injustices done to men whom we consider enemies can, actually, be profoundly repugnant to us. There is only identification of one's destiny with that of others and a choice of sides. Therefore the individual is not, in himself alone, the embodiment of the values he wishes to defend. It needs all humanity, at least, to comprise them. When he rebels, a man identifies himself with other men and so surpasses himself, and from this point of view human solidarity is metaphysical. But for the moment we are only talking of the kind of solidarity that is born in chains.

It would be possible for us to define the positive aspect of the values implicit in every act of rebellion by comparing them with a completely negative concept like that of resentment as defined by Scheler. Rebellion is, in fact, much more than pursuit of a claim, in the strongest sense of the word. Resentment is very well defined by Scheler as an autointoxication—the evil secretion, in a sealed vessel, of prolonged impotence. Rebellion, on the contrary, breaks the seal and allows the whole being to come into play. It liberates stagnant waters and turns them into a raging torrent. Scheler himself emphasizes the passive aspect of resentment and remarks on the prominent place it occupies in the psychology of women who are dedicated to desire and possession. The fountainhead of rebellion, on the contrary, is the principle of superabundant activity and energy. Scheler is also right in saying that resentment is always highly colored by envy. But one envies what one does not have, while the rebel's aim is to defend what he is. He does not merely claim some good that he does not possess or of which he was deprived. His aim is to claim recognition for something which he has and which has already been recognized by him, in almost every case, as more important than anything of which he could be envious. Rebellion is not realistic. According to Scheler, resentment always turns into either unscrupulous ambition or bitterness, depending on whether it is implanted in a strong person or a weak one. But in both cases it is a question of wanting to be something other than what one is. Resentment is always resentment against oneself. The rebel, on the contrary, from his very first step, refuses to allow anyone to touch what he is. He is fighting for the integrity of one part of his being. He does not try, primarily, to conquer, but simply to impose.

Finally, it would seem that resentment takes delight, in advance, in the pain that it would like the object of its envy to feel. Nietzsche and Scheler are right in seeing an excellent example of this in the passage where Tertullian informs his readers that one of the greatest sources of happiness among the blessed will be the spectacle of the Roman emperors consumed in the fires of hell. This kind of happiness is also experienced by the decent people who go to watch executions. The rebel, on the contrary, limits himself, as a matter of principle, to refusing to be humiliated without asking that others should be. He will even accept pain provided his integrity is respected.

It is therefore hard to understand why Scheler completely identifies the spirit of rebellion with resentment. His criticism of the resentment to be found in humanitarianism (which he treats as the non-Christian form of love for mankind) could perhaps be applied to certain indeterminate forms of humanitarian idealism, or to the techniques of terror. But it rings false in relation to man's rebellion against his condition—the movement that enlists the individual in the defense of a dignity common to all men. Scheler wants to demonstrate that humanitarian feelings are always accompanied by a hatred of the world. Humanity is loved in general in order to avoid having to love anybody in particular. This is correct, in some cases, and it is easier to understand Scheler when we realize that for him humanitarianism is represented by Bentham and Rousseau. But man's love for man can be born of other things than a mathematical calculation of the resultant rewards or a theoretical confidence in human nature. In face of the utilitarians, and of Émile's preceptor, there is, for example, the kind of logic, embodied by Dostoievsky in Ivan Karamazov, which progresses from an act of rebellion to metaphysical insurrection. Scheler is aware of this and sums up the concept in the following manner: "There is not enough love in the world to squander it on anything but human beings." Even if this proposition were true, the appalling despair that it implies would merit anything but contempt. In fact, it misunderstands the tortured character of Karamazov's rebellion. Ivan's drama, on the contrary, arises from the fact that there is too much love without an object. This love finding no outlet and God being denied, it is then decided to lavish it on human beings as a generous act of complicity.

Nevertheless, in the act of rebellion as we have envisaged it up to now, an abstract ideal is not chosen through lack of feeling and in pursuit of a sterile demand. We insist that the part of man which cannot be reduced to mere ideas should be taken into consideration—the passionate side of his nature that serves no other purpose than to be part of the act of living. Does this imply that no rebellion is motivated by resentment? No, and we know it only too well in this age of malice. But we must consider the idea of rebellion in its widest sense on pain of betraying it; and in its widest sense rebellion goes far beyond resentment. When Heathcliff, in *Wuthering Heights*, says that he puts his love above God and would willingly go to hell in order to be reunited with the woman he loves, he is prompted not only by youth and humiliation but by the consuming experience of a whole lifetime. The same emotion causes Eckart, in a surprising fit of heresy, to say that he prefers hell with Jesus to heaven without Him. This is the very essence of love. Contrary to Scheler, it would therefore be impossible to overemphasize the passionate affirmation that underlies the act of rebellion and distinguishes it from resentment. Rebellion, though apparently negative, since it creates nothing, is profoundly positive in that it reveals the part of man which must always be defended.

But, to sum up, are not rebellion and the values that it implies relative? Reasons for rebellion do seem to change, in fact, with periods and civilizations. It is obvious that a Hindu pariah, an Inca warrior, a primitive native of central Africa, and a member of one of the first Christian communities had not at all the same ideas about rebellion.

We could even assert, with considerable assurance, that the idea of rebellion has no meaning in these particular cases. However, a Greek slave, a serf, a *condottiere* of the Renaissance, a Parisian bourgeois during the Regency, a Russian intellectual at the beginning of the twentieth century, and a contemporary worker would undoubtedly agree that rebellion is legitimate, even if they differed about the reasons for it. In other words, the problem of rebellion seems to assume a precise meaning only within the confines of Western thought. It is possible to be even more explicit by remarking, like Scheler, that the spirit of rebellion finds few means of expression in societies where inequalities are very great (the Hindu caste system) or, again, in those where there is absolute equality (certain primitive societies). The spirit of rebellion can exist only in a society where a theoretical equality conceals great factual inequalities. The problem of rebellion, therefore, has no meaning except within our own Western society. One might be tempted to affirm that it is relative to the development of individualism if the preceding remarks had not put us on our guard against this conclusion.

On the basis of the evidence, the only conclusion that can be drawn from Scheler's remark is that, thanks to the theory of political freedom, there is, in the very heart of our society, an increasing awareness in man of the idea of man and, thanks to the application of this theory of freedom, a corresponding dissatisfaction. Actual freedom has not increased in proportion to man's awareness of it. We can only deduce from this observation that rebellion is the act of an educated man who is aware of his own rights. But there is nothing which justifies us in saying that it is only a question of individual rights. Because of the sense of solidarity we have already pointed out, it would rather seem that what is at stake is humanity's gradually increasing self-awareness as it pursues its course. In fact, for the Inca and the pariah the problem never arises, because for them it had been solved by a tradition, even before they had had time to raise it—the answer being that tradition is sacred. If in a world where things are held sacred the problem of rebellion does not arise, it is because no real problems are to be found in such a world, all the answers having been given simultaneously. Metaphysic is replaced by myth. There are no more questions, only eternal answers and commentaries, which may be metaphysical. But before man accepts the sacred world and in order that he should be able to accept it— or before he escapes from it and in order that he should be able to escape from it—there is always a period of soul-searching and rebellion. The rebel is a man who is on the point of accepting or rejecting the sacred and determined on laying claim to a human situation in which all the answers are human—in other words, formulated in reasonable terms. From this moment every question, every word, is an act of rebellion while in the sacred world every word is an act of grace. It would be possible to demonstrate in this manner that only two possible worlds can exist for the human mind: the sacred (or, to speak in Christian terms, the world of grace[3]) and the world of rebellion. The disappearance of one is equivalent to the appearance of the other, despite the fact that this appearance can take place in disconcerting forms. There again we rediscover the *All or Nothing*. The present interest of the problem of rebellion only springs from the fact that nowadays whole societies have wanted to discard the sacred. We live in an unsacrosanct moment in history. Insurrection is certainly not the sum total of human experience. But history today, with all its storm and strife, compels us to say that rebellion is one of the essential dimensions of man. It is our historic reality. Unless we choose to ignore reality, we must find our values in it. Is it possible to find a rule of conduct outside the realm of religion and its absolute values? That is the question raised by rebellion.

We have already noted the confused values that are called into play by incipient rebellion. Now we must inquire if these values are to be found again in contemporary forms of rebellious thought and action, and if they are, we must specify their content. But, before going any farther, let us note that the basis of these values is rebellion

[3] There is, of course, an act of metaphysical rebellion at the beginning of Christianity, but the resurrection of Christ and the annunciation of the kingdom of heaven interpreted as a promise of eternal life are the answers that render it futile.

itself. Man's solidarity is founded upon rebellion, and rebellion, in its turn, can only find its justification in this solidarity. We have, then, the right to say that any rebellion which claims the right to deny or destroy this solidarity loses simultaneously its right to be called rebellion and becomes in reality an acquiescence in murder. In the same way, this solidarity, except in so far as religion is concerned, comes to life only on the level of rebellion. And so the real drama of revolutionary thought is announced. In order to exist, man must rebel, but rebellion must respect the limit it discovers in itself—a limit where minds meet and, in meeting, begin to exist. Rebellious thought, therefore, cannot dispense with memory: it is a perpetual state of tension. In studying its actions and its results, we shall have to say, each time, whether it remains faithful to its first noble promise or if, through indolence or folly, it forgets its original purpose and plunges into a mire of tyranny or servitude.

Meanwhile, we can sum up the initial progress that the spirit of rebellion provokes in a mind that is originally imbued with the absurdity and apparent sterility of the world. In absurdist experience, suffering is individual. But from the moment when a movement of rebellion begins, suffering is seen as a collective experience. Therefore the first progressive step for a mind overwhelmed by the strangeness of things is to realize that this feeling of strangeness is shared with all men and that human reality, in its entirety, suffers from the distance which separates it from the rest of the universe. The malady experienced by a single man becomes a mass plague. In our daily trials rebellion plays the same role as does the *"cogito"* in the realm of thought: it is the first piece of evidence. But this evidence lures the individual from his solitude. It founds its first value on the whole human race. I rebel—therefore we exist.

Part Two

Metaphysical Rebellion

Metaphysical rebellion is the movement by which man protests against his condition and against the whole of creation. It is metaphysical because it contests the ends of man and of creation. The slave protests against the condition in which he finds himself within his state of slavery; the metaphysical rebel protests against the condition in which he finds himself as a man. The rebel slave affirms that there is something in him that will not tolerate the manner in which his master treats him; the metaphysical rebel declares that he is frustrated by the universe. For both of them, it is not only a question of pure and simple negation. In both cases, in fact, we find a value judgment in the name of which the rebel refuses to approve the condition in which he finds himself.

The slave who opposes his master is not concerned, let us note, with repudiating his master as a human being. He repudiates him as a master. He denies that he has the right to deny him, a slave, on grounds of necessity. The master is discredited to the exact extent that he fails to respond to a demand which he ignores. If men cannot refer to a common value, recognized by all as existing in each one, then man is incomprehensible to man. The rebel demands that this value should be clearly recognized in himself because he knows or suspects that, without this principle, crime and disorder would reign throughout the world. An act of rebellion on his part seems like a demand for clarity and unity. The most elementary form of rebellion, paradoxically, expresses an aspiration to order.

This description can be applied, word for word, to the metaphysical rebel. He attacks a shattered world in order to demand unity from it. He opposes the principle of justice which he finds in himself to the principle of injustice which he sees being applied in the world. Thus all he wants, originally, is to resolve this contradiction and establish the unitarian reign of justice, if he can, or of injustice, if he is driven to extremes. Meanwhile, he denounces the contradiction. Metaphysical rebellion is a claim, motivated by the concept of a complete unity, against the suffering of life and death and a protest against the human condition both for its incompleteness, thanks to death, and its wastefulness, thanks to evil. If a mass death sentence defines the human condition, then rebellion, in one sense, is its contemporary. At the same time that he rejects his mortality, the rebel refuses to recognize the power that compels him to live in this condition. The metaphysical rebel is therefore not definitely an atheist, as one might think him, but he is inevitably a blasphemer. Quite simply, he blasphemes primarily in the name of order, denouncing God as the father of death and as the supreme outrage.

The rebel slave will help us to throw light on this point. He established, by his protest, the existence of the master against whom he rebelled. But at the same time he demonstrated that his master's power was dependent on his own subordination and he affirmed his own power: the power of continually questioning the superiority of his master. In this respect master and slave are really in the same boat: the temporary sway of the former is as relative as the submission of the latter. The two forces assert themselves alternately at the moment of rebellion until they confront each other for a fight to the death, and one or the other temporarily disappears.

In the same way, if the metaphysical rebel ranges himself against a power whose existence he simultaneously affirms, he only admits the existence of this power at the very instant that he calls it into question. Then he involves this superior being in the same humiliating adventure as mankind's, its ineffectual power being the equivalent of our ineffectual condition. He subjects it to our power of refusal, bends it to the unbending part of human nature, forcibly integrates it into an existence that we render absurd, and finally drags it from its refuge outside time and involves it in history, very far from the eternal stability that it can find only in the unanimous submission of all men. Thus rebellion affirms that, on its own level, any concept of superior existence is contradictory, to say the least.

And so the history of metaphysical rebellion cannot be confused with that of atheism. From a certain point of view it is even confused with the contemporary history of religious sentiment. The rebel defies more than he denies. Originally, at least, he does not suppress God; he merely talks to Him as an equal. But it is not a polite dialogue. It is a polemic animated by the desire to conquer. The slave begins by demanding justice and ends by wanting to wear a crown. He must dominate in his turn. His insurrection against his condition becomes an unlimited campaign against the heavens for the purpose of bringing back a captive king who will first be dethroned and finally condemned to death. Human rebellion ends in metaphysical revolution. It progresses from appearances to acts, from the dandy to the revolutionary. When the throne of God is overturned, the rebel realizes that it is now his own responsibility to create the justice, order, and unity that he sought in vain within his own condition, and in this way to justify the fall of God. Then begins the desperate effort to create, at the price of crime and murder if necessary, the dominion of man. This will not come about without terrible consequences, of which we are so far only aware of a few. But these consequences are in no way due to rebellion itself, or at least they only occur to the extent that the rebel forgets his original purpose, tires of the tremendous tension created by refusing to give a positive or negative answer, and finally abandons himself to complete negation or total submission. Metaphysical insurrection, in its first stages, offers us the same positive content as the slave's rebellion. Our task will be to examine what becomes of this positive content of rebellion in the actions that claim to originate from it and to explain where the fidelity or infidelity of the rebel to the origins of his revolt finally leads him.

The Sons of Cain

*

Metaphysical rebellion, in the real sense of the term, does not appear, in coherent form, in the history of ideas until the end of the eighteenth century—when modern times begin to the accompaniment of the crash of falling ramparts. But from then on, its consequences develop uninterruptedly and it is no exaggeration to say that they have shaped the history of our times. Does this mean that metaphysical rebellion had no significance previous to this date? In any event, its origins must belong to the remote past, in that we like to believe that we live in Promethean times. But is this really a Promethean age?

The first mythologies describe Prometheus as an eternal martyr, chained to a pillar, at the ends of the earth, condemned forever because he refuses to ask forgiveness. Æschylus adds still further to his stature, endows him with lucidity ("no misfortune can fall upon me that I have not myself already foreseen"), makes him cry out his hatred of all the gods, and, plunging him into "a stormy sea of mortal despair," finally abandons him to thunder and lightning: "Ah! see the injustice I endure!"

It cannot be said, therefore, that the ancients were unaware of metaphysical rebellion. Long before Satan, they created a touching and noble image of the Rebel and gave us the most perfect myth of the intelligence in revolt. The inexhaustible genius of the Greeks, which gave such a prominent place to myths of unity and simplicity, was still able to formulate the concept of insurrection. Beyond a doubt, certain characteristics of the Promethean myth still survive in the history of rebellion as we are living it: the fight against death ("I have delivered men from being obsessed by death"), Messianism ("I have instilled blind hopes into men's minds"), philanthropy ("Enemy of Zeus . . . for having loved mankind too much").

But we must not forget that *Prometheus the Fire-bringer*, the last drama of Æschylus' trilogy, proclaimed the reign of the pardoned rebel. The Greeks are never vindictive. In their most audacious flights they always remain faithful to the idea of moderation, a concept they deified. Their rebel does not range himself against all creation, but against Zeus, who is never anything more than one god among many and who himself was mortal. Prometheus himself is a demigod. It is a question of settling a particular account, of a dispute about what is good, and not of a universal struggle between good and evil.

The ancients, even though they believed in destiny, believed primarily in nature, in which they participated wholeheartedly. To rebel against nature amounted to rebelling against oneself. It was butting one's head against a wall. Therefore the only coherent act of rebellion was to commit suicide. Destiny, for the Greeks, was a blind force to which one submitted, just as one submitted to the forces of nature. The acme of excess to the Greek mind was to beat the sea with rods—an act of insanity worthy only of barbarians. Of course, the Greeks described excess, since it exists, but they gave it its proper place and, by doing so, also defined its limits. Achilles' defiance after the death of Patroclus, the imprecations of the Greek tragic heroes cursing their fate, do not imply complete condemnation. Œdipus knows that he is not innocent. He is guilty in spite of himself; he is also part of destiny. He complains, but he says nothing irreparable. Antigone rebels, but she does so in the name of tradition, in order that her brothers may find rest in the tomb and that the appropriate rites may be observed. In her case, rebellion is, in one sense, reactionary. The Greek mind has two aspects and in its meditations almost always re-echoes, as counterpoint to its most tragic melodies, the eternal words of Œdipus, who, blind and desperate, recognizes that all is for the best. Affirmation counterbalances negation. Even when Plato anticipates, with Callicles, the most common type of Nietzschean, even when the latter exclaims: "But when a man appears who has the necessary character . . . he will escape, he will trample on our formulas, our magic spells, our incantations, and the laws, which are all, without exception, contrary to nature. Our slave has rebelled and has shown himself to be the master"—even then, though he rejects law, he speaks in the name of nature.

Metaphysical rebellion presupposes a simplified view of creation—which was inconceivable to the Greeks. In their minds, there were not gods on one side and men on the other, but a series of stages leading from one to the other. The idea of innocence opposed to guilt, the concept of all of history summed up in the struggle between good and evil, was foreign to them. In their universe there were more mistakes than crimes, and the only definitive crime was excess. In a world entirely dominated by history, which ours threatens to become, there are no longer any mistakes, but only crimes, of which the greatest is moderation. This explains the curious mixture of ferocity and forbearance which we find in Greek mythology. The Greeks never made the human mind into an armed camp, and in this respect we are inferior to them. Rebellion, after all, can only be imagined in terms of opposition to someone. The only thing that gives meaning to human protest is the idea of a personal god who has created, and is therefore responsible for, everything. And so we can say, without being paradoxical, that in the Western World the history of rebellion is inseparable from the history of Christianity. We have to wait, in fact, until the very last moments of Greek thought to see rebellion begin to find expression among transitional thinkers—nowhere more profoundly than in the works of Epicurus and Lucretius.

The appalling sadness of Epicurus already strikes a new note. It has its roots, no doubt, in the fear of death, with which the Greek mind was not unfamiliar. But the pathos with which this fear is expressed is very revealing. "We can take precautions against all sorts of things; but so far as death is concerned, we all of us live like the inhabitants of a defenseless citadel." Lucretius is more explicit: "The substance of this vast world is condemned to death and ruin." Therefore why postpone enjoyment? "We spend our lives," writes Epicurus, "in waiting, and we are all condemned to die." Therefore we must all enjoy ourselves. But what a strange form of enjoyment! It consists in sealing up the walls of the citadel, of making sure of a supply of bread and water and of living in darkness and silence. Death hovers over us, therefore we must prove that death is of no importance. Like Epictetus and Marcus Aurelius, Epicurus banishes death from human existence. "Death has no meaning for us, for what is indefinable is incapable of feeling, and what is incapable of feeling has no meaning for us." Is this the equivalent of nothingness? No, for everything in this particular universe is matter, and death only means a return to one's element. Existence is epitomized in a stone. The strange sensual pleasure of which Epicurus speaks consists, above all, in an absence of pain; it is the pleasure of a stone. By an admirable maneuver—which we shall find again in the great French classicists—Epicurus, in order to escape from destiny, destroys sensibility, having first destroyed its primary manifestation: hope. What this Greek philosopher says about the gods cannot be interpreted otherwise. All the unhappiness of human beings springs from the hope that tempts them from the silence of the citadel and exposes them on the ramparts in expectation of salvation. Unreasonable aspirations have no other effect than to reopen carefully bandaged wounds. That is why Epicurus does not deny the gods; he banishes them, and so precipitately that man has no alternative but to retreat once more into the citadel. "The happy and immortal being has no preoccupations of his own and no concern with the affairs of others." Lucretius goes even farther: "It is incontestable that the gods, by their very nature, enjoy their immortality in perfect peace, completely unaware of our affairs, from which they are utterly detached." Therefore let us forget the gods, let us never even think about them, and "neither your thoughts during the day nor your dreams at night will ever be troubled."

Later we shall rediscover this eternal theme of rebellion, but with important modifications. A god who does not reward or punish, a god who turns a deaf ear, is the rebel's only religious conception. But while Vigny will curse the silence of his divinity, Epicurus considers that, as death is inevitable, silence on the part of man is a better preparation for this fate than divine words. This strange mind wears itself out in a sustained attempt to build ramparts around mankind, to fortify the citadel and to stifle the irrepressible cry of human hope. Only when this strategic retreat has been accomplished does Epicurus, like a god among men, celebrate his victory with a song that clearly denotes the defensive aspect of his rebellion. "I have escaped your ambush, O destiny, I have closed all paths by which you might assail me. We shall not be conquered either by you or by any other evil power. And when the inevitable hour of departure strikes, our scorn for those who vainly cling to existence will burst forth in this proud song: 'Ah, with what dignity we have lived.' "

Alone among his contemporaries Lucretius carries this logic much farther and finally brings it to the central problem of modern philosophy. He adds nothing fundamental to Epicurus. He, too, refuses to accept any explanatory principle that cannot be tested by the senses. The atom is only a last refuge where man, reduced to his primary elements, pursues a kind of blind and deaf immortality—an immortal death—which for Lucretius represents, as it does for Epicurus, the only possible form of happiness. He has to admit, however, that atoms do not aggregate of their own accord, and rather than believe in a superior law and, finally, in the destiny he wishes to deny, he accepts the concept of a purely fortuitous mutation, the clinamen, in which the atoms meet and group themselves together. Already, as we can see, the great problem of modern times arises: the discovery that to rescue man from destiny is to deliver him to chance. That is why the contemporary mind is trying so desperately hard to restore destiny to man—a historical destiny this time. Lucretius has not reached this point. His hatred of destiny and death is assuaged by this blind universe where atoms accidentally form human beings and where human beings accidentally return to atoms. But his vocabulary bears witness to a new kind of sensibility. The walled citadel becomes an armed camp. *Mœnia mundi*, the ramparts of the world, is one of the key expressions of Lucretius' rhetoric. The main preoccupation in this armed camp is, of course, to silence hope. But Epicurus' methodical renunciation is transformed into a quivering asceticism, which is sometimes crowned with execrations. Piety, for Lucretius, undoubtedly consists in "being able to contemplate everything with an untroubled mind." But, never-

theless, his mind reels at the injustices done to man.
Spurred on by indignation, he weaves new concepts of
crime, innocence, culpability, and punishment into his
great poem on the nature of things. In it he speaks of
"religion's first crime," Iphigenia's martyred innocence,
and of the tendency of the divinity to "often ignore the
guilty and to mete out undeserved punishment by slaugh-
tering the innocent." If Lucretius scoffs at the fear of
punishment in the next world, it is not as a gesture of
defensive rebellion in the manner of Epicurus, but as a
process of aggressive reasoning: why should evil be punished when we can easily see, here on earth, that goodness
is not rewarded?

In Lucretius' epic poem, Epicurus himself becomes the
proud rebel he never actually was. "When in the eyes of
all mankind humanity was leading an abject existence on
earth, crushed beneath the weight of a religion whose
hideous aspect peered down from the heights of the celestial regions, the first to dare, a Greek, a man, raised his
mortal eyes and challenged the gods. . . . In this way
religion, in its turn, was overthrown and trampled under-
foot, and this victory elevates us to the heavens." Here
we can sense the difference between this new type of
blasphemy and the ancient malediction. The Greek heroes
could aspire to become gods, but simultaneously with
the gods who already existed. At that time it was simply
a matter of promotion. Lucretius' hero, on the other
hand, embarks on a revolution. By repudiating the unworthy and criminal gods, he takes their place himself.
He sallies forth from the armed camp and opens the first
attack on divinity in the name of human suffering. In the
ancient world, murder is both inexplicable and inexpiable.
Already with Lucretius, murder by man is only an answer
to murder by the gods. It is not pure coincidence that
Lucretius' poem ends with a prodigious image of the
sanctuaries of the gods swollen with the accusing corpses
of plague victims.

This new language is incomprehensible without the
concept of a personal god, which is slowly beginning to
form in the minds of Lucretius' and Epicurus' contemporaries. Only a personal god can be asked by the rebel for

a personal accounting. When the personal god begins his reign, rebellion assumes its most resolutely ferocious aspect and pronounces a definitive no. With Cain, the first act of rebellion coincides with the first crime. The history of rebellion, as we are experiencing it today, has far more to do with the children of Cain than with the disciples of Prometheus. In this sense it is the God of the Old Testament who is primarily responsible for mobilizing the forces of rebellion. Inversely, one must submit to the God of Abraham, Isaac, and Jacob when, like Pascal, one has run the full course of intellectual rebellion. The mind most prone to doubt always aspires to the greatest degree of Jansenism.

From this point of view, the New Testament can be considered as an attempt to answer, in advance, every Cain in the world, by painting the figure of God in softer colors and by creating an intercessor between God and man. Christ came to solve two major problems, evil and death, which are precisely the problems that preoccupy the rebel. His solution consisted, first, in experiencing them. The man-god suffers, too—with patience. Evil and death can no longer be entirely imputed to Him since He suffers and dies. The night on Golgotha is so important in the history of man only because, in its shadow, the divinity abandoned its traditional privileges and drank to the last drop, despair included, the agony of death. This is the explanation of the *Lama sabactani* and the heart-rending doubt of Christ in agony. The agony would have been mild if it had been alleviated by hopes of eternity. For God to be a man, he must despair.

Ghosticism, which is the fruit of Greco-Christian collaboration, has tried for two centuries, in reaction against Judaic thought, to promote this concept. We know, for example, the vast number of intercessors invented by Valentinus. But the æons of this particular metaphysical skirmish are the equivalent of the intermediary truths to be found in Hellenism. Their aim is to diminish the absurdity of an intimate relationship between suffering humanity and an implacable god. This is the special role of Marcion's cruel and bellicose second god. This demiurge is responsible for the creation of a finite world and of death. Our duty is to hate him and at the same time to deny everything that he has created, by means of asceticism, to the point of destroying, by sexual abstinence, all creation. This form of asceticism is therefore both proud and rebellious. Marcion simply alters the course of rebellion and directs it toward an inferior god so as to be better able to exalt the superior god. Gnosis, owing to its Greek origins, remains conciliatory and tends to destroy the Judaic heritage in Christianity. It also wanted to avoid Augustinism, by anticipating it, in that Augustinism provides arguments for every form of rebellion. To Basilides, for example, the martyrs were sinners, and so was Christ, because they suffered. A strange conception, but whose aim is to remove the element of injustice from suffering. The Gnostics only wanted to substitute the Greek idea of initiation, which allows mankind every possible chance, for the concept of an all-powerful and arbitrary forgiveness. The enormous number of sects among the second-generation Gnostics indicates how desperate and diversified was the attempt on the part of Greek thought to make the Christian universe more accessible and to remove the motives for a rebellion that Hellenism considered the worst of all evils. But the Church condemned this attempt and, by condemning it, swelled the ranks of the rebels.

In that the children of Cain have triumphed, increasingly, throughout the centuries, the God of the Old Testament can be said to have been incredibly successful. Paradoxically, the blasphemers have injected new life into the jealous God whom Christianity wished to banish from history. One of their most profoundly audacious acts was to recruit Christ into their camp by making His story end on the Cross and on the bitter note of the cry that precedes His agony. By this means it was possible to preserve the implacable face of a God of hate—which coincided far better with creation as the rebels conceived it. Until Dostoievsky and Nietzsche, rebellion is directed only against a cruel and capricious divinity—a divinity who prefers, without any convincing motive, Abel's sacrifice to Cain's and, by so doing, provokes the first murder. Dostoievsky, in the realm of imagination, and Nietzsche, in the realm of fact, enormously increase the field of rebellious thought and demand an accounting from the

God of love Himself. Nietzsche believes that God is dead in the souls of his contemporaries. Therefore he attacks, like his predecessor Stirner, the illusion of God that lingers, under the guise of morality, in the thought of his times. But until they appear upon the scene, the freethinkers, for example, were content to deny the truth of the history of Christ ("that dull story," in Sade's words) and to maintain, by their denials, the tradition of an avenging god.

On the other hand, for as long as the Western World has been Christian, the Gospels have been the interpreter between heaven and earth. Each time a solitary cry of rebellion was uttered, the answer came in the form of an even more terrible suffering. In that Christ had suffered, and had suffered voluntarily, suffering was no longer unjust and all pain was necessary. In one sense, Christianity's bitter intuition and legitimate pessimism concerning human behavior is based on the assumption that over-all injustice is as satisfying to man as total justice. Only the sacrifice of an innocent god could justify the endless and universal torture of innocence. Only the most abject suffering by God could assuage man's agony. If everything, without exception, in heaven and earth is doomed to pain and suffering, then a strange form of happiness is possible.

But from the moment when Christianity, emerging from its period of triumph, found itself submitted to the critical eye of reason—to the point where the divinity of Christ was denied—suffering once more became the lot of man. Jesus profaned is no more than just one more innocent man whom the representatives of the God of Abraham tortured in a spectacular manner. The abyss that separates the master from the slaves opens again and the cry of revolt falls on the deaf ears of a jealous God. The freethinkers have prepared the way for this new dichotomy by attacking, with all the usual precautions, the morality and divinity of Christ. Callot's universe sums up quite satisfactorily this world of hallucination and wretchedness whose inhabitants begin by sniggering up their sleeves and end—with Molière's Don Juan—by laughing to high heaven. During the two centuries which prepare the way for the upheavals, both revolutionary and sacrilegious, of the eighteenth century, all the efforts of the freethinkers are bent on making Christ an innocent, or a simpleton, so as to annex Him to the world of man, endowed with all the noble or derisory qualities of man. Thus the ground will be prepared for the great offensive against a hostile heaven.

Absolute Negation

*

Historically speaking, the first coherent offensive is that of Sade, who musters into one vast war machine the arguments of the freethinkers up to Father Meslier and Voltaire. His negation is also, of course, the most extreme. From rebellion Sade can only deduce an absolute negative. Twenty-seven years in prison do not, in fact, produce a very conciliatory form of intelligence. Such a long period of confinement produces either weaklings or killers and sometimes a combination of both. If the mind is strong enough to construct in a prison cell a moral philosophy that is not one of submission, it will generally be one of domination. Every ethic based on solitude implies the exercise of power. In this respect Sade is the archetype, for in so far as society treated him atrociously, he responded in an atrocious manner. The writer, despite a few happy phrases and the thoughtless praises of our contemporaries, is secondary. He is admired today, with so much ingenuity, for reasons which have nothing to do with literature.

He is exalted as the philosopher in chains and the first theoretician of absolute rebellion. He might well have been. In prison, dreams have no limits and reality is no curb. Intelligence in chains loses in lucidity what it gains in intensity. The only logic known to Sade was the logic of his feelings. He did not create a philosophy, but pursued a monstrous dream of revenge. Only the dream turned out to be prophetic. His desperate demand for freedom led Sade into the kingdom of servitude; his inordinate thirst for a form of life he could never attain was assuaged in the successive frenzies of a dream of universal destruction. In this way, at least, Sade is our contemporary. Let us follow his successive negations.

A Man of Letters

Is Sade an atheist? He says so, and we believe him, before going to prison, in his *Dialogue between a Priest and a Dying Man*; and from then on we are dumbfounded by his passion for sacrilege. One of his cruelest characters, Saint-Fond, does not in any sense deny God. He is content to develop a gnostic theory of a wicked demiurge and to draw the proper conclusions from it. Saint-Fond, it is said, is not Sade. No, of course not. A character is never the author who created him. It is quite likely, however, that an author may be all his characters simultaneously. Now, all Sade's atheists suppose, in principle, the nonexistence of God for the obvious reason that His existence would imply that He was indifferent, wicked, or cruel. Sade's greatest work ends with a demonstration of the stupidity and spite of the divinity. The innocent Justine runs through the storm and the wicked Noirceuil swears that he will be converted if divine retribution consents to spare her life. Justine is struck by lightning, Noirceuil triumphs, and human crime continues to be man's answer to divine crime. Thus there is a freethinker wager that is the answer to the Pascalian wager.

The idea of God which Sade conceives for himself is, therefore, of a criminal divinity who oppresses and denies mankind. That murder is an attribute of the divinity is quite evident, according to Sade, from the history of religions. Why, then, should man be virtuous? Sade's first step as a prisoner is to jump to the most extreme conclusions. If God kills and repudiates mankind, there is nothing to stop one from killing and repudiating one's fellow men. This irritable challenge in no way resembles the tranquil negation that is still to be found in the *Dialogue* of 1782. The man who exclaims: "I have nothing, I give nothing," and who concludes: "Virtue and vice are indistinguishable in the tomb," is neither happy nor tranquil. The concept of God is the only thing, according to him, "which he cannot forgive man." The word *forgive* is already rather strange in the mouth of this expert in torture. But it is himself whom he cannot forgive for an idea that his desperate view of the world, and his condition as a prisoner, completely refute. A double rebellion—against the order of the universe and against himself—is henceforth going to be the guiding principle of Sade's reasoning. In that these two forms of rebellion are contradictory except in the disturbed mind of a victim of persecution, his reasoning is always either ambiguous or legitimate according to whether it is considered in the light of logic or in an attempt at compassion.

He therefore denies man and his morality because God denies them. But he denies God even though He has served as his accomplice and guarantor up to now. For what reason? Because of the strongest instinct to be found in one who is condemned by the hatred of mankind to live behind prison walls: the sexual instinct. What is this instinct? On the one hand, it is the ultimate expression of nature,[1] and, on the other, the blind force that demands the total subjection of human beings, even at the price of their destruction. Sade denies God in the name of nature—the ideological concepts of his time presented it in mechanistic form—and he makes nature a power bent on destruction. For him, nature is sex; his logic leads him to a lawless universe where the only master is the inordinate energy of desire. This is his delirious kingdom, in which he finds his finest means of expression: "What are all the creatures of the earth in comparison with a single one of our desires!" The long arguments by which Sade's heroes demonstrate that nature has need of crime, that it must destroy in order to create, and that we help nature create from the moment we destroy it ourselves, are only aimed at establishing absolute freedom for the prisoner, Sade, who is too unjustly punished not to long for the explosion that will blow everything to pieces. In this respect he goes against his times: the freedom he demands is not one of principles, but of instincts.

Sade dreamed, no doubt, of a universal republic, whose scheme he reveals through his wise reformer, Zamé. He

---

[1] Sade's great criminals excuse their crimes on the ground that they were born with uncontrollable sexual appetites about which they could do nothing.

shows us, by this means, that one of the purposes of rebellion is to liberate the whole world, in that, as the movement accelerates, rebellion is less and less willing to accept limitations. But everything about him contradicts this pious dream. He is no friend of humanity, he hates philanthropists. The equality of which he sometimes speaks is a mathematical concept: the equivalence of the objects that comprise the human race, the abject equality of the victims. Real fulfillment, for the man who allows absolutely free rein to his desires and who must dominate everything, lies in hatred. Sade's republic is not founded on liberty but on libertinism. "Justice," this peculiar democrat writes, "has no real existence. It is the divinity of all the passions."

Nothing is more revealing in this respect than the famous lampoon, read by Dolmancé in the *Philosophie du Boudoir*, which has the curious title: *People of France, one more effort if you want to be republicans.* Pierre Klossowski[2] is right in attaching so much importance to it, for this lampoon demonstrates to the revolutionaries that their republic is founded on the murder of the King —who was King by divine right— and that by guillotining God on January 21, 1793 they deprived themselves forever of the right to outlaw crime or to censure malevolent instincts. The monarchy supported the concept of a God who, in conjunction with itself, created all laws. As for the Republic, it stands alone, and morality was supposed to exist without benefit of the Commandments. It is doubtful, however, that Sade, as Klossowski maintains, had a profound sense of sacrilege and that an almost religious horror led him to the conclusions that he expresses. It is much more likely that he came to these conclusions first and afterwards perceived the correct arguments to justify the absolute moral license that he wanted the government of his time to sanction. Logic founded on passions reverses the traditional sequence of reasoning and places the conclusions before the premises. To be convinced of this we only have to appraise the admirable sequence of sophisms by which Sade, in this passage, justifies calumny, theft, and murder and demands that they be tolerated under the new dispensation.

[2] *Sade, mon prochain.*

It is then, however, that his thoughts are most profound. He rejects, with exceptional perspicacity for his times, the presumptuous alliance of freedom with virtue. Freedom, particularly when it is a prisoner's dream, cannot endure limitations. It must sanction crime or it is no longer freedom. On this essential point Sade never varies. This man who never preached anything but contradictions only achieves coherence—and of a most complete kind—when he talks of capital punishment. An addict of refined ways of execution, a theoretician of sexual crime, he was never able to tolerate legal crime. "My imprisonment by the State, with the guillotine under my very eyes, was far more horrible to me than all the Bastilles imaginable." From this feeling of horror he drew the strength to be moderate, publicly, during the Terror, and to intervene generously on behalf of his mother-in-law, despite the fact that she had had him imprisoned. A few years later Nodier summed up, perhaps without knowing it, the position obstinately defended by Sade: "To kill a man in a paroxysm of passion is understandable. To have him killed by someone else after calm and serious meditation and on the pretext of duty honorably discharged is incomprehensible." Here we find the germ of an idea which again will be developed by Sade: he who kills must pay with his own life. Sade is more moral, we see, than our contemporaries.

But his hatred for the death penalty is at first no more than a hatred for men who are sufficiently convinced of their own virtue to dare to inflict capital punishment, when they themselves are criminals. You cannot simultaneously choose crime for yourself and punishment for others. You must open the prison gates or give an impossible proof of your own innocence. From the moment you accept murder, even if only once, you must allow it universally. The criminal who acts according to nature cannot, without betraying his office, range himself on the side of the law. "One more effort if you want to be republicans" means: "Accept the freedom of crime, the only reasonable attitude, and enter forever into a state of insurrection as you enter into a state of grace." Thus total submission to evil leads to an appalling penitence, which cannot fail to horrify the Republic of enlightenment and of natural goodness. By a significant coincidence, the manuscript of *One Hundred and Twenty Days of Sodom* was burned during the first riot of the Republic, which could hardly fail to denounce Sade's heretical theories of freedom and to throw so compromising a supporter into prison once more. By so doing, it gave him the regrettable opportunity of developing his rebellious logic still further.

The universal republic could be a dream for Sade, but never a temptation. In politics his real position is cynicism. In his *Society of the Friends of Crime* he declares himself ostensibly in favor of the government and its laws, which he meanwhile has every intention of violating. It is the same impulse that makes the lowest form of criminal vote for conservative candidates. The plan that Sade had in mind assures the benevolent neutrality of the authorities. The republic of crime cannot, for the moment at least, be universal. It must pretend to obey the law. In a world that knows no other rule than murder, beneath a criminal heaven, and in the name of a criminal nature, however, Sade, in reality, obeys no other law than that of inexhaustible desire. But to desire without limit is the equivalent of being desired without limit. License to destroy supposes that you yourself can be destroyed. Therefore you must struggle and dominate. The law of this world is nothing but the law of force; its driving force, the will to power.

The advocate of crime really only respects two kinds of power: one, which he finds among his own class, founded on the accident of birth, and the other by which, through sheer villainy, an underdog raises himself to the level of the libertines of noble birth whom Sade makes his heroes. This powerful little group of initiates knows that it has all the rights. Anyone who doubts, even for a second, these formidable privileges is immediately driven from the flock, and once more becomes a victim. Thus a sort of aristocratic morality is created through which a little group of men and women manage to entrench themselves above a caste of slaves because they possess the secret of a strange knowledge. The only problem for them consists in organizing themselves so as to be able to exercise fully their rights which have the terrifying scope of desire.

They cannot hope to dominate the entire universe

until the law of crime has been accepted by the universe. Sade never believed that his fellow countrymen would be capable of the additional effort needed to make it "republican." But if crime and desire are not the law of the entire universe, if they do not reign at least over a specified territory, they are no longer unifying principles, but ferments of conflict. They are no longer the law, and man returns to chaos and confusion. Thus it is necessary to create from all these fragments a world that exactly coincides with the new law. The need for unity, which Creation leaves unsatisfied, is fulfilled, at all costs, in a microcosm. The law of power never has the patience to await complete control of the world. It must fix the boundaries, without delay, of the territory where it holds sway, even if it means surrounding it with barbed wire and observation towers.

For Sade, the law of power implies barred gates, castles with seven circumvallations from which it is impossible to escape, and where a society founded on desire and crime functions unimpeded, according to the rules of an implacable system. The most unbridled rebellion, insistence on complete freedom, lead to the total subjection of the majority. For Sade, man's emancipation is consummated in these strongholds of debauchery where a kind of bureaucracy of vice rules over the life and death of the men and women who have committed themselves forever to the hell of their desires. His works abound with descriptions of these privileged places where feudal libertines, to demonstrate to their assembled victims their absolute impotence and servitude, always repeat the Duc de Blangis's speech to the common people of the *One Hundred and Twenty Days of Sodom:* "You are already dead to the world."

Sade himself also inhabited the tower of Freedom, but in the Bastille. Absolute rebellion took refuge with him in a sordid fortress from which no one, either persecuted or persecutors, could ever escape. To establish his freedom, he had to create absolute necessity. Unlimited freedom of desire implies the negation of others and the suppression of pity. The heart, that "weak spot of the intellect," must be exterminated; the locked room and the system will see to that. The system, which plays a role of capital importance in Sade's fabulous castles, perpetuates a universe of mistrust. It helps to anticipate everything so that no unexpected tenderness or pity occur to upset the plans for complete enjoyment. It is a curious kind of pleasure, no doubt, which obeys the commandment: "We shall rise every morning at ten o'clock"! But enjoyment must be prevented from degenerating into attachment, it must be put in parentheses and toughened. Objects of enjoyment must also never be allowed to appear as persons. If man is "an absolutely material species of plant," he can only be treated as an object, and as an object for experiment. In Sade's fortress republic, there are only machines and mechanics. The system, which dictates the method of employing the machines, puts everything in its right place. His infamous convents have their rule—significantly copied from that of religious communities. Thus the libertine indulges in public confession. But the process is changed: "If his conduct is pure, he is censured."

Sade, as was the custom of his period, constructed ideal societies. But, contrary to the custom of his period, he codifies the natural wickedness of mankind. He meticulously constructs a citadel of force and hatred, pioneer that he is, even to the point of calculating mathematically the amount of the freedom he succeeded in destroying. He sums up his philosophy with an unemotional accounting of crimes: "Massacred before the first of March: 10. After the first of March: 20. To come: 16. Total: 46." A pioneer, no doubt, but a limited one, as we can see.

If that were all, Sade would be worthy only of the interest that attaches to all misunderstood pioneers. But once the drawbridge is up, life in the castle must go on. No matter how meticulous the system, it cannot foresee every eventuality. It can destroy, but it cannot create. The masters of these tortured communities do not find the satisfaction they so desperately desire. Sade often evokes the "pleasant habit of crime." Nothing here, however, seems very pleasant—more like the fury of a man in chains. The point, in fact, is to enjoy oneself, and the maximum of enjoyment coincides with the maximum of destruction. To possess what one is going to kill, to copulate with suffering—those are the moments of freedom toward which the entire organization of Sade's castles is directed. But from the moment when sexual crime destroys the object of desire, it also destroys desire, which exists only at the precise moment of destruction. Then another object must be brought under subjection and killed again, and then another, and so on to an infinity of all possible objects. This leads to that dreary accumulation of erotic and criminal scenes in Sade's novels, which, paradoxically, leaves the reader with the impression of a hideous chastity.

What part, in this universe, could pleasure play or the exquisite joy of acquiescent and accomplice bodies? In it we find an impossible quest for escape from despair—a quest that finishes, nevertheless, in a desperate race from servitude to servitude and from prison to prison. If only nature is real and if, in nature, only desire and destruction are legitimate, then, in that all humanity does not suffice to assuage the thirst for blood, the path of destruction must lead to universal annihilation. We must become, according to Sade's formula, nature's executioner. But even that position is not achieved too easily. When the accounts are closed, when all the victims are massacred, the executioners are left face to face in the deserted castle. Something is still missing. The tortured bodies return, in their elements, to nature and will be born again. Even murder cannot be fully consummated: "Murder only deprives the victim of his first life; a means must be found of depriving him of his second. . . ." Sade contemplates an attack on creation: "I abhor nature. . . . I should like to upset its plans, to thwart its progress, to halt the stars in their courses, to overturn the floating spheres of space, to destroy what serves nature and to succor all that harms it; in a word, to insult it in all its works, and I cannot succeed in doing so." It is in vain that he dreams of a technician who can pulverize the universe: he knows that, in the dust of the spheres, life will continue. The attack against creation is doomed to failure. It is impossible to destroy everything, there is always a remainder. "I cannot succeed in doing so . . ." the icy and implacable universe suddenly relents at the appalling melancholy by which Sade, in the end and quite unwillingly, always moves us. "We could perhaps attack the sun, deprive the universe of it, or use it to set fire to the world— those would be real crimes. . . ." Crimes, yes, but not the definitive crime. It is necessary to go farther. The executioners eye each other with suspicion.

They are alone, and one law alone governs them: the law of power. As they accepted it when they were masters, they cannot reject it if it turns against them. All power tends to be unique and solitary. Murder must be repeated: in their turn the masters will tear one another to pieces. Sade accepts this consequence and does not flinch. A curious kind of stoicism, derived from vice, sheds a little light in the dark places of his rebellious soul. He will not try to live again in the world of affection and compromise. The drawbridge will not be lowered; he will accept personal annihilation. The unbridled force of his refusal achieves, at its climax, an unconditional acceptance that is not without nobility. The master consents to be the slave in his turn and even, perhaps, wishes to be. "The scaffold would be for me the throne of voluptuousness."

Thus the greatest degree of destruction coincides with the greatest degree of affirmation. The masters throw themselves on one another, and Sade's work, dedicated to the glory of libertinism, ends by being "strewn with corpses of libertines struck down at the height of their powers." [3] The most powerful, the one who will survive, is the solitary, the Unique, whose glorification Sade has undertaken—in other words, himself. At last he reigns supreme, master and God. But at the moment of his greatest victory the dream vanishes. The Unique turns back toward the prisoner whose unbounded imagination gave birth to him, and they become one. He is in fact alone, imprisoned in a bloodstained Bastille, entirely constructed around a still unsatisfied, and henceforth undirected, desire for pleasure. He has only triumphed in a dream and those ten volumes crammed with philosophy and atrocities recapitulate an unhappy form of asceticism, an illusory advance from the total no to the absolute yes, an acquiescence in death at last, which transfigures the assassination of everything and everyone into a collective suicide.

Sade was executed in effigy; he, too, only killed in his imagination. Prometheus ends in Onan. Sade is still a prisoner when he dies, but this time in a lunatic asylum,

[3] Maurice Blanchot: *Lautréamont et Sade.*

acting plays on an improvised stage with other lunatics. A derisory equivalent of the satisfaction that the order of the world failed to give him was provided for him by dreams and by creative activity. The writer, of course, has no need to refuse himself anything. For him, at least, boundaries disappear and desire can be allowed free rein. In this respect Sade is the perfect man of letters. He created a fable in order to give himself the illusion of existing. He put "the moral crime that one commits by writing" above everything else. His merit, which is incontestable, lies in having immediately demonstrated, with the unhappy perspicacity of accumulated rage, the extreme consequences of rebellious logic—at least when it forgets the truth to be found in its origins. These consequences are a complete totalitarianism, universal crime, an aristocracy of cynicism, and the desire for an apocalypse. They will be found again many years after his death. But having tasted them, he was caught, it seems, on the horns of his own dilemma and could only escape the dilemma in literature. Strangely enough, it is Sade who sets rebellion on the path of literature down which it will be led still farther by the romantics. He himself is one of those writers of whom he says: "their corruption is so dangerous, so active, that they have no other aim in printing their monstrous works than to extend beyond their own lives the sum total of their crimes; they can commit no more, but their accursed writings will lead others to do so, and this comforting thought which they carry with them to the tomb consoles them for the obligation that death imposes on them of renouncing this life." Thus his rebellious writings bear witness to his desire for survival. Even if the immortality he longs for is the immortality of Cain, at least he longs for it, and despite himself bears witness to what is most true in metaphysical rebellion.

Moreover, even his followers compel us to do him homage. His heirs are not all writers. Of course, there is justification for saying that he suffered and died to stimulate the imagination of the intelligentsia in literary cafés. But that is not all. Sade's success in our day is explained by the dream that he had in common with contemporary thought: the demand for total freedom, and dehumanization coldly planned by the intelligence. The reduction of man to an object of experiment, the rule that specifies the relation between the will to power and man as an object, the sealed laboratory that is the scene of this monstrous experiment, are lessons which the theoreticians of power will discover again when they come to organizing the age of slavery.

Two centuries ahead of time and on a reduced scale, Sade extolled totalitarian societies in the name of unbridled freedom—which, in reality, rebellion does not demand. The history and the tragedy of our times really begin with him. He only believed that a society founded on freedom of crime must coincide with freedom of morals, as though servitude had its limits. Our times have limited themselves to blending, in a curious manner, his dream of a universal republic and his technique of degradation. Finally, what he hated most, legal murder, has availed itself of the discoveries that he wanted to put to the service of instinctive murder. Crime, which he wanted to be the exotic and delicious fruit of unbridled vice, is no more today than the dismal habit of a police-controlled morality. Such are the surprises of literature.

The Dandies' Rebellion

Even after Sade's time, men of letters still continue to dominate the scene. Romanticism, Lucifer-like in its rebellion, is really only useful for adventures of the imagination. Like Sade, romanticism is separated from earlier forms of rebellion by its preference for evil and the individual. By putting emphasis on its powers of defiance and refusal, rebellion, at this stage, forgets its positive content. Since God claims all that is good in man, it is necessary to deride what is good and choose what is evil. Hatred of death and of injustice will lead, therefore, if not to the exercise, at least to the vindication, of evil and murder.

The struggle between Satan and death in *Paradise Lost*, the favorite poem of the romantics, symbolizes this drama; all the more profoundly in that death (with, of course, sin) is the child of Satan. In order to combat evil, the rebel renounces good, because he considers himself innocent, and once again gives birth to evil. The romantic hero first of all brings about the profound and, so to speak, religious blending of good and evil.[4] This type of hero is "fatal" because fate confounds good and evil without man being able to prevent it. Fate does not allow judgments of value. It replaces them by the statement that "It is so"—which excuses everything, with the exception of the Creator, who alone is responsible for this scandalous state of affairs. The romantic hero is also "fatal" because, to the extent that he increases in power and genius, the power of evil increases in him. Every manifestation of power, every excess, is thus covered by this "It is so." That the artist, particularly the poet, should be demoniac is a very ancient idea, which is formulated provocatively in the work of the romantics. At this period there is even an imperialism of evil, whose aim is to annex everything, even the most orthodox geniuses. "What made Milton write with constraint," Blake observes, "when he spoke of angels and of God, and with audacity when he spoke of demons and of hell, is that he was a real poet and on the side of the demons, without knowing it." The poet, the genius, man himself in his most exalted image, therefore cry out simultaneously with Satan: "So farewell hope, and with hope farewell fear, farewell remorse. . . . Evil, be thou my good." It is the cry of outraged innocence.

The romantic hero, therefore, considers himself compelled to do evil by his nostalgia for an unrealizable good. Satan rises against his Creator because the latter employed force to subjugate him. "Whom reason hath equal'd," says Milton's Satan, "force hath made supreme above his equals." Divine violence is thus explicitly condemned. The rebel flees from this aggressive and unworthy God, "Farthest from him is best," and reigns over all the forces hostile to the divine order. The Prince of Darkness has only chosen this path because good is a notion defined and utilized by God for unjust purposes. Even innocence irritates the Rebel in so far as it implies being duped. This "dark spirit of evil who is enraged by innocence" creates a human injustice parallel to divine injustice. Since violence is at the root of all creation, deliberate violence shall be its answer. The fact that there is an excess of despair

---

[4] A dominant theme in William Blake, for example.

adds to the causes of despair and brings rebellion to that
state of indignant frustration which follows the long experience of injustice and where the distinction between
good and evil finally disappears. Vigny's Satan can

> . . . no longer find in good or evil any pleasure
> nor of the sorrow that he causes take the measure.

This defines nihilism and authorizes murder.

Murder, in fact, is on the way to becoming acceptable. It is enough to compare the Lucifer of the painters
of the Middle Ages with the Satan of the romantics. An
adolescent "young, sad, charming" (Vigny) replaces the
horned beast. "Beautiful, with a beauty unknown on this
earth" (Lermontov), solitary and powerful, unhappy and
scornful, he is offhand even in oppression. But his excuse
is sorrow. "Who here," says Milton's Satan, "will envy
whom the highest place . . . condemns to greatest share
of endless pain." So many injustices suffered, a sorrow so
unrelieved, justify every excess. The rebel therefore allows
himself certain advantages. Murder, of course, is not recommended for its own sake. But it is implicit in the value—
supreme for the romantic—attached to frenzy. Frenzy is
the reverse of boredom: Lorenzaccio dreams of Han of
Iceland. Exquisite sensibilities evoke the elementary furies
of the beast. The Byronic hero, incapable of love, or capable only of an impossible love, suffers endlessly. He is
solitary, languid, his condition exhausts him. If he wants
to feel alive, it must be in the terrible exaltation of a brief
and destructive action. To love someone whom one will
never see again is to give a cry of exultation as one perishes in the flames of passion. One lives only in and for the
moment, in order to achieve "the brief and vivid union of a
tempestuous heart united to the tempest" (LERMONTOV).
The threat of mortality which hangs over us makes everything abortive. Only the cry of anguish can bring us to
life; exaltation takes the place of truth. To this extent the
apocalypse becomes an absolute value in which everything is confounded—love and death, conscience and
culpability. In a chaotic universe no other life exists but
that of the abyss where, according to Alfred Le Poittevin,
human beings come "trembling with rage and exulting in

their crimes" to curse the Creator. The intoxication of frenzy and, ultimately, some suitable crime reveal in a moment the whole meaning of a life. Without exactly advocating crime, the romantics insist on paying homage to a basic system of privileges which they illustrate with the conventional images of the outlaw, the criminal with the heart of gold, and the kind brigand. Their works are bathed in blood and shrouded in mystery. The soul is delivered, at a minimum expenditure, of its most hideous desires—desires that a later generation will assuage in extermination camps. Of course these works are also a challenge to the society of the times. But romanticism, at the source of its inspiration, is chiefly concerned with defying moral and divine law. That is why its most original creation is not, primarily, the revolutionary, but, logically enough, the dandy.

Logically, because this obstinate persistence in Satanism can only be justified by the endless affirmation of injustice and, to a certain extent, by its consolidation. Pain, at this stage, is acceptable only on condition that it is incurable. The rebel chooses the metaphysic of inevitable evil, which is expressed in the literature of damnation from which we have not yet escaped. "I was conscious of my power and I was conscious of my chains" (Petrus Borel). But these chains are valuable objects. Without them it would be necessary to prove, or to exercise, this power which, after all, one is not very sure of having. It is only too easy to end up by becoming a government employee in Algiers, and Prometheus, like the above-mentioned Borel, will devote the rest of his days to closing the cabarets and reforming morals in the colonies. All the same, every poet to be received into the fold must be damned.[5] Charles Lassailly, the same who planned a philosophic novel, *Robespierre and Jesus Christ*, never went to bed without uttering several fervent blasphemies to give himself courage. Rebellion puts on mourning and exhibits itself for public admiration. Much more than the cult of the individual, romanticism inaugurates the cult of

---

[5] French literature still feels the effects of this. "Poets are no longer damned," says Malraux. There are fewer. But the others all suffer from bad consciences.

the "character." It is at this point that it is logical. No longer hoping for the rule or the unity of God, determined to take up arms against an antagonistic destiny, anxious to preserve everything of which the living are still capable in a world dedicated to death, romantic rebellion looked for a solution in the attitude that it itself assumed. The attitude assembled, in æsthetic unity, all mankind who were in the hands of fate and about to be destroyed by divine violence. The human being who is condemned to death is, at least, magnificent before he disappears, and his magnificence is his justification. It is an established fact, the only one that can be thrown in the petrified face of the God of hate. The impassive rebel does not flinch before the eyes of God. "Nothing," says Milton, "will change this determined mind, this high disdain born of an offended conscience." Everything is drawn or rushes toward the void, but even though man is humiliated, he is obstinate and at least preserves his pride. A baroque romantic, discovered by Raymond Queneau, claims that the aim of all intellectual life is to become God. This romantic is really a little ahead of his time. The aim, at that time, was only to equal God and remain on His level. He is not destroyed, but by incessant effort He is refused any act of submission. Dandyism is a degraded form of asceticism.

The dandy creates his own unity by æsthetic means. But it is an æsthetic of singularity and of negation. "To live and die before a mirror": that, according to Baudelaire, was the dandy's slogan. It is indeed a coherent slogan. The dandy is, by occupation, always in opposition. He can only exist by defiance. Up to now man derived his coherence from his Creator. But from the moment that he consecrates his rupture with Him, he finds himself delivered over to the fleeting moment, to the passing days, and to wasted sensibility. Therefore he must take himself in hand. The dandy rallies his forces and creates a unity for himself by the very violence of his refusal. Profligate, like all people without a rule of life, he is coherent as an actor. But an actor implies a public; the dandy can only play a part by setting himself up in opposition. He can only be sure of his own existence by finding it in the expression of others' faces. Other people are his mirror. A mirror that

quickly becomes clouded, it is true, since human capacity
for attention is limited. It must be ceaselessly stimulated,
spurred on by provocation. The dandy, therefore, is always compelled to astonish. Singularity is his vocation,
excess his way to perfection. Perpetually incomplete, always on the fringe of things, he compels others to create
him, while denying their values. He plays at life because
he is unable to live it. He plays at it until he dies, except
for the moments when he is alone and without a mirror.
For the dandy, to be alone is not to exist. The romantics
talked so grandly about solitude only because it was their
real horror, the one thing they could not bear. Their rebellion thrusts its roots deep, but from the Abbé Prévost's
Cleveland up to the time of the Dadaists—including the
frenetics of 1830 and Baudelaire and the decadents of
1880—more than a century of rebellion was completely
glutted by the audacities of "eccentricity." If they were all
able to talk of unhappiness, it is because they despaired of
ever being able to conquer it, except in futile parodies, and
because they instinctively felt that it remained their sole
excuse and their real claim to nobility.

That is why the heritage of romanticism was not
claimed by Victor Hugo, the epitome of France, but by
Baudelaire and Lacenaire, the poets of crime. "Everything
in this world exudes crime," says Baudelaire, "the newspaper, the walls, and the face of man." Nevertheless crime,
which is the law of nature, singularly fails to appear distinguished. Lacenaire, the first of the gentleman criminals,
exploits it effectively; Baudelaire displays less tenacity, but
is a genius. He creates the garden of evil where crime
figures only as one of the rarer species. Terror itself becomes an exquisite sensation and a collector's item. "Not
only would I be happy to be a victim, but I would not
even hate being an executioner in order to *feel* the revolution from both sides." Even Baudelaire's conformity has
the odor of crime. If he chose Maistre as his master, it is
to the extent that this conservative goes to extremes and
centers his doctrine on death and on the executioner. "The
real saint," Baudelaire pretends to think, "is he who flogs
and kills people for their own good." His argument will be
heard. A race of real saints is beginning to spread over
the earth for the purpose of confirming these curious con-

clusions about rebellion. But Baudelaire, despite his satanic arsenal, his taste for Sade, his blasphemies, remains too much of a theologian to be a proper rebel. His real drama, which made him the greatest poet of his time, was something else. Baudelaire can be mentioned here only to the extent that he was the most profound theoretician of dandyism and gave definite form to one of the conclusions of romantic revolt.

Romanticism demonstrates, in fact, that rebellion is part and parcel of dandyism: one of its objectives is appearances. In its conventional forms, dandyism admits a nostalgia for ethics. It is only honor degraded as a point of honor. But at the same time it inaugurates an æsthetic which is still valid in our world, an æsthetic of solitary creators, who are obstinate rivals of a God they condemn. From romanticism onward, the artist's task will not only be to create a world, or to exalt beauty for its own sake, but also to define an attitude. Thus the artist becomes a model and offers himself as an example: art is his ethic. With him begins the age of the directors of conscience. When the dandies fail to commit suicide or do not go mad, they make a career and pursue prosperity. Even when, like Vigny, they exclaim that they are going to retire into silence, their silence is piercing.

But at the very heart of romanticism, the sterility of this attitude becomes apparent to a few rebels who provide a transitional type between the eccentrics (or the Incredible) and our revolutionary adventurers. Between the times of the eighteenth-century eccentric and the "conquerors" of the twentieth century, Byron and Shelley are already fighting, though only ostensibly, for freedom. They also expose themselves, but in another way. Rebellion gradually leaves the world of appearances for the world of action, where it will completely commit itself. The French students in 1830 and the Russian Decembrists will then appear as the purest incarnations of a rebellion which is at first solitary and which then tries, through sacrifice, to find the path to solidarity. But, inversely, the taste for the apocalypse and a life of frenzy will reappear among present-day revolutionaries. The endless series of treason trials, the terrible game played out between the judge and the accused, the elaborate staging of cross-examinations, sometimes lead us to believe that there is a tragic resemblance to the old subterfuge by which the romantic rebel, in refusing to be what he was, provisionally condemned himself to a make-believe world in the desperate hope of achieving a more profound existence.

The Rejection of Salvation

＊

If the romantic rebel extols evil and the individual, this does not mean that he sides with mankind, but merely with himself. Dandyism, of whatever kind, is always dandyism in relation to God. The individual, in so far as he is a created being, can oppose himself only to the Creator. He has need of God, with whom he carries on a kind of a gloomy flirtation. Armand Hoog[1] rightly says that, despite its Nietzschean atmosphere, God is not yet dead even in romantic literature. Damnation, so clamorously demanded, is only a clever trick played on God. But with Dostoievsky the description of rebellion goes a step farther. Ivan Karamazov sides with mankind and stresses human innocence. He affirms that the death sentence which hangs over them is unjust. Far from making a plea for evil, his first impulse, at least, is to plead for justice, which he ranks above the divinity. Thus he does not absolutely deny the existence of God. He refutes Him in the name of a moral value. The romantic rebel's ambition was to talk to God as one equal to another. Evil was the answer to evil, pride the answer to cruelty. Vigny's ideal, for example, is to answer silence with silence. Obviously, the point is to raise oneself to the level of God, which already is blasphemy. But there is no thought of disputing the power or position of the deity. The blasphemy is reverent, since every blasphemy is, ultimately, a participation in holiness.

With Ivan, however, the tone changes. God, in His turn, is put on trial. If evil is essential to divine creation, then creation is unacceptable. Ivan will no longer have recourse to this mysterious God, but to a higher principle

[1] *Les Petits Romantiques.*

—namely, justice. He launches the essential undertaking of rebellion, which is that of replacing the reign of grace by the reign of justice. He simultaneously begins the attack on Christianity. The romantic rebels broke with God Himself, on the principle of hatred. Ivan explicitly rejects the mystery and, consequently, God, on the principle of love. Only love can make us consent to the injustice done to Martha, to the exploitation of workers, and, finally, to the death of innocent children.

"If the suffering of children," says Ivan, "serves to complete the sum of suffering necessary for the acquisition of truth, I affirm from now onward that truth is not worth such a price." Ivan rejects the basic interdependence, introduced by Christianity, between suffering and truth. Ivan's most profound utterance, the one which opens the deepest chasms beneath the rebel's feet, is his *even if:* "I would persist in my indignation even if I were wrong." Which means that even if God existed, even if the mystery cloaked a truth, even if the starets Zosime were right, Ivan would not admit that truth should be paid for by evil, suffering, and the death of innocents. Ivan incarnates the refusal of salvation. Faith leads to immortal life. But faith presumes the acceptance of the mystery and of evil, and resignation to injustice. The man who is prevented by the suffering of children from accepting faith will certainly not accept eternal life. Under these conditions, even if eternal life existed, Ivan would refuse it. He rejects this bargain. He would accept grace only unconditionally, and that is why he makes his own conditions. Rebellion wants all or nothing. "All the knowledge in the world is not worth a child's tears." Ivan does not say that there is no truth. He says that if truth does exist, it can only be unacceptable. Why? Because it is unjust. The struggle between truth and justice is begun here for the first time; and it will never end. Ivan, by nature a solitary and therefore a moralist, will satisfy himself with a kind of metaphysical Don Quixotism. But a few decades more and an immense political conspiracy will attempt to prove that justice is truth.

In addition, Ivan is the incarnation of the refusal to be the only one saved. He throws in his lot with the damned and, for their sake, rejects eternity. If he had faith, he could, in fact, be saved, but others would be damned and suffering would continue. There is no possible salvation for the man who feels real compassion. Ivan will continue to put God in the wrong by doubly rejecting faith as he would reject injustice and privilege. One step more and from *All or Nothing* we arrive at *Everyone or No One*.

This extreme determination, and the attitude that it implies, would have sufficed for the romantics. But Ivan,[2] even though he also gives way to dandyism, really lives his problems, torn between the negative and the affirmative. From this moment onward, he accepts the consequences. If he rejects immortality, what remains for him? Life in its most elementary form. When the meaning of life has been suppressed, there still remains life. "I live," says Ivan, "in spite of logic." And again: "If I no longer had any faith in life, if I doubted a woman I loved, or the universal order of things, if I were persuaded, on the contrary, that everything was only an infernal and accursed chaos—even then I would want to live." Ivan will live, then, and will love as well "without knowing why." But to live is also to act. To act in the name of what? If there is no immortality, then there is neither reward nor punishment. "I believe that there is no virtue without immortality." And also: "I only know that suffering exists, that no one is guilty, that everything is connected, that everything passes away and equals out." But if there is no virtue, there is no law: "Everything is permitted."

With this "everything is permitted" the history of contemporary nihilism really begins. The romantic rebellion did not go so far. It limited itself to saying, in short, that everything was not permitted, but that, through insolence, it allowed itself to do what was forbidden. With the Karamazovs, on the contrary, the logic of indignation turned rebellion against itself and confronted it with a desperate contradiction. The essential difference is that the romantics allowed themselves moments of complacence, while Ivan compelled himself to do evil so as to be coherent. He would not allow himself to be good. Nihilism is not only despair and negation but, above all, the de-

[2] It is worth noting that Ivan is, in a certain way, Dostoievsky, who is more at ease in this role than in the role of Aliosha.

sire to despair and to negate. The same man who so violently took the part of innocence, who trembled at the suffering of a child, who wanted to see "with his own eyes" the lamb lie down with the lion, the victim embrace his murderer, from the moment that he rejects divine coherence and tries to discover his own rule of life, recognizes the legitimacy of murder. Ivan rebels against a murderous God; but from the moment that he begins to rationalize his rebellion, he deduces the law of murder. If all is permitted, he can kill his father or at least allow him to be killed. Long reflection on the condition of mankind as people sentenced to death only leads to the justification of crime. Ivan simultaneously hates the death penalty (describing an execution, he says furiously: "His head fell, in the name of divine grace") and condones crime, in principle. Every indulgence is allowed the murderer, none is allowed the executioner. This contradiction, which Sade swallowed with ease, chokes Ivan Karamazov.

He pretends to reason, in fact, as though immortality did not exist, while he only goes so far as to say that he would refuse it even if it did exist. In order to protest against evil and death, he deliberately chooses to say that virtue exists no more than does immortality and to allow his father to be killed. He consciously accepts his dilemma; to be virtuous and illogical, or logical and criminal. His prototype, the devil, is right when he whispers: "You are going to commit a virtuous act and yet you do not believe in virtue; that is what angers and torments you." The question that Ivan finally poses, the question that constitutes the real progress achieved by Dostoievsky in the history of rebellion, is the only one in which we are interested here: can one live and stand one's ground in a state of rebellion?

Ivan allows us to guess his answer: one can live in a state of rebellion only by pursuing it to the bitter end. What is the bitter end of metaphysical rebellion? Metaphysical revolution. The master of the world, after his legitimacy has been contested, must be overthrown. Man must occupy his place. "As God and immortality do not exist, the new man is permitted to become God." But what does becoming God mean? It means, in fact, recognizing that everything is permitted and refusing to recognize any other law but one's own. Without it being necessary to develop the intervening arguments, we can see that to become God is to accept crime (a favorite idea of Dostoievsky's intellectuals). Ivan's personal problem is, then, to know if he will be faithful to his logic and if, on the grounds of an indignant protest against innocent suffering, he will accept the murder of his father with the indifference of a man-god. We know his solution: Ivan allows his father to be killed. Too profound to be satisfied with appearances, too sensitive to perform the deed himself, he is content to allow it to be done. But he goes mad. The man who could not understand how one could love one's neighbor cannot understand either how one can kill him. Caught between unjustifiable virtue and unacceptable crime, consumed with pity and incapable of love, a recluse deprived of the benefits of cynicism, this man of supreme intelligence is killed by contradiction. "My mind is of this world," he said; "what good is it to try to understand what is not of this world?" But he lived only for what is not of this world, and his proud search for the absolute is precisely what removed him from the world of which he loved no part.

The fact that Ivan was defeated does not obviate the fact that once the problem is posed, the consequence must follow: rebellion is henceforth on the march toward action. This has already been demonstrated by Dostoievsky, with prophetic intensity, in his legend of the Grand Inquisitor. Ivan, finally, does not distinguish the creator from his creation. "It is not God whom I reject," he says, "it is creation." In other words, it is God the father, indistinguishable from what He has created.[3] His plot to usurp the throne, therefore, remains completely moral. He does not want to reform anything in creation. But creation being what it is, he claims the right to free himself morally and to free all the rest of mankind with him. On the other hand, from the moment when the spirit of rebellion, having accepted the concept of "everything is permitted" and

[3] Ivan allows his father to be killed and thus chooses a direct attack against nature and procreation. Moreover, this particular father is infamous. The repugnant figure of old Karamazov is continually coming between Ivan and the God of Aliosha.

"everyone or no one," aims at reconstructing creation in order to assert the sovereignty and divinity of man, and from the moment when metaphysical rebellion extends itself from ethics to politics, a new undertaking, of incalculable import, begins, which also springs, we must note, from the same nihilism. Dostoievsky, the prophet of the new religion, had foreseen and announced it: "If Aliosha had come to the conclusion that neither God nor immortality existed, he would immediately have become an atheist and a socialist. For socialism is not only a question of the working classes; it is above all, in its contemporary incarnation, a question of atheism, a question of the tower of Babel, which is constructed without God's help, not to reach to the heavens, but to bring the heavens down to earth." [4]

After that, Aliosha can, in fact, treat Ivan with compassion as a "real simpleton." The latter only made an attempt at self-control and failed. Others will appear, with more serious intentions, who, on the basis of the same despairing nihilism, will insist on ruling the world. These are the Grand Inquisitors who imprison Christ and come to tell Him that His method is not correct, that universal happiness cannot be achieved by the immediate freedom of choosing between good and evil, but by the domination and unification of the world. The first step is to conquer and rule. The kingdom of heaven will, in fact, appear on earth, but it will be ruled over by men—a mere handful to begin with, who will be the Cæsars, because they were the first to understand—and later, with time, by all men. The unity of all creation will be achieved by every possible means, since everything is permitted. The Grand Inquisitor is old and tired, for the knowledge he possesses is bitter. He knows that men are lazy rather than cowardly and that they prefer peace and death to the liberty of discerning between good and evil. He has pity, a cold pity, for the silent prisoner whom history endlessly deceives. He urges him to speak, to recognize his misdeeds, and, in one sense, to approve the actions of the Inquisitors and of the Cæsars. But the prisoner does not speak. The enterprise will continue, therefore, without him; he will be killed.

[4] These questions (God and immortality) are the same questions that socialism poses, but seen from another angle.

Legitimacy will come at the end of time, when the kingdom of men is assured. "The affair has only just begun, it is far from being terminated, and the world has many other things to suffer, but we shall achieve our aim, we shall be Cæsar, and then we shall begin to think about universal happiness."

By then the prisoner has been executed; the Grand Inquisitors reign alone, listening to "the profound spirit, the spirit of destruction and death." The Grand Inquisitors proudly refuse freedom and the bread of heaven and offer the bread of this earth without freedom. "Come down from the cross and we will believe in you," their police agents are already crying on Golgotha. But He did not come down and, even, at the most tortured moment of His agony, He protested to God at having been forsaken. There are, thus, no longer any proofs, but faith and the mystery that the rebels reject and at which the Grand Inquisitors scoff. Everything is permitted and centuries of crime are prepared in that cataclysmic moment. From Paul to Stalin, the popes who have chosen Cæsar have prepared the way for Cæsars who quickly learn to despise popes. The unity of the world, which was not achieved with God, will henceforth be attempted in defiance of God.

But we have not yet reached that point. For the moment, Ivan offers us only the tortured face of the rebel plunged in the abyss, incapable of action, torn between the idea of his own innocence and the desire to kill. He hates the death penalty because it is the image of the human condition, and, at the same time, he is drawn to crime. Because he has taken the side of mankind, solitude is his lot. With him the rebellion of reason culminates in madness.

*

From the moment that man submits God to moral judgment, he kills Him in his own heart. And then what is the basis of morality? God is denied in the name of justice, but can the idea of justice be understood without the idea of God? At this point are we not in the realm of absurdity? Absurdity is the concept that Nietzsche meets face to face. In order to be able to dismiss it, he pushes it to extremes: morality is the ultimate aspect of God, which must be destroyed before reconstruction can begin. Then God no longer exists and is no longer responsible for our existence; man must resolve to act, in order to exist.

The Unique

Even before Nietzsche, Stirner wanted to eradicate the very idea of God from man's mind, after he had destroyed God Himself. But, unlike Nietzsche, his nihilism was gratified. Stirner laughs in his blind alley; Nietzsche beats his head against the wall. In 1845, the year when *Der Einziger und sein Eigentum* (*The Unique and Its Characteristics*) appeared, Stirner begins to define his position. Stirner, who frequented the "Society of Free Men" with the young Hegelians of the left (of whom Marx was one), had an account to settle not only with God, but also with Feuerbach's Man, Hegel's Spirit, and its historical incarnation, the State. All these idols, to his mind, were offsprings of the same "mongolism"—the belief in the eternity of ideas. Thus he was able to write: "I have constructed my case on nothing." Sin is, of course, a "mongol scourge," but it is also the law of which we are prisoners. God is the enemy; Stirner goes as far as he can in blasphemy ("digest the Host and you are rid of it"). But God is only one of the aberrations of the I, or more precisely of what I am. Socrates, Jesus, Descartes, Hegel, all the prophets and philosophers, have done nothing but invent new methods of deranging what I am, the I that Stirner is so intent on distinguishing from the absolute I of Fichte by reducing it to its most specific and transitory aspect. "It has no name," it is the Unique.

For Stirner the history of the universe up to the time of Jesus is nothing but a sustained effort to idealize reality. This effort is incarnated in the ideas and rites of purification which the ancients employed. From the time of Jesus, the goal is reached, and another effort is embarked upon which consists, on the contrary, in attempting to realize the ideal. The passion of the incarnation takes the place of purification and devastates the world, to a greater and greater degree, as socialism, the heir of Christ, extends its sway. But the history of the universe is nothing but a continual offense to the unique principle that "I am"—a living, concrete principle, a triumphant principle that the world has always wanted to subject to the yoke of successive abstractions—God, the State, society, humanity. For Stirner, philanthropy is a hoax. Atheistic philosophies, which culminate in the cult of the State and of Man, are only "theological insurrections." "Our atheists," says Stirner, "are really pious folk." There is only one religion that exists throughout all history, the belief in eternity. This belief is a deception. The only truth is the Unique, the enemy of eternity and of everything, in fact, which does not further its desire for domination.

With Stirner, the concept of negation which inspires his rebellion irresistibly submerges every aspect of affirmation. It also sweeps away the substitutes for divinity with which the moral conscience is encumbered. "External eternity is swept away," he says, "but internal eternity has become a new heaven." Even revolution, revolution in particular, is repugnant to this rebel. To be a revolutionary, one must continue to believe in something, even where there is nothing in which to believe. "The [French] Revolution ended in reaction and that demonstrates what the

Revolution was in *reality*." To dedicate oneself to humanity is no more worth while than serving God. Moreover, fraternity is only "Communism in its Sunday best." During the week, the members of the fraternity become slaves. Therefore there is only one form of freedom for Stirner, "my power," and only one truth, "the magnificent egotism of the stars."

In this desert everything begins to flower again. "The terrifying significance of an unpremeditated cry of joy cannot be understood while the long night of faith and reason endures." This night is drawing to a close, and a dawn will break which is not the dawn of revolution but of insurrection. Insurrection is, in itself, an asceticism which rejects all forms of consolation. The insurgent will not be in agreement with other men except in so far as, and as long as, their egotism coincides with his. His real life is led in solitude where he will assuage, without restraint, his appetite for existing, which is his only reason for existence.

In this respect individualism reaches a climax. It is the negation of everything that denies the individual and the glorification of everything that exalts and ministers to the individual. What, according to Stirner, is good? "Everything of which I can make use." What am I, legitimately, authorized to do? "Everything of which I am capable." Once again, rebellion leads to the justification of crime. Stirner not only has attempted to justify crime (in this respect the terrorist forms of anarchy are directly descended from him), but is visibly intoxicated by the perspectives that he thus reveals. "To break with what is sacred, or rather to destroy the sacred, could become universal. It is not a new revolution that is approaching—but is not a powerful, proud, disrespectful, shameless, conscienceless crime swelling like a thundercloud on the horizon, and can you not see that the sky, heavy with foreboding, is growing dark and silent?" Here we can feel the somber joy of those who create an apocalypse in a garret. This bitter and imperious logic can no longer be held in check, except by an I which is determined to defeat every form of abstraction and which has itself become abstract and nameless through being isolated and cut off from its roots. There are no more crimes and no more imperfections, and therefore no more sinners. We are all perfect.

Since every I is, in itself, fundamentally criminal in its attitude toward the State and the people, we must recognize that to live is to transgress. Unless we accept death, we must be willing to kill in order to be unique. "You are not as noble as a criminal, you who do not desecrate anything." Moreover Stirner, still without the courage of his convictions, specifies: "Kill them, do not martyr them."

But to decree that murder is legitimate is to decree mobilization and war for all the Unique. Thus murder will coincide with a kind of collective suicide. Stirner, who either does not admit or does not see this, nevertheless does not recoil at the idea of any form of destruction. The spirit of rebellion finally discovers one of its bitterest satisfactions in chaos. "You [the German nation] will be struck down. Soon your sister nations will follow you; when all of them have gone your way, humanity will be buried, and on its tomb I, sole master of myself at last, I, heir to all the human race, will shout with laughter." And so, among the ruins of the world, the desolate laughter of the individual-king illustrates the last victory of the spirit of rebellion. But at this extremity nothing else is possible but death or resurrection. Stirner, and with him all the nihilist rebels, rush to the utmost limits, drunk with destruction. After which, when the desert has been disclosed, the next step is to learn how to live there. Nietzsche's exhaustive search then begins.

Nietzsche and Nihilism

"We deny God, we deny the responsibility of God, it is only thus that we will deliver the world." With Nietzsche, nihilism seems to become prophetic. But we can draw no conclusions from Nietzsche except the base and mediocre cruelty that he hated with all his strength, unless we give first place in his work—well ahead of the prophet—to the diagnostician. The provisional, methodical—in a word, strategic—character of his thought cannot be doubted for a moment. With him nihilism becomes conscious for the first time. Surgeons have this in common with prophets: they think and operate in terms of the future. Nietzsche never thought except in terms of an apocalypse to come, not in order to extol it, for he guessed the sordid and calculating aspect that this apocalypse would finally assume, but in order to avoid it and to transform it into a renaissance. He recognized nihilism for what it was and examined it like a clinical fact.

He said of himself that he was the first complete nihilist of Europe. Not by choice, but by condition, and because he was too great to refuse the heritage of his time. He diagnosed in himself, and in others, the inability to believe and the disappearance of the primitive foundation of all faith—namely, the belief in life. The "can one live as a rebel?" became with him "can one live believing in nothing?" His reply is affirmative. Yes, if one creates a system out of absence of faith, if one accepts the final consequences of nihilism, and if, on emerging into the desert and putting one's confidence in what is going to come, one feels, with the same primitive instinct, both pain and joy.

Instead of methodical doubt, he practiced methodical negation, the determined destruction of everything that still hides nihilism from itself, of the idols that camouflage God's death. "To raise a new sanctuary, a sanctuary must be destroyed, that is the law." According to Nietzsche, he who wants to be a creator of good or of evil must first of all destroy all values. "Thus the supreme evil becomes part of the supreme good, but the supreme good is creative." He wrote, in his own manner, the *Discours de la Méthode* of his period, without the freedom and exactitude of the seventeenth-century French he admired so much, but with the mad lucidity that characterizes the twentieth century, which, according to him, is the century of genius. We must return to the examination of this system of rebellion.[1]

Nietzsche's first step is to accept what he knows. Atheism for him goes without saying and is "constructive and radical." Nietzsche's supreme vocation, so he says, is to provoke a kind of crisis and a final decision about the problem of atheism. The world continues on its course at

[1] We are obviously concerned here with Nietzsche's final philosophic position, between 1880 and his collapse. This chapter can be considered as a commentary on *Der Wille zur Macht* (*The Will to Power*).

random and there is nothing final about it. Thus God is useless, since He wants nothing in particular. If He wanted something—and here we recognize the traditional formulation of the problem of evil—He would have to assume the responsibility for "a sum total of pain and inconsistency which would debase the entire value of being born." We know that Nietzsche was publicly envious of Stendahl's epigram: "The only excuse for God is that he does not exist." Deprived of the divine will, the world is equally deprived of unity and finality. That is why it is impossible to pass judgment on the world. Any attempt to apply a standard of values to the world leads finally to a slander on life. Judgments are based on what is, with reference to what should be—the kingdom of heaven, eternal concepts, or moral imperatives. But what should be does not exist; and this world cannot be judged in the name of nothing. "The advantages of our times: nothing is true, everything is permitted." These magnificent or ironic formulas which are echoed by thousands of others, at least suffice to demonstrate that Nietzsche accepts the entire burden of nihilism and rebellion. In his somewhat puerile reflections on "training and selection" he even formulated the extreme logic of nihilistic reasoning: "Problem: by what means could we obtain a strict form of complete and contagious nihilism which would teach and practice, with complete scientific awareness, voluntary death?"

But Nietzsche enlists values in the cause of nihilism which, traditionally, have been considered as restraints on nihilism—principally morality. Moral conduct, as explained by Socrates, or as recommended by Christianity, is in itself a sign of decadence. It wants to substitute the mere shadow of a man for a man of flesh and blood. It condemns the universe of passion and emotion in the name of an entirely imaginary world of harmony. If nihilism is the inability to believe, then its most serious symptom is not found in atheism, but in the inability to believe in what is, to see what is happening, and to live life as it is offered. This infirmity is at the root of all idealism. Morality has no faith in the world. For Nietzsche, real morality cannot be separated from lucidity. He is severe on the "calumniators of the world" because he discerns in the calumny a shameful taste for evasion. Traditional morality, for him, is only a special type of immorality. "It is virtue," he says, "which has need of justification." And again: "It is for moral reasons that good, one day, will cease to be done."

Nietzsche's philosophy, undoubtedly, revolves around the problem of rebellion. More precisely, it begins by being a rebellion. But we sense the change of position that Nietzsche makes. With him, rebellion begins with "God is dead," which is assumed as an established fact; then it turns against everything that aims at falsely replacing the vanished deity and reflects dishonor on a world which doubtless has no direction but which remains nevertheless the only proving-ground of the gods. Contrary to the opinion of certain of his Christian critics, Nietzsche did not form a project to kill God. He found Him dead in the soul of his contemporaries. He was the first to understand the immense importance of the event and to decide that this rebellion on the part of men could not lead to a renaissance unless it was controlled and directed. Any other attitude toward it, whether regret or complacency, must lead to the apocalypse. Thus Nietzsche did not formulate a philosophy of rebellion, but constructed a philosophy on rebellion.

If he attacks Christianity in particular, it is only in so far as it represents morality. He always leaves intact the person of Jesus on the one hand, and on the other the cynical aspects of the Church. We know that, from the point of view of the connoisseur, he admired the Jesuits. "Basically," he writes, "only the God of morality is rejected." Christ, for Nietzsche as for Tolstoy, is not a rebel. The essence of His doctrine is summed up in total consent and in nonresistance to evil. Thou shalt not kill, even to prevent killing. The world must be accepted as it is, nothing must be added to its unhappiness, but you must consent to suffer personally from the evil it contains. The kingdom of heaven is within our immediate reach. It is only an inner inclination which allows us to make our actions coincide with these principles and which can give us immediate salvation. Not faith but deeds—that, according to Nietzsche, is Christ's message. From then on, the history of Christianity is nothing but a long betrayal of this message. The New Testament is already corrupted, and from the time of Paul to the Councils, subservience to faith leads to the neglect of deeds.

What is the profoundly corrupt addition made by Christianity to the message of its Master? The idea of judgment, completely foreign to the teachings of Christ, and the correlative notions of punishment and reward. From that moment nature becomes history, and significant history expressed by the idea of human totality is born. From the Annunciation until the Last Judgment, humanity has no other task but to conform to the strictly moral ends of a narrative that has already been written. The only difference is that the characters, in the epilogue, separate themselves into the good and the bad. While Christ's sole judgment consists in saying that the sins of nature are unimportant, historical Christianity makes nature the source of sin. "What does Christ deny? Everything that at present bears the name Christian." Christianity believes that it is fighting against nihilism because it gives the world a sense of direction, while it is really nihilist itself in so far as, by imposing an imaginary meaning on life, it prevents the discovery of its real meaning: "Every Church is a stone rolled onto the tomb of the man-god; it tries to prevent the resurrection, by force." Nietzsche's paradoxical but significant conclusion is that God has been killed by Christianity, in that Christianity has secularized the sacred. Here we must understand historical Christianity and "its profound and contemptible duplicity."

The same process of reasoning leads to Nietzsche's attitude toward socialism and all forms of humanitarianism. Socialism is only a degenerate form of Christianity. In fact, it preserves a belief in the finality of history which betrays life and nature, which substitutes ideal ends for real ends, and contributes to enervating both the will and the imagination. Socialism is nihilistic, in the henceforth precise sense that Nietzsche confers on the word. A nihilist is not one who believes in nothing, but one who does not believe in what exists. In this sense, all forms of socialism are manifestations, degraded once again, of Christian decadence. For Christianity, reward and punishment implied the existence of history. But, by inescapable logic, all history ends by implying punishment and reward; and, from this day on, collectivist Messianism is born. Similarly, the equality of souls before God leads, now that God is dead, to equality pure and simple. There again, Nietzsche wages war against socialist doctrines in so far as they are moral doctrines. Nihilism, whether manifested in religion or in socialist preachings, is the logical conclusion of our so-called superior values. The free mind will destroy these values and denounce the illusions on which they are built, the bargaining that they imply, and the crime they commit in preventing the lucid intelligence from accomplishing its mission: to transform passive nihilism into active nihilism.

In this world rid of God and of moral idols, man is now alone and without a master. No one has been less inclined than Nietzsche (and in this way he distinguishes himself from the romantics) to let it be believed that such freedom would be easy. This complete liberation put him among the ranks of those of whom he himself said that they suffered a new form of anguish and a new form of happiness. But, at the beginning, it is only anguish that makes him cry out: "Alas, grant me madness. . . . Unless I am above the law, I am the most outcast of all outcasts." He who cannot maintain his position above the law must in fact find another law or take refuge in madness. From the moment that man believes neither in God nor in immortal life, he becomes "responsible for everything alive, for everything that, born of suffering, is condemned to suffer from life." It is he, and he alone, who must discover law and order. Then the time of exile begins, the endless search for justification, the aimless nostalgia, "the most painful, the most heartbreaking question, that of the heart which asks itself: where can I feel at home?"

Because his mind was free, Nietzsche knew that freedom of the mind is not a comfort, but an achievement to which one aspires and at long last obtains after an exhausting struggle. He knew that in wanting to consider oneself above the law, there is a great risk of finding oneself beneath the law. That is why he understood that only the mind found its real emancipation in the acceptance of new obligations. The essence of his discovery consists in saying that if the eternal law is not freedom, the absence of law is still less so. If nothing is true, if the world is without order, then nothing is forbidden; to prohibit an action, there must, in fact, be a standard of values and an aim. But, at the same time, nothing is authorized; there must also be values and aims in order to choose another course of action. Absolute domination by the law does not represent liberty, but no more does absolute anarchy. The sum total of every possibility does not amount to liberty, but to attempt the impossible amounts to slavery. Chaos is also a form of servitude. Freedom exists only in a world where what is possible is defined at the same time as what is not possible. Without law there is no freedom. If fate is not guided by superior values, if chance is king, then there is nothing but the step in the dark and the appalling freedom of the blind. On the point of achieving the most complete liberation, Nietzsche therefore chooses the most complete subordination. "If we do not make of God's death a great renunciation and a perpetual victory over ourselves, we shall have to pay for that omission." In other words, with Nietzsche, rebellion ends in asceticism. A profounder logic replaces the "if nothing is true, everything is permitted" of Karamazov by "if nothing is true, nothing is permitted." To deny that one single thing is forbidden in this world amounts to renouncing everything that is permitted. At the point where it is no longer possible to say what is black and what is white, the light is extinguished and freedom becomes a voluntary prison.

It can be said that Nietzsche, with a kind of frightful joy, rushes toward the impasse into which he methodically drives his nihilism. His avowed aim is to render the situation untenable to his contemporaries. His only hope seems to be to arrive at the extremity of contradiction. Then if man does not wish to perish in the coils that strangle him, he will have to cut them at a single blow and create his own values. The death of God accomplishes nothing and can only be endured in terms of preparing a resurrection. "If we fail to find grandeur in God," says Nietzsche, "we find it nowhere; it must be denied or created." To deny it was the task of the world around him, which he saw rushing toward suicide. To create was the superhuman task for which he was willing to die. He knew in fact that creation is only possible in the extremity of solitude and that man would only commit himself to this staggering task if, in the most extreme distress of mind, he was compelled to undertake it or perish. Nietzsche cries out to man that the only truth is the world, to which he must be faithful and in which he must live and find his salvation. But at the same time he teaches him that to live in a lawless world is impossible because to live explicitly implies a law. How can one live freely and without law? To this enigma man must find an answer, on pain of death.

Nietzsche at least does not flinch. He answers and his answer is bold: Damocles never danced better than beneath the sword. One must accept the unacceptable and hold to the untenable. From the moment that it is admitted that the world pursues no end, Nietzsche proposes to concede its innocence, to affirm that it accepts no judgment since it cannot be judged on any intention, and consequently to replace all judgments based on values by absolute assent, and by a complete and exalted allegiance to this world. Thus from absolute despair will spring infinite joy, from blind servitude, unbounded freedom. To be free is, precisely, to abolish ends. The innocence of the ceaseless change of things, as soon as one consents to it, represents the maximum liberty. The free mind willingly accepts what is necessary. Nietzsche's most profound concept is that the necessity of phenomena, if it is absolute, without rifts, does not imply any kind of restraint. Total acceptance of total necessity is his paradoxical definition of freedom. The question "free of what?" is thus replaced by "free for what?" Liberty coincides with heroism. It is the asceticism of the great man, "the bow bent to the breaking-point."

This magnificent consent, born of abundance and fullness of spirit, is the unreserved affirmation of human imperfection and suffering, of evil and murder, of all that is problematic and strange in our existence. It is born of an arrested wish to be what one is in a world that is what it is. "To consider oneself a fatality, not to wish to be other than one is . . ." Nietzschean asceticism, which begins with the recognition of fatality, ends in a deification of fate. The more implacable destiny is, the more it becomes worthy of adoration. A moral God, pity, and love are enemies of fate to the extent that they try to counterbalance it. Nietzsche wants no redemption. The joy of self-realization is the joy of annihilation. But only the individual is annihilated. The movement of rebellion, by which man demanded his own existence, disappears in the individual's absolute submission to the inevitable. *Amor fati* replaces what was an *odium fati*. "Every individual collaborates with the entire cosmos, whether we know it or not, whether we want it or not." The individual is lost in the destiny of the species and the eternal movement of the spheres. "Everything that has existed is eternal, the sea throws it back on the shore."

Nietzsche then turns to the origins of thought—to the pre-Socratics. These philosophers suppressed ultimate causes so as to leave intact the eternal values of the principles they upheld. Only power without purpose, only Heraclitus' "chance," is eternal. Nietzsche's whole effort is directed toward demonstrating the existence of the law that governs the eternal flux and of the element of chance in the inevitable: "A child is innocence and forgetfulness, a new beginning, a gamble, a wheel that spins automatically, a first step, the divine gift of being able to consent." The world is divine because the world is inconsequential. That is why art alone, by being equally inconsequential, is capable of grasping it. It is impossible to give a clear account of the world, but art can teach us to reproduce it—just as the world reproduces itself in the course of its eternal gyrations. The primordial sea indefatigably repeats the same words and casts up the same astonished beings on the same seashore. But at least he who consents to his own return and to the return of all things, who becomes an echo and an exalted echo, participates in the divinity of the world.

By this subterfuge, the divinity of man is finally introduced. The rebel, who at first denies God, finally aspires to replace Him. But Nietzsche's message is that the rebel can only become God by renouncing every form of rebellion, even the type of rebellion that produces gods to chastise humanity. "If there is a God, how can one tolerate not being God oneself?" There is, in fact, a god—namely, the world. To participate in its divinity, all that is necessary is to consent. "No longer to pray, but to give one's blessing," and the earth will abound in men-gods. To say yes to the world, to reproduce it, is simultaneously to re-create the world and oneself, to become the great artist, the creator. Nietzsche's message is summed up in the word *creation*, with the ambiguous meaning it has assumed. Nietzsche's sole admiration was for the egotism and severity proper to all creators. The transmutation of values consists only in replacing critical values by creative values; by respect and admiration for what exists. Divinity without immortality defines the extent of the creator's freedom. Dionysos, the earth-god, shrieks eternally as he is torn limb from limb. But at the same time he represents the agonized beauty that coincides with suffering. Nietzsche thought that to accept this earth and Dionysos was to accept his own sufferings. And to accept everything, both suffering and the supreme contradiction simultaneously, was to be king of all creation. Nietzsche agreed to pay the price for his kingdom. Only the "sad and suffering" world is true—the world is the only divinity. Like Empedocles, who threw himself into the crater of Mount Etna to find truth in the only place where it exists— namely, in the bowels of the earth—Nietzsche proposed that man should allow himself to be engulfed in the cosmos in order to rediscover his eternal divinity and to become Dionysos. *The Will to Power* ends, like Pascal's *Pensées*, of which it so often reminds us, with a wager. Man does not yet obtain assurance but only the wish for assurance, which is not at all the same thing. Nietzsche, too, hesitated on this brink: "That is what is unforgivable in you. You have the authority and you refuse to sign." Yet finally he had to sign. But the name of Dionysos immortalized only the notes to Ariadne, which he wrote when he was mad.

In a certain sense, rebellion, with Nietzsche, ends again in the exaltation of evil. The difference is that evil is no longer a revenge. It is accepted as one of the possible aspects of good and, with rather more conviction, as part of destiny. Thus he considers it as something to be avoided and also as a sort of remedy. In Nietzsche's mind, the only problem was to see that the human spirit bowed proudly to the inevitable. We know, however, his posterity and what kind of politics were to claim the authorization of the man who claimed to be the last antipolitical German. He dreamed of tyrants who were artists. But tyranny comes more naturally than art to mediocre men. "Rather Cesare Borgia than Parsifal," he exclaimed. He begat both Cæsar and Borgia, but devoid of the distinction of feeling which he attributed to the great men of the Renaissance. As a result of his insistence that the individual should bow before the eternity of the species and should submerge himself in the great cycle of time, race has been turned into a special aspect of the species, and the individual has been made to bow before this sordid god. The life of which he spoke with fear and trembling has been degraded to a sort of biology for domestic use. Finally, a race of vulgar overlords, with a blundering desire for power, adopted, in his name, the "anti-Semitic deformity" on which he never ceased to pour scorn.

. He believed in courage combined with intelligence, and that was what he called strength. Courage has been turned in his name against intelligence, and the virtues that were really his have thus been transformed into their opposite: blind violence. He confused freedom and solitude, as do all proud spirits. His "profound solitude at midday and at midnight" was nevertheless lost in the mechanized hordes that finally inundated Europe. Advocate of classic taste, of irony, of frugal defiance, aristocrat who had the courage to say that aristocracy consisted in practicing virtue without asking for a reason and that a man who had to have reasons for being honest was not to be trusted, addict of integrity ("integrity that has become an instinct, a passion"), stubborn supporter of the "supreme equity of the supreme intelligence that is the mortal enemy of fanaticism," he was set up, thirty-three years after his death, by his own countrymen as the master of lies and violence, and his ideas and virtues, made admirable by his sacrifice, have been rendered detestable. In the history of the intelligence, with the exception of Marx, Nietzsche's adventure has no equivalent; we shall never finish making reparation for the injustice done to him. Of course history records other philosophies that have been misconstrued and betrayed. But up to the time of Nietzsche and National

Socialism, it was quite without parallel that a process of thought—brilliantly illuminated by the nobility and by the sufferings of an exceptional mind—should have been demonstrated to the eyes of the world by a parade of lies and by the hideous accumulation of corpses in concentration camps. The doctrine of the superman led to the methodical creation of sub-men—a fact that doubtless should be denounced, but which also demands interpretation. If the final result of the great movement of rebellion in the nineteenth and twentieth centuries was to be this ruthless bondage, then surely rebellion should be rejected and Nietzsche's desperate cry to his contemporaries taken up: "My conscience and yours are no longer the same conscience."

We must first of all realize that we can never confuse Nietzsche with Rosenberg. We must be the advocates of Nietzsche. He himself has said so, denouncing in advance his bastard progeny: "he who has liberated his mind still has to purify himself." But the question is to find out if the liberation of the mind, as he conceived it, does not preclude purification. The very movement that comes to a head with Nietzsche, and that sustains him, has its laws and its logic, which, perhaps, explain the bloody travesty of his philosophy. Is there nothing in his work that can be used in support of definitive murder? Cannot the killers, provided they deny the spirit in favor of the letter (and even all that remains of the spirit in the letter), find their pretext in Nietzsche? The answer must be yes. From the moment that the methodical aspect of Nietzschean thought is neglected (and it is not certain that he himself always observed it), his rebellious logic knows no bounds.

We also remark that it is not in the Nietzschean refusal to worship idols that murder finds its justification, but in the passionate approbation that distinguishes Nietzsche's work. To say yes to everything supposes that one says yes to murder. Moreover, it expresses two ways of consenting to murder. If the slave says yes to everything, he consents to the existence of a master and to his own sufferings: Jesus teaches nonresistance. If the master says yes to everything, he consents to slavery and to the suffering of others; and the result is the tyrant and the glorification of murder. "Is it not laughable that we believe in a sacred, infrangible law—thou shalt not lie, thou shalt not kill—in an existence characterized by perpetual lying and perpetual murder?" Actually metaphysical rebellion, in its initial stages, was only a protest against the lie and the crime of existence. The Nietzschean affirmative, forgetful of the original negative, disavows rebellion at the same time that it disavows the ethic that refuses to accept the world as it is. Nietzsche clamored for a Roman Cæsar with the soul of Christ. To his mind, this was to say yes to both slave and master. But, in the last analysis, to say yes to both was to give one's blessing to the stronger of the two—namely, the master. Cæsar must inevitably renounce the domination of the mind and choose to rule in the realm of fact. "How can one make the best of crime?" asks Nietzsche, as a good professor faithful to his system. Cæsar must answer: by multiplying it. "When the ends are great," Nietzsche wrote to his own detriment, "humanity employs other standards and no longer judges crime as such even if it resorts to the most frightful means." He died in 1900, at the beginning of the century in which that pretension was to become fatal. It was in vain that he exclaimed in his hour of lucidity, "It is easy to talk about all sorts of immoral acts; but would one have the courage to carry them through? For example, I could not bear to break my word or to kill; I should languish, and eventually I should die as a result—that would be my fate." From the moment that assent was given to the totality of human experience, the way was open to others who, far from languishing, would gather strength from lies and murder. Nietzsche's responsibility lies in having legitimized, for reasons of method—and even if only for an instant—the opportunity for dishonesty of which Dostoievsky had already said that if one offered it to people, one could always be sure of seeing them rushing to seize it. But his involuntary responsibility goes still farther.

Nietzsche is exactly what he recognized himself as being: the most acute manifestation of nihilism's conscience. The decisive step that he compelled rebellion to take consists in making it jump from the negation of the ideal to the secularization of the ideal. Since the salvation of man is not achieved in God, it must be achieved on earth. Since the world has no direction, man, from the moment he accepts this, must give it one that will eventually lead to a superior type of humanity. Nietzsche laid claim to the direction of the future of the human race. "The task of governing the world is going to fall to our lot." And elsewhere: "The time is approaching when we shall have to struggle for the domination of the world, and this struggle will be fought in the name of philosophical principles." In these words he announced the twentieth century. But he was able to announce it because he was warned by the interior logic of nihilism and knew that one of its aims was ascendancy; and thus he prepared the way for this ascendancy.

There is freedom for man without God, as Nietzsche imagined him; in other words, for the solitary man. There is freedom at midday when the wheel of the world stops spinning and man consents to things as they are. But *what is* becomes *what will be,* and the ceaseless change of things must be accepted. The light finally grows dim, the axis of the day declines. Then history begins again and freedom must be sought in history; history must be accepted. Nietzscheism—the theory of the individual's will to power—was condemned to support the universal will to power. Nietzscheism was nothing without world domination. Nietzsche undoubtedly hated freethinkers and humanitarians. He took the words *freedom of thought* in their most extreme sense: the divinity of the individual mind. But he could not stop the freethinkers from partaking of the same historical fact as himself—the death of God—nor could he prevent the consequences being the same. Nietzsche saw clearly that humanitarianism was only a form of Christianity deprived of superior justification, which preserved final causes while rejecting the first cause. But he failed to perceive that the doctrines of socialist emancipation must, by an inevitable logic of nihilism, lead to what he himself had dreamed of: superhumanity.

Philosophy secularizes the ideal. But tyrants appear who soon secularize the philosophies that give them the right to do so. Nietzsche had already predicted this development in discussing Hegel, whose originality, according to him, consisted in inventing a pantheism in which evil, error, and suffering could no longer serve as arguments against the divinity. "But the State, the powers that be, immediately made use of this grandiose initiative." He himself, however, had conceived of a system in which crime could no longer serve as an argument and in which the only value resided in the divinity of man. This grandiose initiative also had to be put to use. National Socialism in this respect was only a transitory heir, only the speculative and rabid outcome of nihilism. In all other respects those who, in correcting Nietzsche with the help of Marx, will choose to assent only to history, and no longer to all of creation, will be perfectly logical. The rebel whom Nietzsche set on his kness before the cosmos will, from now on, kneel before history. What is surprising about that? Nietzsche, at least in his theory of super-humanity, and Marx before him, with his classless society, both replace the Beyond by the Later On. In that way Nietzsche betrayed the Greeks and the teachings of Jesus, who, according to him, replaced the Beyond by the Immediate. Marx, like Nietzsche, thought in strategic terms, and like Nietzsche hated formal virtue. Their two rebellions, both of which finish similarly in adhesion to a certain aspect of reality, end by merging into Marxism-Leninism and being incarnated in that caste, already mentioned by Nietzsche, which would "replace the priest, the teacher, the doctor." The fundamental difference is that Nietzsche, in awaiting the superman, proposed to assent to what exists and Marx to what is to come. For Marx, nature is to be subjugated in order to obey history; for Nietzsche, nature is to be obeyed in order to subjugate history. It is the difference between the Christian and the Greek. Nietzsche, at least, foresaw what was going to happen: "Modern socialism tends to create a form of secular Jesuitism, to make instruments of all men"; and again: "What we desire is well-being. . . . As a result we march toward a spiritual slavery such as has never been seen. . . . Intellectual Cæsarism hovers over every activity of the businessman and the philosopher." Placed in the crucible of Nietzschean philosophy, rebellion, in the intoxication of freedom, ends in biological or historical Cæsarism. The absolute negative had driven Stirner to deify crime simultaneously with the individual. But the absolute affirmative leads to universalizing murder and mankind simultaneously. Marxism-Leninism has really accepted the burden of Nietzsche's freewill by means of ignoring several Nietzschean virtues. The great rebel thus creates with his own hands, and for his own imprisonment, the implacable reign of necessity. Once he had escaped from God's prison, his first care was to construct the prison of history and of reason, thus putting the finishing touch to the camouflage and consecration of the nihilism whose conquest he claimed.

The Poets' Rebellion

*

If metaphysical rebellion refuses to assent and restricts itself to absolute negation, it condemns itself to passive acceptance. If it prostrates itself in adoration of what exists and renounces its right to dispute any part of reality, it is sooner or later compelled to act. Ivan Karamazov—who represents non-interference, but in a dolorous aspect—stands halfway between the two positions. Rebel poetry, at the end of the nineteenth and the beginning of the twentieth century, constantly oscillated between these two extremes: between literature and the will to power, between the irrational and the rational, the desperate dream and ruthless action. The rebel poets—above all, the surrealists—light the way that leads from passive acceptance to action, along a spectacular short-cut.

Hawthorne was able to say of Melville that, as an unbeliever, he was extremely uneasy in his unbelief. It can equally well be said of the poets who rushed to assault the heavens, with the intent of turning everything upside down, that by so doing they affirmed their desperate nostalgia for order. As an ultimate contradiction, they wanted to extract reason from unreason and to systematize the irrational. These heirs of romanticism claimed to make poetry exemplary and to find, in its most harrowing aspects, the real way of life. They deified blasphemy and transformed poetry into experience and into a means of action. Until their time those who claimed to influence men and events, at least in the Occident, did so in the name of rational rules. On the contrary, surrealism, after Rimbaud, wanted to find constructive rules in insanity and destruction. Rimbaud, through his work and only through his work, pointed out the path, but with the blinding, momentary illumination of a flash of lightning. Surrealism excavated this path and codified its discoveries. By its excesses as well as by its retreats, it gave the last and most magnificent expression to a practical theory of irrational rebellion at the very same time when, on another path, rebellious thought was founding the cult of absolute reason. Lautréamont and Rimbaud—its sources of inspiration—demonstrate by what stages the irrational desire to accept appearances can lead the rebel to adopt courses of action completely destructive to freedom.

Lautréamont and Banality

Lautréamont demonstrates that the rebel dissimulates the desire to accept appearance behind the desire for banality. In either case, whether he abases or vaunts himself, the rebel wants to be other than he is, even when he is prepared to be recognized for what he really is. The blasphemies and the conformity of Lautréamont illustrate this unfortunate contradiction, which is resolved in his case in the desire to be nothing at all. Far from being a recantation, as is generally supposed, the same passion for annihilation explains Maldoror's invocation of the primeval night and the laborious banalities of the *Poésies*.

Lautréamont makes us understand that rebellion is adolescent. Our most effective terrorists, whether they are armed with bombs or with poetry, hardly escape from infancy. The *Songs of Maldoror* are the works of a highly talented schoolboy; their pathos lies precisely in the contradictions of a child's mind ranged against creation and against itself. Like the Rimbaud of the *Illuminations*, beating against the confines of the world, the poet chooses the apocalypse and destruction rather than accept the impossible principles that make him what he is in a world such as it is.

"I offer myself to defend mankind," says Lautréamont, without wishing to be ingenuous. Is Maldoror, then, the angel of pity? In a certain sense he is, in that he pities himself. Why? That remains to be seen. But pity deceived, outraged, inadmissible, and unadmitted will lead him to strange extremities. Maldoror, in his own words, received life like a wound and forbade suicide to heal the scar (*sic*). Like Rimbaud he is the one who suffers and who rebelled; each, being strangely reluctant to say that he is rebelling against what he is, gives the rebel's eternal alibi: love of mankind.

The man who offers himself to defend mankind at the same time writes: "Show me one man who is good." This perpetual vacillation is part of nihilist rebellion. We rebel against the injustice done to ourselves and to mankind. But in the moment of lucidity, when we simultaneously perceive the legitimacy of this rebellion and its futility, the frenzy of negation is extended to the very thing that we claimed to be defending. Not being able to atone for injustice by the elevation of justice, we choose to submerge it in an even greater injustice, which is finally confounded with annihilation. "The evil you have done me is too great, too great the evil I have done you, for it to be involuntary." In order not to be overcome with self-hatred, one's innocence must be proclaimed, an impossibly bold step for one man alone, for self-knowledge will prevent him. But at least one can declare that everyone is innocent, though they may be treated as guilty. God is then the criminal.

From the romantics to Lautréamont, there is, therefore, no real progress, except in style. Lautréamont resuscitates, once again, with a few improvements, the figure of the God of Abraham and the image of the Luciferian rebel. He places God "on a throne built of excrement, human and golden," on which sits, "with imbecile pride, his body covered with a shroud made of unwashed sheets, he who styles himself the Creator." "The horrible Eternal One with the features of a viper," "the crafty bandit" who can be seen "stoking the fires in which young and old perish," rolls drunkenly in the gutter, or seeks base pleasures in the brothel. God is not dead, he has fallen. Face to face with the fallen deity, Maldoror appears as a conventional cavalier in a black cloak. He is the Accursed. "Eyes must not witness the hideous aspect which the Supreme Being, with a smile of intense hatred, has granted me." He has forsworn everything—"father, mother, Providence, love, ideals—so as to think no longer of anything

else but himself." Racked with pride, this hero has all
the illusions of the metaphysical dandy: "A face that is
more than human, sad with the sadness of the universe,
beautiful as an act of suicide." Like the romantic rebel,
Maldoror, despairing of divine justice, will take the side
of evil. To cause suffering and, in causing it, to suffer,
that is his lot. The *Songs* are veritable litanies of evil.

At this point mankind is no longer even defended.
On the contrary, "to attack that wild beast, man, with
every possible weapon, and to attack the creator . . ." that
is the intention announced by the *Songs*. Overwhelmed at
the thought of having God as an enemy, intoxicated with
the solitude experienced by great criminals ("I alone
against humanity"), Maldoror goes to war against creation and its author. The *Songs* exalt "the sanctity of
crime," announce an increasing series of "glorious crimes,"
and stanza 20 of Song II even inaugurates a veritable
pedagogy of crime and violence.

Such a burning ardor is, at this period, merely conventional. It costs nothing. Lautréamont's real originality
lies elsewhere.[1] The romantics maintained with the greatest
care the fatal opposition between human solitude and
divine indifference—the literary expressions of this solitude
being the isolated castle and the dandy. But Lautréamont's
work deals with a more profound drama. It is quite apparent that he found this solitude insupportable and that,
ranged against creation, he wished to destroy its limits.
Far from wanting to fortify the reign of humanity with
crenelated towers, he wishes to merge it with all other
reigns. He brought back creation to the shores of the
primeval seas where morality, as well as every other problem, loses all meaning—including the problem, which
he considers so terrifying, of the immortality of the soul.
He had no desire to create a spectacular image of the
rebel, or of the dandy, opposed to creation, but to mingle
mankind and the world together in the same general destruction. He attacked the very frontier that separates
mankind from the universe. Total freedom, the freedom
of crime in particular, supposes the destruction of human

[1] It accounts for the difference between Song I, published
separately, which is Byronic in a rather banal way, and the
other Songs, which resound with a monstrous rhetoric.

frontiers. It is not enough to condemn oneself and all mankind to execration. The reign of mankind must still be brought back to the level of the reign of the instinct. We find in Lautréamont this refusal to recognize rational consciousness, this return to the elementary which is one of the marks of a civilization in revolt against itself. It is no longer a question of recognizing appearances, by making a determined and conscious effort, but of no longer existing at all on the conscious level.

All the creatures that appear in the *Songs* are amphibious, because Maldoror rejects the earth and its limitations. The flora is composed of algæ and seaweed. Maldoror's castle is built on the waters. His native land is the timeless sea. The sea—a double symbol—is simultaneously the place of annihilation and of reconciliation. It quenches, in its own way, the thirst of souls condemned to scorn themselves and others, and the thirst for oblivion. Thus the *Songs* replace the *Metamorphoses*, and the timeless smile is replaced by the laughter of a mouth slashed with a razor, by the image of a gnashing, frantic, travesty of humor. This bestiary cannot contain all the meanings that have been given to it, but undoubtedly it discloses a desire for annihilation which has its origins in the very darkest places of rebellion. The "stultify yourselves" of Pascal takes on a literal sense with Lautréamont. Apparently he could not bear the cold and implacable clarity one must endure in order to live. "My subjectivity and one creator—that is too much for one brain." And so he chose to reduce life, and his work, to the flash of a cuttlefish's fin in the midst of its cloud of ink. The beautiful passage where Maldoror couples with a female shark on the high seas "in a long, chaste, and frightful copulation" —above all, the significant passage in which Maldoror, transformed into an octopus, attacks the Creator—are clear expressions of an escape beyond the frontiers of existence and of a convulsive attack on the laws of nature.

Those who see themselves banished from the harmonious fatherland where justice and passion finally strike an even balance still prefer, to solitude, the barren kingdoms where words have no more meaning and where force and the instincts of blind creatures reign. This challenge is, at the same time, a mortification. The battle with the angel, in Song II, ends in the defeat and putrefaction of the angel. Heaven and earth are then brought back and intermingled in the liquid chasms of primordial life. Thus the man-shark of the *Songs* "only acquired the new change in the extremities of his arms and legs as an expiatory punishment for some unknown crime." There is, in fact, a crime, or the illusion of a crime (is it homosexuality?) in Maldoror's virtually unknown life. No reader of the *Songs* can avoid the idea that this book is in need of a *Stavrogin's Confession*.

But there is no confession and we find in the *Poésies* a redoubling of that mysterious desire for expiation. The spirit appropriate to certain forms of rebellion which consists, as we shall see, in re-establishing reason at the end of the irrational adventure, of rediscovering order by means of disorder and of voluntarily loading oneself down with chains still heavier than those from which release was sought, is described in this book with such a desire for simplification and with such cynicism that this change of attitude must definitely have a meaning. The *Songs*, which exalted absolute negation, are followed by a theory of absolute assent, and uncompromising rebellion is succeeded by complete conformity—all this with total lucidity. The *Poésies*, in fact, give us the best explanation of the *Songs*. "Despair, fed by the prejudices of hallucination, imperturbably leads literature to the mass abrogation of laws both social and divine, and to theoretical and practical wickedness." The *Poésies* also denounce "the culpability of a writer who rolls on the slopes of the void and pours scorn on himself with cries of joy." But they prescribe no other remedy for this evil than metaphysical conformity: "Since the poetry of doubt arrives, in this way, at such a point of theoretical wickedness and mournful despair, it is poetry that is radically false; for the simple reason that it discusses principles, and principles should not be discussed" (letter to Darassé). In short, his reasoning recapitulates the morality of a choirboy or of an infantry manual. But conformity can be passionate, and thereby out of the ordinary. When the victory of the malevolent eagle over the dragon hope has been proclaimed, Maldoror can still obstinately repeat that the burden of his song is nothing but hope, and can write: "With my voice and with the solemnity of the days of my glory, I recall you, O blessed Hope, to my deserted dwelling"—he must still try to convince. To console humanity, to treat it as a brother, to return to Confucius, Buddha, Socrates, Jesus Christ, "moralists who wandered through villages, dying of hunger" (which is of doubtful historical accuracy), are still the projects of despair. Thus virtue and an ordered life have a nostalgic appeal in the midst of vice. For Lautréamont refuses to pray, and Christ for him is only a moralist. What he proposes, or rather what he proposes to himself, is agnosticism and the fulfillment of duty. Such a sound program, unhappily, supposes surrender, the calm of evening, a heart untouched by bitterness, and untroubled contemplation. Lautréamont rebels when he suddenly writes: "I know no other grace but that of being born." But one can sense his clenched teeth when he adds: "An impartial mind finds that enough." But no mind is impartial when confronted with life and death. With Lautréamont, the rebel flees to the desert. But this desert of conformity is as dreary as Rimbaud's Harrar. The taste for the absolute and the frenzy of annihilation sterilize him again. Just as Maldoror wanted total rebellion, Lautréamont, for the same reasons, demands absolute banality. The exclamation of awareness which he tried to drown in the primeval seas, to confuse with the howl of the beast, which at another moment he tried to smother in the adoration of mathematics, he now wants to stifle by applying a dismal conformity. The rebel now tries to turn a deaf ear to the call that urges him toward the being who lies at the heart of his rebellion. The important thing is to exist no longer—either by refusing to be anything at all or by accepting to be no matter what. In either case it is a purely artificial convention. Banality, too, is an attitude.

Conformity is one of the nihilistic temptations of rebellion which dominate a large part of our intellectual history. It demonstrates how the rebel who takes to action is tempted to succumb, if he forgets his origins, to the most absolute conformity. And so it explains the twentieth century. Lautréamont, who is usually hailed as the bard of pure rebellion, on the contrary proclaims the advent of the taste for intellectual servitude which flourishes in

the contemporary world. The *Poésies* are only a preface
to a "future work" of which we can only surmise the con-
tents and which was to have been the ideal end-result of
literary rebellion. But this book is being written today,
despite Lautréamont, in millions of copies, by bureaucratic order. Of course, genius cannot be separated from
banality. But it is not a question of the banality of others
—the banality that we vainly try to capture and which
itself captures the creative writer, where necessary, with
the help of the censors. For the creative writer it is a
question of his own form of banality, which must be completely created. Every genius is at once extraordinary and
banal. He is nothing if he is only one or the other. We
must remember this when thinking of rebellion. It has
its dandies and its menials, but it does not recognize its
legitimate sons.

Surrealism and Revolution

This is not the place to deal at length with Rimbaud.
Everything that can be said about him—and even more,
unfortunately—has already been said. It is worth pointing
out, however, for it concerns our subject, that only in his
work was Rimbaud the poet of rebellion. His life, far from
justifying the myth it created, only illustrates (an objective
perusal of the letters from Harrar suffices to prove this)
the fact that he surrendered to the worst form of nihilism
imaginable. Rimbaud has been deified for renouncing his
genius, as if his renunciation implied superhuman virtue.
It must be pointed out, however, despite the fact that by
doing so we disqualify the alibis of our contemporaries,
that genius alone—and not the renunciation of genius—
implies virtue. Rimbaud's greatness does not lie in the
first poems from Charleville nor in his trading at Harrar.
It shines forth at the moment when, in giving the most
peculiarly appropriate expression to rebellion that it has
ever received, he simultaneously proclaims his triumph and
his agony, his conception of a life beyond the confines of
this world and the inescapability of the world, the yearning
for the unattainable and reality brutally determined on

restraint, the rejection of morality and the irresistible compulsion to duty. At the moment when he carries in his breast both illumination and the darkness of hell, when he hails and insults beauty, and creates, from an insoluble conflict, the intricate counterpoint of an exquisite song, he is the poet of rebellion—the greatest of all. The order in which he wrote his two great works is of no importance. In any case there was very little time between the conception of the two books, and any artist knows, with the certainty born of experience, that Rimbaud simultaneously carried the seeds of the *Season in Hell (Une Saison en Enfer)* and the *Illuminations* within him. Though he wrote them one after the other, there is no doubt that he experienced the suffering of both of them at the same time. This contradiction, which killed him, was the real source of his genius.

But where, then, is the virtue of someone who refuses to face the contradiction and betrays his own genius before having drunk it to the last bitter drop? Rimbaud's silence is not a new method of rebelling; at least, we can no longer say so after the publication of the Harrar letters. His metamorphosis is undoubtedly mysterious. But there is also a mystery attached to the banality achieved by brilliant young girls whom marriage transforms into adding or knitting machines. The myth woven around Rimbaud supposes and affirms that nothing was possible after the *Season in Hell*. But what is impossible for the supremely gifted poet or for the inexhaustibly creative writer? How can we imagine anything to follow *Moby Dick, The Trial, Zarathustra, The Possessed?* Nevertheless, they were followed by great works, which instruct, implement, and bear witness to what is finest in the writer, and which only come to an end at his death. Who can fail to regret the work that would have been greater than the *Season in Hell* and of which we have been deprived by Rimbaud's abdication?

Can Abyssinia be considered as a monastery; is it Christ who shut Rimbaud's mouth? Such a Christ would be the kind of man who nowadays lords it over the cashier's desk in a bank, to judge by the letters in which the unhappy poet talks only about his money which he wants

to see "wisely invested" and "bringing in regular divi
dends." [2] The man who exulted under torture, who
hurled curses at God and at beauty, who hardened himself
in the harsh atmosphere of crime, now only wants to
marry someone "with a future." The mage, the seer, the
convict who lived perpetually in the shadow of the penal
colony, the man-king on a godless earth, always carried
seventeen pounds of gold in a belt worn uncomfortably
round his stomach, which he complained gave him dysen-
tery. Is this the mythical hero, worshipped by so many
young men who, though they do not spit in the face of
the world, would die of shame at the mere idea of such
a belt? To maintain the myth, those decisive letters must
be ignored. It is easy to see why they have been so little
commented upon. They are a sacrilege, as truth sometimes
is. A great and praiseworthy poet, the greatest of his time,
a dazzling oracle—Rimbaud is all of these things. But he
is not the man-god, the burning inspiration, the monk
of poetry as he is often presented. The man only recap-
tured his greatness in the hospital bed in which, at the
hour of his painful end, even his mediocrity becomes
moving: "How unlucky I am, how very unlucky I am . . .
and I've money on me that I can't even keep an eye on!"
The defiant cry of those last wretched moments: "No, no,
now I rebel against death!" happily restores Rimbaud to
that part of common human experience which involun-
tarily coincides with greatness. The young Rimbaud comes
to life again on the brink of the abyss and with him revives the rebellion of the times when his imprecations
against life were only expressions of despair at the thought
of death. It is at this point that the bourgeois trader once
more rejoins the tortured adolescent whom we so much
admired. He recaptures his youth in the terror and bitter
pain finally experienced by those who do not know how
to attain happiness. Only at this point does his passion,
and with it his truth, begin.

Moreover, Harrar was actually foretold in his work,
but in the form of his final abdication. "And best of all,

[2] It is only fair to note that the tone of these letters might
be explained by the people to whom they are written. But they
do not suggest that Rimbaud is making a great effort to lie. Not
one word betrays the Rimbaud of former times.

a drunken sleep on the beach." The fury of annihilation, appropriate to every rebel, then assumes its most common form. The apocalypse of crime—as conceived by Rimbaud in the person of the prince who insatiably slaughters his subjects—and endless licentiousness are rebellious themes that will be taken up again by the surrealists. But finally, even with Rimbaud, nihilist dejection prevailed; the struggle, the crime itself, proved too exacting for his exhausted mind. The seer who drank, if we may venture to say so, in order not to forget ended by finding in drunkenness the heavy sleep so well known to our contemporaries. One can sleep on the beach, or at Aden. And one consents, no longer actively, but passively, to accept the order of the world, even if the order is degrading. Rimbaud's silence is also a preparation for the silence of authority, which hovers over minds resigned to everything save to the necessity of putting up a fight. Rimbaud's great intellect, suddenly subordinated to money, proclaims the advent of other demands, which are at first excessive and which will later be put to use by the police. To be nothing—that is the cry of the mind exhausted by its own rebellion. This leads to the problem of suicide of the mind, which, after all, is less respectable than the surrealists' suicide, and more fraught with consequences. Surrealism itself, coming at the end of this great act of rebellion, is only significant because it attempted to perpetuate that aspect of Rimbaud which alone evokes our sympathy. Deriving the rules for a rebellious asceticism from the letter about the seer and the system it implies, he illustrates the struggle between the will to be and the desire for annihilation, between the yes and the no, which we have discovered again and again at every stage of rebellion. For all these reasons, rather than repeat the endless commentaries that surround Rimbaud's work, it seemed preferable to rediscover him and to follow him among his successors.

Absolute rebellion, total insubordination, sabotage on principle, the humor and cult of the absurd—such is the nature of surrealism, which defines itself, in its primary intent, as the incessant examination of all values. The refusal to draw any conclusions is flat, decisive, and provocative. "We are specialists in rebellion." Surrealism, which,

according to Aragon, is a machine for capsizing the mind,
was first conjured up by the Dadaist movement, whose
romantic origins and anemic dandyism must be noted.[3]
Non-signification and contradiction are therefore culti-
vated for their own sakes. "The real Dadaists are against
Dada. Everyone is a director of Dada." Or again: "What
is good? What is ugly? What is great, strong, weak . . . ?
Don't know! Don't know!" These parlor nihilists were
obviously threatened with having to act as slaves to the
strictest orthodoxies. But there is something more in surrealism than standard nonconformism, the legacy left by
Rimbaud, which, in fact, Breton recapitulates as follows:
"Must we abandon all hope at that particular point?"

An urgent appeal to absent life is reinforced by a
total rejection of the present world, as Breton's arrogant
statement indicates: "Incapable of accepting the fate
assigned to me, my highest perceptions outraged by this
denial of justice, I refrain from adapting my existence to
the ridiculous conditions of existence here below." The
mind, according to Breton, can find no point of rest
either in this life or beyond it. Surrealism wants to find a
solution to this endless anxiety. It is "a cry of the mind
which turns against itself and finally takes the desperate
decision to throw off its bonds." It protests against death
and "the laughable duration" of a precarious condition.
Thus surrealism places itself at the mercy of impatience.
It exists in a condition of wounded frenzy: at once inflexible and self-righteous, with the consequent implication
of a moral philosophy. Surrealism, the gospel of chaos,
found itself compelled, from its very inception, to create
an order. But at first it only dreamed of destruction—by
poetry, to begin with—on the plane of imprecation, and
later by the use of actual weapons. The trial of the real
world has become, by logical development, the trial of
creation.

Surrealist irreligion is methodical and rational. At
first it established itself on the idea of the absolute non-
culpability of man, to whom one should render "all the
power that he has been capable of putting into the word
God." As in every history of rebellion, this idea of abso-

[3] Jarry, one of the masters of Dadaism, is the last incarnation, peculiar rather than brilliant, of the metaphysical dandy.

lute non-culpability, springing from despair, was little by little transformed into a mania for punishment. The surrealists, while simultaneously exalting human innocence, believed that they could exalt murder and suicide. They spoke of suicide as a solution and Crevel, who considered this solution "the most probable, just, and definitive," killed himself, as did Rigaut and Vaché. Later Aragon was to condemn the "babblers about suicide." Nevertheless the fact remains that to extol annihilation, without personal involvement, is not a very honorable course. On this point surrealism has retained, from the *"littérature"* it despised, the most facile excuses and has justified Rigaud's staggering remark: "You are all poets, and I myself am on the side of death."

Surrealism did not rest there. It chose as its hero Violette Nozière or the anonymous common-law criminal, affirming in this way, in the face of crime, the innocence of man. But it also was rash enough to say—and this is the statement that André Breton must have regretted ever since 1933—that the simplest surrealist act consisted in going out into the street, revolver in hand, and shooting at random into the crowd. Whoever refuses to recognize any other determining factor apart from the individual and his desires, any priority other than that of the unconscious, actually succeeds in rebelling simultaneously against society and against reason. The theory of the gratuitous act is the culmination of the demand for absolute freedom. What does it matter if this freedom ends by being embodied in the solitude defined by Jarry: "When I'll have collected all the ready cash, in the world, I'll kill everybody and go away." The essential thing is that every obstacle should be denied and that the irrational should be triumphant. What, in fact, does this apology for murder signify if not that, in a world without meaning and without honor, only the desire for existence, in all its forms, is legitimate? The instinctive joy of being alive, the stimulus of the unconscious, the cry of the irrational, are the only pure truths that must be professed. Everything that stands in the way of desire—principally society—must therefore be mercilessly destroyed. Now we can understand André Breton's remark about Sade: "Certainly man no longer consents to unite with nature except in crime; it remains to be seen if this is not one of the wildest, the most incontestable, ways of loving." It is easy to see that he is talking of love without an object, which is love as experienced by people who are torn asunder. But this empty, avid love, this insane desire for possession, is precisely the love that society inevitably thwarts. That is why Breton, who still bears the stigma of his declarations, was able to sing the praises of treason and declare (as the surrealists have tried to prove) that violence is the only adequate mode of expression.

But society is not only composed of individuals. It is also an institution. Too well-mannered to kill everybody, the surrealists, by the very logic of their attitude, came to consider that, in order to liberate desire, society must first be overthrown. They chose to serve the revolutionary movement of their times. From Walpole and Sade—with an inevitability that comprises the subject of this book—surrealists passed on to Helvétius and Marx. But it is obvious that it is not the study of Marxism that led them to revolution.[4] Quite the contrary: surrealism is involved in an incessant effort to reconcile, with Marxism, the inevitable conclusions that led it to revolution. We can say, without being paradoxical, that the surrealists arrived at Marxism on account of what, today, they most detest in Marx. Knowing the basis and the nobility of the motives that compelled him, particularly when one has shared the same lacerating experiences, one hesitates to remind André Breton that his movement implied the establishment of "ruthless authority" and of dictatorship, of political fanaticism, the refusal of free discussion, and the necessity of the death penalty. The peculiar vocabulary of that period is also astonishing ("sabotage," "informer," etc.) in that it is the vocabulary of a police-dominated revolution. But these frenetics wanted "any sort of revolution," no matter what as long as it rescued them from the world of shopkeepers and compromise in which they were forced to live. In that they could not have the best, they still preferred the worst. In that respect they were nihilists. They were not aware of the fact that those among them who were, in

[4] The Communists who joined the party as a result of having studied Marx can be counted on the fingers of one hand. They are first converted and then they read the Scriptures.

the future, to remain faithful to Marxism were faithful
at the same time to their initial nihilism. The real destruction of language, which the surrealists so obstinately
wanted, does not lie in incoherence or automatism. It lies
in the word *order*. It was pointless for Aragon to begin
with a denunciation of the "shameful pragmatic attitude,"
for in that attitude he finally found total liberation from
morality, even if that liberation coincided with another
form of servitude. The surrealist who meditated most
profoundly about this problem, Pierre Naville, in trying
to find the denominator common to revolutionary action
and surrealist action, localized it, with considerable pene-
tration, in pessimism, meaning in "the intention of accom-
panying man to his downfall and of overlooking nothing
that could ensure that his perdition might be useful."
This mixture of Machiavellianism and Augustinism in
fact explains twentieth-century rebellion; no more audacious expression can be given to the nihilism of the times.
The renegades of surrealism were faithful to most of the
principles of nihilism. In a certain way, they wanted to
die. If André Breton and a few others finally broke with
Marxism, it was because there was something in them
beyond nihilism, a second loyalty to what is purest in
the origins of rebellion: they did not want to die.

Certainly, the surrealists wanted to profess materialism. "We are pleased to recognize as one of the prime
causes of the mutiny on board the battleship *Potemkin*
that terrible piece of meat." But there is not with them,
as with the Marxists, a feeling of friendship, even intellectual, for that piece of meat. Putrid meat typifies only the
real world, which in fact gives birth to revolt, but against
itself. It explains nothing, even though it justifies everything. Revolution, for the surrealists, was not an end to be
realized day by day, in action, but an absolute and consolatory myth. It was "the real life, like love," of which
Eluard spoke, who at that time had no idea that his friend
Kalandra would die of that sort of life. They wanted the
"communism of genius," not the other form of Communism. These peculiar Marxists declared themselves in
rebellion against history and extolled the heroic individual.
"History is governed by laws, which are conditioned by the
cowardice of individuals." André Breton wanted revolu-

tion and love together—and they are incompatible. Revolution consists in loving a man who does not yet exist. But he who loves a living being, if he really loves, can only consent to die for the sake of the being he loves. In reality, revolution for André Breton was only a particular aspect of rebellion, while for Marxists and, in general, for all political persuasions, only the contrary is true. Breton was not trying to create, by action, the promised land that was supposed to crown history. One of the fundamental theses of surrealism is, in fact, that there is no salvation. The advantage of revolution was not that it gives mankind happiness, "abominable material comfort." On the contrary, according to Breton, it should purify and illuminate man's tragic condition. World revolution and the terrible sacrifices it implies would only bring one advantage: "preventing the completely artificial precariousness of the social condition from screening the real precariousness of the human condition." Quite simply, for Breton, this form of progress was excessive. One might as well say that revolution should be enrolled in the service of the inner asceticism by which individual men can transfigure reality into the supernatural, "the brilliant revenge of man's imagination." With André Breton, the supernatural holds the same place as the rational does with Hegel. Thus it would be impossible to imagine a more complete antithesis to the political philosophy of Marxism. The lengthy hesitations of those whom Artaud called the Amiels of revolution are easily explained. The surrealists were more different from Marx than were reactionaries like Joseph de Maistre, for example. The reactionaries made use of the tragedy of existence to reject revolution—in other words, to preserve a historical situation. The Marxists made use of it to justify revolution—in other words, to create another historical situation. Both make use of the human tragedy to further their pragmatic ends. But Breton made use of revolution to consummate the tragedy and, in spite of the title of his magazine, made use of revolution to further the surrealist adventure.

Finally, the definitive rupture is explained if one considers that Marxism insisted on the submission of the irrational, while the surrealists rose to defend irrationality to the death. Marxism tended toward the conquest of totality, and surrealism, like all spiritual experiences, tended toward unity. Totality can demand the submission of the irrational, if rationalism suffices to conquer the world. But the desire for unity is more demanding. It does not suffice that everything should be rational. It wants, above all, the rational and the irrational to be reconciled on the same level. There is no unity that supposes any form of mutilation.

For André Breton, totality could be only a stage, a necessary stage perhaps, but certainly inadequate, on the way that leads to unity. Here we find once again the theme of All or Nothing. Surrealism tends toward universality, and the curious but profound reproach that Breton makes to Marx consists in saying quite justifiably that the latter is not universal. The surrealists wanted to reconcile Marx's "let us transform the world" with Rimbaud's "let us change life." But the first leads to the conquest of the totality of the world and the second to the conquest of the unity of life. Paradoxically, every form of totality is restrictive. In the end, the two formulas succeeded in splitting the surrealist group. By choosing Rimbaud, Breton demonstrated that surrealism was not concerned with action, but with asceticism and spiritual experience. He again gave first place to what composed the profound originality of his movement: the restoration of the sacred and the conquest of unity, which make surrealism so invaluable for a consideration of the problem of rebellion. The more he elaborated on this original concept, the more irreparably he separated himself from his political companions, and at the same time from some of his first manifestoes.

André Breton never, actually, wavered in his support of surrealism—the fusion of a dream and of reality, the sublimation of the old contradiction between the ideal and the real. We know the surrealist solution: concrete irrationality, objective risk. Poetry is the conquest, the only possible conquest, of the "supreme position." "A certain position of the mind from where life and death, the real and the imaginary, the past and the future . . . cease to be perceived in a contradictory sense." What is this supreme position that should mark the "colossal abortion of the Hegelian system"? It is the search for the summit-abyss, familiar to the mystics. Actually, it is the mysticism without God which demonstrates and quenches the rebel's thirst for the absolute. The essential enemy of surrealism is rationalism. Breton's method, moreover, presents the peculiar spectacle of a form of Occidental thought in which the principle of analogy is continually favored to the detriment of the principles of identity and contradiction. More precisely, it is a question of dissolving contradictions in the fires of love and desire and of demolishing the walls of death. Magic rites, primitive or naïve civilizations, alchemy, the language of flowers, fire, or sleepless nights, are so many miraculous stages on the way to unity and the philosophers' stone. If surrealism did not change the world, it furnished it with a few strange myths which partly justified Nietzsche's announcement of the return of the Greeks. Only partly, because he was referring to unenlightened Greece, the Greece of mysteries and dark gods. Finally, just as Nietzsche's experience culminated in the acceptance of the light of day, surrealist experience culminates in the exaltation of the darkness of night, the agonized and obstinate cult of the tempest. Breton, according to his own statements, understood that, despite everything, life was a gift. But his compliance could never shed the full light of day, the light that all of us need. "There is too much of the north in me," he said, "for me to be a man who complies entirely."

He nevertheless often diminished, to his own detriment, the importance of negation and advanced the positive claims of rebellion. He chose severity rather than silence and retained only the "demand for morality," which, according to Bataille, first gave life to surrealism: "To substitute a new morality for current morality, which is the cause of all our evils." Of course he did not succeed (nor has anybody in our time) in the attempt to found a new morality. But he never despaired of being able to do so. Confronted with the horror of a period in which man, whom he wanted to magnify, has been persistently degraded in the name of certain principles that surrealism adopted, Breton felt constrained to propose, provisionally, a return to traditional morality. That represents a hesitation perhaps. But it is the hesitation of nihilism and the real progress of rebellion. After all, when he could not give himself the morality and the values of whose necessity he was clearly aware, we know very well that Breton chose love. In the general meanness of his times—and this cannot be forgotten—he is the only person who wrote profoundly above love. Love is the entranced morality that served this exile as a native land. Of course, a dimension is still missing here. Surrealism, in that it is neither politics nor religion, is perhaps only an unbearable form of wisdom. But it is also the absolute proof that there is no comfortable form of wisdom: "We want, we shall have, the hereafter in our lifetime," Breton has admirably exclaimed. While reason embarks on action and sets its armies marching on the world, the splendid night in which Breton delights announces dawns that have not yet broken, and, as well, the advent of the poet of our renaissance: René Char.

Nihilism and History

✳

One hundred and fifty years of metaphysical rebellion and of nihilism have witnessed the persistent reappearance, under different guises, of the same ravaged countenance: the face of human protest. All of them, decrying the human condition and its creator, have affirmed the solitude of man and the nonexistence of any kind of morality. But at the same time they have all tried to construct a purely terrestrial kingdom where their chosen principles will hold sway. As rivals of the Creator, they have inescapably been led to the point of reconstructing creation according to their own concepts. Those who rejected, for the sake of the world they had just created, all other principles but desire and power, have rushed to suicide or madness and have proclaimed the apocalypse. As for the rest, who wanted to create their own principles, they have chosen pomp and ceremony, the world of appearances, or banality, or again murder and destruction. But Sade and the romantics, Karamazov or Nietzsche only entered the world of death because they wanted to discover the true life. So that by a process of inversion, it is the desperate appeal for order that rings through this insane universe. Their conclusions have only proved disastrous or destructive to freedom from the moment they laid aside the burden of rebellion, fled the tension that it implies, and chose the comfort of tyranny or of servitude.

Human insurrection, in its exalted and tragic forms, is only, and can only be, a prolonged protest against death, a violent accusation against the universal death penalty. In every case that we have come across, the protest is always directed at everything in creation which is dissonant, opaque, or promises the solution of continuity. Essentially, then, we are dealing with a perpetual demand for unity. The rejection of death, the desire for immortality and for clarity, are the mainsprings of all these extravagances, whether sublime or puerile. Is it only a cowardly and personal refusal to die? No, for many of these rebels have paid the ultimate price in order to live up to their own demands. The rebel does not ask for life, but for reasons for living. He rejects the consequences implied by death. If nothing lasts, then nothing is justified; everything that dies is deprived of meaning. To fight against death amounts to claiming that life has a meaning, to fighting for order and for unity.

The protest against evil which is at the very core of metaphysical revolt is significant in this regard. It is not the suffering of a child, which is repugnant in itself, but the fact that the suffering is not justified. After all, pain, exile, or confinement are sometimes accepted when dictated by good sense or by the doctor. In the eyes of the rebel, what is missing from the misery of the world, as well as from its moments of happiness, is some principle by which they can be explained. The insurrection against evil is, above all, a demand for unity. The rebel obstinately confronts a world condemned to death and the impenetrable obscurity of the human condition with his demand for life and absolute clarity. He is seeking, without knowing it, a moral philosophy or a religion. Rebellion, even though it is blind, is a form of asceticism. Therefore, if the rebel blasphemes, it is in the hope of finding a new god. He staggers under the shock of the first and most profound of all religious experiences, but it is a disenchanted religious experience. It is not rebellion itself that is noble, but its aims, even though its achievements are at times ignoble.

At least we must know how to recognize the ignoble ends it achieves. Each time that it deifies the total rejection, the absolute negation, of what exists, it destroys. Each time that it blindly accepts what exists and gives voice to absolute assent, it destroys again. Hatred of the creator can turn to hatred of creation or to exclusive and defiant love of what exists. But in both cases it ends in murder and loses the right to be called rebellion. One can be nihilist in two ways, in both by having an intemperate recourse to absolutes. Apparently there are rebels who want to die and those who want to cause death. But they are identical, consumed with desire for the true life, frustrated by their desire for existence and therefore preferring generalized injustice to mutilated justice. At this pitch of indignation, reason becomes madness. If it is true that the instinctive rebellion of the human heart advances gradually through the centuries toward its most complete realization, it has also grown, as we have seen, in blind audacity, to the inordinate extent of deciding to answer universal murder by metaphysical assassination.

The *even if*, which we have already recognized as marking the most important moment of metaphysical rebellion, is in any case only fulfilled in absolute destruction. It is not the nobility of rebellion that illuminates the world today, but nihilism. And it is the consequences of nihilism that we must retrace, without losing sight of the truth innate in its origins. Even if God existed, Ivan would never surrender to Him in the face of the injustice done to man. But a longer contemplation of this injustice, a more bitter approach, transformed the "even if you exist" into "you do not deserve to exist," therefore "you do not exist." The victims have found in their own innocence the justification for the final crime. Convinced of their condemnation and without hope of immortality, they decided to murder God. If it is false to say that from that day began the tragedy of contemporary man, neither is it true to say that there was where it ended. On the contrary, this attempt indicates the highest point in a drama that began with the end of the ancient world and of which the final words have not yet been spoken. From this moment, man decides to exclude himself from grace and to live by his own means. Progress, from the time of Sade up to the present day, has consisted in gradually enlarging the stronghold where, according to his own rules, man without God brutally wields power. In defiance of the divinity, the frontiers of this stronghold have been gradually extended, to the point of making the entire universe into a fortress erected against the fallen and exiled deity. Man, at the culmination of his rebellion, incarcerated himself; from Sade's lurid castle to the concentration camps, man's greatest liberty consisted only in building the prison of his crimes. But the state of siege gradually spreads, the demand for freedom wants to embrace all mankind. Then the only kingdom that is opposed to the kingdom of grace must be founded —namely, the kingdom of justice—and the human community must be reunited among the debris of the fallen City of God. To kill God and to build a Church are the constant and contradictory purpose of rebellion. Absolute freedom finally becomes a prison of absolute duties, a collective asceticism, a story to be brought to an end. The nineteenth century, which is the century of rebellion, thus merges into the twentieth, the century of justice and ethics, in which everyone indulges in self-recrimination. Chamfort, the moralist of rebellion, had already provided the formula: "One must be just before being generous, as one must have bread before having cake." Thus the ethic of luxury will be renounced in favor of the bitter morality of the empire-builders.

We must now embark on the subject of this convulsive effort to control the world and to introduce a universal rule. We have arrived at the moment when rebellion, rejecting every aspect of servitude, attempts to annex all creation. Every time it experiences a setback, we have already seen that the political solution, the solution of conquest, is formulated. Henceforth, with the introduction of moral nihilism, it will retain, of all its acquisitions, only the will to power. In principle, the rebel only wanted to conquer his own existence and to maintain it in the face of God. But he forgets his origins and, by the law of spiritual imperialism, he sets out in search of world conquest by way of an infinitely multiplied series of murders. He drove God from His heaven, but now that the spirit of metaphysical rebellion openly joins forces with revolutionary movements, the irrational claim for freedom paradoxically adopts reason as a weapon, and as the only means of conquest which appears entirely human. With the death of God, mankind remains; and by this we mean the history that we must understand and shape. Nihilism, which, in the very midst of rebellion, smothers the force of creation, only adds that one is justified in using every means at one's disposal. Man, on an earth that he knows is henceforth solitary, is going to add, to irrational crimes, the crimes of reason that are bent on the triumph of man. To the "I rebel, therefore we exist," he adds, with prodigious plans in mind which even include the death of rebellion: "And we are alone."

Part Three

Historical Rebellion

∗

Freedom, "that terrible word inscribed on the chariot of the storm," [1] is the motivating principle of all revolutions. Without it, justice seems inconceivable to the rebel's mind. There comes a time, however, when justice demands the suspension of freedom. Then terror, on a grand or small scale, makes its appearance to consummate the revolution. Every act of rebellion expresses a nostalgia for innocence and an appeal to the essence of being. But one day nostalgia takes up arms and assumes the responsibility of total guilt; in other words, adopts murder and violence. The servile rebellions, the regicide revolutions, and those of the twentieth century have thus, consciously, accepted a burden of guilt which increased in proportion to the degree of liberation they proposed to introduce. This contradiction, which has become only too obvious, prevents our contemporary revolutionaries from displaying that aspect of happiness and optimism which shone forth from the faces and the speeches of the members of the Constituent Assembly in 1789. Is this contradiction inevitable? Does it characterize or betray the value of rebellion? These questions are bound to arise about revolution as they are bound to arise about metaphysical rebellion. Actually, revolution is only the logical consequence of metaphysical rebellion, and we shall discover, in our analysis of the revolutionary movement, the same desperate and bloody effort to affirm the dignity of man in defiance of the things that deny its existence. The revolutionary spirit thus undertakes the defense of that part of man which refuses to submit. In other words, it tries to assure him

[1] Philothée O'Neddy.

his crown in the realm of time, and, rejecting God, it chooses history with an apparently inevitable logic.

In theory, the word *revolution* retains the meaning that it has in astronomy. It is a movement that describes a complete circle, that leads from one form of government to another after a complete transition. A change of regulations concerning property without a corresponding change of government is not a revolution, but a reform. There is no kind of economic revolution, whether its methods are violent or pacific, which is not, at the same time, manifestly political. Revolution can already be distinguished, in this way, from rebellion. The warning given to Louis XVI: "No, sire, this is not a rebellion, it is a revolution," accents the essential difference. It means precisely that "it is the absolute certainty of a new form of government." Rebellion is, by nature, limited in scope. It is no more than an incoherent pronouncement. Revolution, on the contrary, originates in the realm of ideas. Specifically, it is the injection of ideas into historical experience, while rebellion is only the movement that leads from individual experience into the realm of ideas. While even the collective history of a movement of rebellion is always that of a fruitless struggle with facts, of an obscure protest which involves neither methods nor reasons, a revolution is an attempt to shape actions to ideas, to fit the world into a theoretic frame. That is why rebellion kills men while revolution destroys both men and principles. But, for the same reasons, it can be said that there has not yet been a revolution in the course of history. There could only be one, and that would be the definitive revolution. The movement that seems to complete the circle already begins to describe another at the precise moment when the new government is formed. The anarchists, with Varlet as their leader, were made well aware of the fact that government and revolution are incompatible in the direct sense. "It implies a contradiction," says Proudhon, "that a government could ever be revolutionary, for the very simple reason that it is the government." Now that the experiment has been made, let us qualify that statement by adding that a government can be revolutionary only in opposition to other governments. Revolutionary governments are obliged, most of the time, to be war governments. The more extensive the revolution, the more considerable the chances of the war that it implies. The society born of the revolution of 1789 wanted to fight for Europe. The society born of the 1917 revolution is fighting for universal dominion. Total revolution ends by demanding—we shall see why—the control of the world.

While waiting for this to happen, if happen it must, the history of man, in one sense, is the sum total of his successive rebellions. In other words, the movement of transition which can be clearly expressed in terms of space is only an approximation in terms of time. What was devoutly called, in the nineteenth century, the progressive emancipation of the human race appears, from the outside, like an uninterrupted series of rebellions, which overreach themselves and try to find their formulation in ideas, but which have not yet reached the point of definitive revolution where everything in heaven and on earth would be stabilized. A superficial examination seems to imply, rather than any real emancipation, an affirmation of mankind by man, an affirmation increasingly broad in scope, but always incomplete. In fact, if there had ever been one real revolution, there would be no more history. Unity would have been achieved, and death would have been satiated. That is why all revolutionaries finally aspire to world unity and act as though they believed that history was concluded. The originality of twentieth-century revolution lies in the fact that, for the first time, it openly claims to realize the ancient dream of Anarchasis Cloots of unity of the human race and, at the same time, the definitive consummation of history. Just as the movement of rebellion led to the point of "All or Nothing" and just as metaphysical rebellion demanded the unity of the world, the twentieth-century revolutionary movement, when it arrived at the most obvious conclusions of its logic, insisted with threats of force on arrogating to itself the whole of history. Rebellion is therefore compelled, on pain of appearing futile or out of date to become revolutionary. It no longer suffices for the rebel to deify himself like Stirner or to look to his own salvation by adopting a certain attitude of mind. The species must be deified, as Nietzsche attempted to do, and his ideal of the superman must be adopted so as to assure salvation for all—as Ivan

Karamazov wanted. For the first time, the Possessed appear
on the scene and proceed to give the answer to one of the
secrets of the times: the identity of reason and of the will
to power. Now that God is dead, the world must be
changed and organized by the forces at man's disposal.
The force of imprecation alone is not enough; weapons are
needed and totality must be conquered. Even revolution,
particularly revolution, which claims to be materialist, is
only a limitless metaphysical crusade. But can totality
claim to be unity? That is the question which this book
must answer. So far we can only say that the purpose of
this analysis is not to give, for the hundredth time, a
description of the revolutionary phenomenon, nor once
more to examine the historic or economic causes of great
revolutions. Its purpose is to discover in certain revolutionary data the logical sequence, the explanations, and the
invariable themes of metaphysical rebellion.

The majority of revolutions are shaped by, and derive their originality from, murder. All, or almost all, have
been homicidal. But some, in addition, have practiced
regicide and deicide. Just as the history of metaphysical
rebellion began with Sade, so our real inquiry only begins
with his contemporaries, the regicides, who attack the
incarnation of divinity without yet daring to destroy the
principle of eternity. (But before this the history of mankind also demonstrates the equivalent of the first movement of rebellion—the rebellion of the slave.)

When a slave rebels against his master, the situation
presented is of one man pitted against another, under a
cruel sky, far from the exalted realms of principles. The
final result is merely the murder of a man. The servile
rebellions, peasant risings, beggar outbreaks, rustic revolts,
all advance the concept of a principle of equality, a life for
a life, which despite every kind of mystification and
audacity will always be found in the purest manifestations
of the revolutionary spirit—Russian terrorism in 1905, for
example.

Spartacus' rebellion, which took place as the ancient
world was coming to an end, a few decades before the
Christian era, is an excellent illustration of this point.

First we note that this is a rebellion of gladiators—that is to say, of slaves consecrated to single combat and condemned, for the delectation of their masters, to kill or be killed. Beginning with seventy men, this rebellion ended with an army of seventy thousand insurgents, which crushed the best Roman legions and advanced through Italy to march on the Eternal City itself. However, as André Prudhommeaux remarks (in *The Tragedy of Spartacus*), this rebellion introduced no new principle into Roman life. The proclamation issued by Spartacus goes no farther than to offer "equal rights" to the slaves. The transition from fact to right, which we analyzed in the first stage of rebellion, is, indeed, the only logical acquisition that one can find on this level of rebellion. The insurgent rejects slavery and affirms his equality with his master. He wants to be master in his turn.

Spartacus' rebellion is a continual illustration of this principle of positive claims. The slave army liberates the slaves and immediately hands over their former masters to them in bondage. According to one tradition, of doubtful veracity it is true, gladiatorial combats were even organized between several hundred Roman citizens, while the slaves sat in the grandstands delirious with joy and excitement. But to kill men leads to nothing but killing more men. For one principle to triumph, another principle must be overthrown. The city of light of which Spartacus dreamed could only have been built on the ruins of eternal Rome, of its institutions and of its gods. Spartacus' army marches to lay siege to a Rome paralyzed with fear at the prospect of having to pay for its crimes. At the decisive moment, however, within sight of the sacred walls, the army halts and wavers, as if it were retreating before the principles, the institutions, the city of the gods. When these had been destroyed, what could be put in their place except the brutal desire for justice, the wounded and exacerbated love that until this moment had kept these wretches on their feet.[2] In any case, the army retreated without having

---

[2] Spartacus' rebellion recapitulates the program of the servile rebellions that preceded it. But this program is limited to the distribution of land and the abolition of slavery. It is not directly concerned with the gods of the city.

fought, and then made the curious move of deciding to return to the place where the slave rebellion originated, to retrace the long road of its victories and to return to Sicily. It was as though these outcasts, forever alone and helpless before the great tasks that awaited them and too daunted to assail the heavens, returned to what was purest and most heartening in their history, to the land of their first awakening, where it was easy and right to die.

Then began their defeat and martyrdom. Before the last battle, Spartacus crucified a Roman citizen to show his men the fate that was in store for them. During the battle, Spartacus himself tried with frenzied determination, the symbolism of which is obvious, to reach Crassus, who was commanding the Roman legions. He wanted to perish, but in single combat with the man who symbolized, at that moment, every Roman master; it was his dearest wish to die, but in absolute equality. He did not reach Crassus: principles wage war at a distance and the Roman general kept himself apart. Spartacus died, as he wished, but at the hands of mercenaries, slaves like himself, who killed their own freedom with his. In revenge for the one crucified citizen, Crassus crucified thousands of slaves. The six thousand crosses which, after such a just rebellion, staked out the road from Capua to Rome demonstrated to the servile crowd that there is no equality in the world of power and that the masters calculate, at a usurious rate, the price of their own blood.

The cross is also Christ's punishment. One might imagine that He chose a slave's punishment, a few years later, only so as to reduce the enormous distance that henceforth would separate humiliated humanity from the implacable face of the Master. He intercedes, He submits to the most extreme injustice so that rebellion shall not divide the world in two, so that suffering will also light the way to heaven and preserve it from the curses of mankind. What is astonishing in the fact that the revolutionary spirit, when it wanted to affirm the separation of heaven and earth, should begin by disembodying the divinity by killing His representatives on earth? In certain aspects, the period of rebellions comes to an end in 1793 and revolutionary times begin—on a scaffold.[3]

[3] In that this book is not concerned with the spirit of rebellion inside Christianity, the Reformation has no place here, nor the numerous rebellions against ecclesiastical authority which preceded it. But we can say, at least, that the Reformation prepares the way for Jacobinism and in one sense initiates the reforms that 1789 carries out.

The Regicides

*

Kings were put to death long before January 21, 1793, and before the regicides of the nineteenth century. But Ravaillac, Damiens, and their followers were interested in attacking the person, not the principle, of the king. They wanted another king and that was all. It never occurred to them that the throne could remain empty forever. 1789 is the starting-point of modern times, because the men of that period wished, among other things, to overthrow the principle of divine right and to introduce to the historical scene the forces of negation and rebellion which had become the essence of intellectual discussion in the previous centuries. Thus they added to traditional tyrannicide the concept of calculated deicide. The so-called freethinkers, the philosophers and jurists, served as levers for this revolution.[1] In order for such an undertaking to enter into the realms of possibility and to be considered legitimate, it was first necessary for the Church, whose infinite responsibility it is, to place itself on the side of the masters by compromising with the executioner—a step that developed into the Inquisition and was perpetuated by complicity with the temporal powers. Michelet is quite correct in wanting to recognize only two outstanding characters in the revolutionary saga: Christianity and the French Revolution. In fact, for him, 1789 is explained by the struggle between divine grace and justice. Although Michelet shared the taste for all-embracing abstractions

---

[1] The kings themselves collaborated in this by allowing political power gradually to encroach on religious power, thus threatening the very principle of their legitimacy.

with his intemperate period, he saw that this taste was one of the profound causes of the revolutionary crisis.

Even if the monarchy of the *ancien régime* was not always arbitrary in its manner of governing, it was undoubtedly arbitrary in principle. It was founded on divine right, which means that its legitimacy could never be questioned. Its legitimacy often was questioned, however, in particular by various parliaments. But those who exercised it considered and presented it as an axiom. Louis XIV, as is well known, rigidly adhered to the principle of divine right.[2] Bossuet gave him considerable help in this direction by saying to the kings of France: "You are gods." The king, in one of his aspects, is the divine emissary in charge of human affairs and therefore of the administration of justice. Like God Himself, he is the last recourse of the victims of misery and injustice. In principle, the people can appeal to the king for help against their oppressors. "If the King only knew, if the Czar only knew . . ." was the frequently expressed sentiment of the French and Russian people during periods of great distress. It is true in France, at least, that, when the monarchy did know, it often tried to defend the lower classes against the oppressions of the aristocracy and the bourgeoisie. But was this, essentially, justice? From the absolute point of view, which was the point of view of the writers of the period, it was not. Even though it is possible to appeal to the king, it is impossible to appeal against him in so far as he is the embodiment of a principle. He dispenses his protection and his assistance if and when he wants to. One of the attributes of grace is that it is discretionary. Monarchy in its theocratic form is a type of government which wants to put grace before justice by always letting it have the last word. Rousseau in his Savoyard curate's declaration, on the other hand, is only original in so far as he submits God to justice and in this way inaugurates, with the rather naïve solemnity of the period, contemporary history.

From the moment that the freethinkers began to question the existence of God, the problem of justice

[2] Charles I clung so tenaciously to the principle of divine right that he considered it unnecessary to be just and loyal to those who denied it.

became of primary importance. The justice of the period was, quite simply, confused with equality. The throne of God totters and justice, to confirm its support of equality, must give it the final push by making a direct attack on His representative on earth. Divine right to all intents and purposes was already destroyed by being opposed and forced to compromise with natural right for three years, from 1789 to 1792. In the last resort, grace is incapable of compromise. It can give in on certain points, but never on the final point. But that does not suffice. According to Michelet, Louis XVI still wanted to be king in prison. In a France entirely governed by new principles, the principle that had been defeated still survived behind prison walls through the mere power of faith and through the existence of one human being. Justice has this in common with grace, and this alone, that it wants to be total and to rule absolutely. From the moment they conflict, they fight to the death. "We do not want to condemn the King," said Danton, who had not even the good manners of a lawyer, "we want to kill him." In fact, if God is denied, the King must die. Saint-Just, it seems, was responsible for Louis XVI's death; but when he exclaims: "To determine the principle in virtue of which the accused is perhaps to die, is to determine the principle by which the society that judges him lives," he demonstrates that it is the philosophers who are going to kill the King: the King must die in the name of the social contract.[3] But this demands an explanation.

The New Gospel

The Social Contract is, primarily, an inquiry into the legitimacy of power. But it is a book about rights, not about facts, and at no time is it a collection of sociological observations. It is concerned with principles and for this very reason is bound to be controversial. It presumes that traditional legitimacy, which is supposedly of divine origin,

[3] Rousseau would not, of course, have wanted this. It must be remembered, before proceeding with this analysis and in order to set its limits, that Rousseau firmly declared: "Nothing on this earth is worth buying at the price of human blood."

is not acquired. Thus it proclaims another sort of legitimacy and other principles. *The Social Contract* is also a catechism, of which it has both the tone and the dogmatic language. Just as 1789 completes the conquests of the English and American revolutions, so Rousseau pushes to its limits the theory of the social contract to be found in Hobbes. *The Social Contract* amplifies and dogmatically explains the new religion whose god is reason, confused with nature, and whose representative on earth, in place of the king, is the people considered as an expression of the general will.

The attack on the traditional order is so evident that, from the very first chapter, Rousseau is determined to demonstrate the precedence of the citizens' pact, which established the people, over the pact between the people and the king, which founded royalty. Until Rousseau's time, God created kings, who, in their turn, created peoples. After *The Social Contract*, peoples create themselves before creating kings. As for God, there is nothing more to be said, for the time being. Here we have, in the political field, the equivalent of Newton's revolution. Power, therefore, is no longer arbitrary, but derives its existence from general consent. In other words, power is no longer what is, but what should be. Fortunately, according to Rousseau, what cannot be separated from what should be. The people are sovereign "only because they are always everything that they should be." Confronted with this statement of principle, it is perfectly justifiable to say that reason, which was always obstinately invoked at that period, is not particularly well treated in the context. It is evident that, with *The Social Contract*, we are assisting at the birth of a new *mystique*—the will of the people being substituted for God Himself. "Each of us," says Rousseau, "places his person and his entire capabilities under the supreme guidance of the will of the people, and we receive each individual member into the body as an indivisible part of the whole."

This political entity, proclaimed sovereign, is also defined as a divine entity. Moreover, it has all the attributes of a divine entity. It is, in fact, infallible in that, in its role of sovereign, it cannot even wish to commit abuses. "Under the law of reason, nothing is done without cause."

It is totally free, if it is true that absolute freedom is freedom in regard to oneself. Thus Rousseau declares that it is against the nature of the body politic for the sovereign power to impose a law upon itself that it cannot violate. It is also inalienable, indivisible; and, finally, it even aims at solving the great theological problem, the contradiction between absolute power and divine innocence. The will of the people is, in fact, coercive; its power has no limits. But the punishment it inflicts on those who refuse to obey it is nothing more than a means of "compelling them to be free." The deification is completed when Rousseau, separating the sovereign from his very origins, reaches the point of distinguishing between the general will and the will of all. This can be logically deduced from Rousseau's premises. If man is naturally good, if nature as expressed in him is identified with reason,[4] he will express the pre-eminence of reason, on the one condition that he expresses himself freely and naturally. He can no longer, therefore, go back on his decision, which henceforth hovers over him. The will of the people is primarily the expression of universal reason, which is categorical. The new God is born.

That is why the words that are to be found most often in *The Social Contract* are the words *absolute, sacred, inviolable*. The body politic thus defined, whose laws are sacred commandments, is only a by-product of the mystic body of temporal Christianity. *The Social Contract*, moreover, terminates with a description of a civil religion and makes of Rousseau a harbinger of contemporary forms of society which exclude not only opposition but even neutrality. Rousseau is, in fact, the first man in modern times to institute the profession of civil faith. He is also the first to justify the death penalty in a civil society and the absolute submission of the subject to the authority of the sovereign. "It is in order not to become victim of an assassin that we consent to die if we become assassins." A strange justification, but one which firmly establishes the fact that you must know how to die if the sovereign commands, and must, if necessary, concede that he is right and you are wrong. This mystic idea explains Saint-Just's silence from the time of his arrest until he goes to the

Every ideology is contrary to human psychology.

scaffold. Suitably developed, it equally well explains the enthusiasm of the defendants in the Moscow trials.

We are witnessing the dawn of a new religion with its martyrs, its ascetics, and its saints. To be able to estimate the influence achieved by this gospel, one must have some idea of the inspired tones of the proclamations of 1789. Fauchet, confronted with the skeletons discovered in the Bastille, exclaims: "The day of revelation is upon us. . . . The very bones have risen at the sound of the voice of French freedom; they bear witness against the centuries of oppression and death, and prophesy the regeneration of human nature and of the life of nations." Then he predicts: "We have reached the heart of time. The tyrants are ready to fall." It is the moment of astonished and generous faith when a remarkably enlightened mob overthrows the scaffold and the wheel at Versailles.[5] Scaffolds seemed to be the very altars of religion and injustice. The new faith could not tolerate them. But a moment comes when faith, if it becomes dogmatic, erects its own altars and demands unconditional adoration. Then scaffolds reappear and despite the altars, the freedom, the oaths, and the feasts of Reason, the Masses of the new faith must now be celebrated with blood. In any case, in order that 1789 shall mark the beginning of the reign of "holy humanity" [6] and of "Our Lord the human race," [7] the fallen sovereign must first of all disappear. The murder of the King-priest will sanction the new age—which endures to this day.

The Execution of the King

Saint-Just introduced Rousseau's ideas into the pages of history. At the King's trial, the essential part of his arguments consisted in saying that the King is not inviolable and should be judged by the Assembly and not by

[5] The same idyl takes place in Russia, in 1905, where the soviet of St. Petersburg parades through the streets carrying placards demanding the abolition of the death penalty, and again in 1917.

[6] Vergniaud.

[7] Anarchasis Cloots.

a special tribunal. His arguments he owed to Rousseau. A tribunal cannot be the judge between the king and the sovereign people. The general will cannot be cited before ordinary judges. It is above everything. The inviolability and the transcendence of the general will are thus proclaimed. We know that the predominant theme of the trial was the inviolability of the royal person. The struggle between grace and justice finds its most provocative illustration in 1793 when two different conceptions of transcendence meet in mortal combat. Moreover, Saint-Just is perfectly aware of how very much is at stake: "The spirit in which the King is judged will be the same as the spirit in which the Republic is established."

Saint-Just's famous speech has, therefore, all the earmarks of a theological treatise. "Louis, the stranger in our midst," is the thesis of this youthful prosecutor. If a contract, either civil or natural, could still bind the king and his people, there would be a mutual obligation; the will of the people could not set itself up as absolute judge to pronounce absolute judgment. Therefore it is necessary to prove that no agreement binds the people and the king. In order to prove that the people are themselves the embodiment of eternal truth it is necessary to demonstrate that royalty is the embodiment of eternal crime. Saint-Just, therefore, postulates that every king is a rebel or a usurper. He is a rebel against the people whose absolute sovereignty he usurps. Monarchy is not a king, "it is crime." Not *a* crime, but crime itself, says Saint-Just; in other words, absolute profanation. That is the precise, and at the same time ultimate, meaning of Saint-Just's remark, the import of which has been stretched too far:[8] "No one can rule innocently." Every king is guilty, because any man who wants to be king is automatically on the side of death. Saint-Just says exactly the same thing when he proceeds to demonstrate that the sovereignty of the people is a "sacred matter." Citizens are inviolable and sacred and can be constrained only by the law, which is an expression of their common will. Louis alone does not benefit by this particular inviolability or by the assistance of the

[8] Or at least the significance of which has been anticipated. When Saint-Just made this remark, he did not know that he was already speaking for himself.

law, for he is placed outside the contract. He is not part of the general will; on the contrary, by his very existence he is a blasphemer against this all-powerful will. He is not a "citizen," which is the only way of participating in the new divine dispensation. "What is a king in comparison with a Frenchman?" Therefore, he should be judged and nothing more.

But who will interpret the will of the people and pronounce judgment? The Assembly, which by its origin has retained the right to administer this will, and which participates as an inspired council in the new divinity. Should the people be asked to ratify the judgment? We know that the efforts of the monarchists in the Assembly were finally concentrated on this point. In this way the life of the King could be rescued from the logic of the bourgeois jurists and at least entrusted to the spontaneous emotions and compassion of the people. But here again Saint-Just pushes his logic to its extremes and makes use of the conflict, invented by Rousseau, between the general will and the will of all. Even though the will of all would pardon, the general will cannot do so. Even the people cannot efface the crime of tyranny. Cannot the victims, according to law, withdraw their complaint? We are not dealing with law, we are dealing with theology. The crime of the king is, at the same time, a sin against the ultimate nature of things. A crime is committed; then it is pardoned, punished, or forgotten. But the crime of royalty is permanent; it is inextricably bound to the person of the king, to his very existence. Christ Himself, though He can forgive sinners, cannot absolve false gods. They must disappear or conquer. If the people forgive today, they will find the crime intact tomorrow, even though the criminal sleeps peacefully in prison. Therefore there is only one solution: "To avenge the murder of the people by the death of the King."

The only purpose of Saint-Just's speech is, once and for all, to block every egress for the King except the one leading to the scaffold. If, in fact, the premises of *The Social Contract* are accepted, this is logically inevitable. At last, after Saint-Just, "kings will flee to the desert, and nature will resume her rights." It was quite pointless of the Convention to vote a reservation and say that it did not intend to create a precedent if it passed judgment on Louis XVI or if it pronounced a security measure. In doing so, it refused to face the consequences of its own principles and tried to camouflage, with shocking hypocrisy, its real purpose, which was to found a new form of absolutism. Jacques Roux, at least, was speaking the truth of the times when he called the King Louis the Last, thus indicating that the real revolution, which had already been accomplished on the economic level, was then taking place on the philosophic plane and that it implied a twilight of the gods. Theocracy was attacked in principle in 1789 and killed in its incarnation in 1793. Brissot was right in saying: "The most solid monument to our revolution is philosophy." [9]

On January 21, with the murder of the King-priest, was consummated what has significantly been called the passion of Louis XVI. It is certainly a crying scandal that the public assassination of a weak but goodhearted man has been presented as a great moment in French history. That scaffold marked no climax—far from it. But the fact remains that, by its consequences, the condemnation of the King is at the crux of our contemporary history. It symbolizes the secularization of our history and the disincarnation of the Christian God. Up to now God played a part in history through the medium of the kings. But His representative in history has been killed, for there is no longer a king. Therefore there is nothing but a semblance of God, relegated to the heaven of principles.[1]

The revolutionaries may well refer to the Gospel, but in fact they dealt a terrible blow to Christianity, from which it has not yet recovered. It really seems as if the execution of the King, followed, as we know, by hysterical scenes of suicide and madness, took place in complete awareness of what was being done. Louis XVI seems, sometimes, to have doubted his divine right, though he systematically rejected any projected legislation which threatened his faith. But from the moment that he suspected or knew his fate, he seemed to identify himself, as his language betrayed, with his divine mission, so that

[9] The religious Wars of the Vendée showed him to be right again.
[1] This will become the god of Kant, Jacobi, and Fichte.

there would be no possible doubt that the attempt on his person was aimed at the King-Christ, the incarnation of the divinity, and not at the craven flesh of a mere man. His bedside book in the Temple was the *Imitation*. The calmness and perfection that this man of rather average sensibility displayed during his last moments, his indifference to everything of this world, and, finally, his brief display of weakness on the solitary scaffold, so far removed from the people whose ears he had wanted to reach, while the terrible rolling of the drum drowned his voice, give us the right to imagine that it was not Capet who died, but Louis appointed by divine right, and that with him, in a certain manner, died temporal Christianity. To emphasize this sacred bond, his confessor sustained him, in his moment of weakness, by reminding him of his "resemblance" to the God of Sorrows. And Louis XVI recovers himself and speaks in the language of this God: "I shall drink," he says, "the cup to the last dregs." Then he commits himself, trembling, into the ignoble hands of the executioner.

The Religion of Virtue

A religion that executes its obsolete sovereign must now establish the power of its new sovereign; it closes the churches, and this leads to an endeavor to build a temple. The blood of the gods, which for a second bespatters the confessor of Louis XVI, announces a new baptism. Joseph de Maistre qualified the Revolution as satanic. We can see why and in what sense. Michelet, however, was closer to the truth when he called it a purgatory. An era blindly embarks down this tunnel on an attempt to discover a new illumination, a new happiness, and the face of the real God. But what will this new god be? Let us ask Saint-Just once more.

The year 1789 does not yet affirm the divinity of man, but the divinity of the people, to the degree in which the will of the people coincides with the will of nature and of reason. If the general will is freely expressed, it can only be the universal expression of reason. If the people are free, they are infallible. Once the King is dead, and the chains of the old despotism thrown off, the people are going to express what, at all times and in all places, is, has been, and will be the truth. They are the oracle that must be consulted to know what the eternal order of the world demands. *Vox populi, vox naturæ.* Eternal principles govern our conduct: Truth, Justice, finally Reason. There we have the new God. The Supreme Being, whom cohorts of young girls come to adore at the Feast of Reason, is only the ancient god disembodied, peremptorily deprived of any connection with the earth, and launched like a balloon into a heaven empty of all transcendent principles. Deprived of all his representatives, of any intercessor, the god of the lawyers and philosophers only has the value of a demonstration. He is not very strong, in fact, and we can see why Rousseau, who preached tolerance, thought that atheists should be condemned to death. To ensure the adoration of a theorem for any length of time, faith is not enough; a police force is needed as well. But that will only come later. In 1793 the new faith is still intact, and it will suffice, to take Saint-Just's word, to govern according to the dictates of reason. The art of ruling, according to him, has produced only monsters because, before his time, no one wished to govern according to nature. The period of monsters has come to an end with the termination of the period of violence. "The human heart advances from nature to violence, from violence to morality." Morality is, therefore, only nature finally restored after centuries of alienation. Man only has to be given law "in accord with nature and with his heart," and he will cease to be unhappy and corrupt. Universal suffrage, the foundation of the new laws, must inevitably lead to a universal morality. "Our aim is to create an order of things which establishes a universal tendency toward good."

The religion of reason quite naturally establishes the Republic of law and order. The general will is expressed in laws codified by its representatives. "The people make the revolution, the legislator makes the Republic." "Immortal, impassive" institutions, "sheltered from the temerity of man," will govern in their turn the lives of all men by universal accord and without possibility of contradiction since by obeying the laws all will only be obeying themselves. "Outside the law," says Saint-Just, "everything is sterile and dead." It is the formal and legalistic Republic of the Romans. We know the passion of Saint-Just and his contemporaries for ancient Rome. The decadent young man who, in Reims, spent hours in a room painted black and decorated with white teardrops, with the shutters closed, dreamed of the Spartan Republic. The author of *Organt*, a long and licentious poem, was absolutely convinced of the necessity for frugality and virtue. In the institutions that he invented, Saint-Just refused to allow children to eat meat until the age of sixteen, and he dreamed of a nation that was both vegetarian and revolutionary. "The world has been empty since the Romans," he exclaimed. But heroic times were at hand. Cato, Brutus, Scævola, had become possible once more. The rhetoric of the Latin moralists flourished once again. *Vice, virtue, corruption*, were terms that constantly recurred in the oratory of the times, and even more in the speeches of Saint-Just, of which they were the perpetual burden. The reason for this is simple. This perfect edifice, as Montesquieu had already seen, could not exist without virtue. The French Revolution, by claiming to build history on the principle of absolute purity, inaugurates modern times simultaneously with the era of formal morality.

What, in fact, is virtue? For the bourgeois philosopher of the period it is conformity with nature[2] and, in politics, conformity with the law, which expresses the general will. "Morality," says Saint-Just, "is stronger than tyrants." It has, in fact, just killed Louis XVI. Every form of disobedience to law therefore comes, not from an imperfection in the law, which is presumed to be impossible, but from a lack of virtue in the refractory citizen. That is why the Republic not only is an assembly, as Saint-Just forcibly says, but is also virtue itself. Every form of moral corruption is at the same time political corruption, and vice versa. A principle of infinite repression, derived from this very doctrine, is then established. Undoubtedly Saint-Just was sincere in his desire for a universal idyl. He really dreamed of a republic of ascetics, of humanity reconciled

[2] But nature itself, as we encounter it in the works of Bernardin de Saint-Pierre, conforms to a pre-established virtue. Nature is also an abstract principle.

and dedicated to the chaste pursuits of the age of innocence, under the watchful eye of those wise old men whom
he decked out in advance with a tricolor scarf and a white
plume. We also know that, at the beginning of the Revolution, Saint-Just declared himself, at the same time as
Robespierre, against the death penalty. He only demanded
that murderers should be dressed in black for the rest of
their lives. He wanted to establish a form of justice which
did not attempt "to find the culprit guilty, but to find him
weak"—an admirable ambition. He also dreamed of a
republic of forgiveness which would recognize that though
the fruits of crime are bitter, its roots are nevertheless
tender. One of his outbursts, at least, came from the heart
and is not easily forgotten: "it is a frightful thing to torment the people." Yes indeed, it is a frightful thing. But a
man can realize this and yet submit to principles that
imply, in the final analysis, the torment of the people.

Morality, when it is formal, devours. To paraphrase
Saint-Just, no one is virtuous innocently. From the moment that laws fail to make harmony reign, or when the
unity which should be created by adherence to principles
is destroyed, who is to blame? Factions. Who compose the
factions? Those who deny by their very actions the necessity of unity. Factions divide the sovereign; therefore they
are blasphemous and criminal. They, and they alone, must
be combated. But what if there are many factions? All
shall be fought to the death. Saint-Just exclaims: "Either
the virtues or the Terror." Freedom must be guaranteed,
and the draft constitution presented to the Convention,
already mentions the death penalty. Absolute virtue is
impossible, and the republic of forgiveness leads, with implacable logic, to the republic of the guillotine. Montesquieu had already denounced this logic as one of the
causes of the decadence of societies, saying that the abuse
of power is greatest when laws do not anticipate it. The
pure law of Saint-Just did not take into account the truth,
which is as old as history itself, that law, in its essence, is
bound to be transgressed.

The Terror

Saint-Just, the contemporary of Sade, finally arrives at the justification of crime, though he starts from very different principles. Saint-Just is, of course, the anti-Sade. If Sade's formula were "Open the prisons or prove your virtue," then Saint-Just's would be: "Prove your virtue or go to prison." Both, however, justify terrorism—the libertine justifies individual terrorism, the high priest of virtue State terrorism. Absolute good and absolute evil, if the necessary logic is applied, both demand the same degree of passion. Of course, there is a certain ambiguity in the case of Saint-Just. The letter which he wrote to Vilain d'Aubigny in 1792 has something really insane about it. It is a profession of faith by a persecuted persecutor which ends with a hysterical avowal: "If Brutus does not kill others, he will kill himself." A personality so obstinately serious, so voluntarily cold, logical, and imperturbable, leads one to imagine every kind of aberration and disorder. Saint-Just invented the kind of seriousness which makes the history of the last two centuries so tedious and depressing. "He who makes jokes as the head of a government," he said, "has a tendency to tyranny." An astonishing maxim, above all if one thinks of the penalty for the mere accusation of tyranny, one which, in any case, prepared the way for the pedant Cæsars. Saint-Just sets the example; even his tone is definitive. That cascade of peremptory affirmatives, that axiomatic and sententious style, portrays him better than the most faithful painting. His sentences drone on; his definitions follow one another with the coldness and precision of commandments. "Principles should be moderate, laws implacable, principles without redress." It is the style of the guillotine.

Such pertinacity in logic, however, implies a profound passion. Here, as elsewhere, we again find the passion for unity. Every rebellion implies some kind of unity. The rebellion of 1789 demands the unity of the whole country. Saint-Just dreams of an ideal city where manners and customs, in final agreement with the law, will proclaim the innocence of man and the identity of his nature with reason. And if factions arise to interrupt this dream, passion will exaggerate its logic. No one will dare to imagine that, since factions exist, the principles are perhaps wrong. Factions will be condemned as criminal because principles remain intangible. "It is time that everyone returned to morality and the aristocracy to the Terror." But the aristocratic factions are not the only ones to be reckoned with; there are the republicans, too, and anyone else who criticizes the actions of the legislature and of the Convention. They, too, are guilty, since they threaten unity. Saint-Just, then, proclaims the major principle of twentieth-century tyrannies. "A patriot is he who supports the Republic in general; whoever opposes it in detail is a traitor." Whoever criticizes it is a traitor, whoever fails to give open support is a suspect. When neither reason nor the free expression of individual opinion succeeds in systematically establishing unity, it must be decided to suppress all alien elements. Thus the guillotine becomes a logician whose function is refutation. "A rogue who has been condemned to death by the tribunal says he wants to resist oppression simply because he wants to resist the scaffold!" Saint-Just's indignation is hard to understand in that, until his time, the scaffold was precisely nothing else but one of the most obvious symbols of oppression. But at the heart of this logical delirium, at the logical conclusion of this morality of virtue, the scaffold represents freedom. It assures rational unity, and harmony in the ideal city. It purifies (the word is apt) the Republic and eliminates malpractices that arise to contradict the general will and universal reason. "They question my right to the title of philanthropist," Marat exclaims, in quite a different style. "Ah, what injustice! Who cannot see that I want to cut off a few heads to save a great number?" A few—a faction? Naturally—and all historic actions are performed at this price. But Marat, making his final calculations, claimed two hundred and seventy-three thousand heads. But he compromised the therapeutic aspect of the operation by screaming during the massacre: "Brand them with hot irons, cut off their thumbs, tear out their tongues." This philanthropist wrote day and night, in the most monotonous vocabulary imaginable, of the necessity of killing in order to create. He wrote again, by candlelight deep down in his cellar, during the September nights while his henchmen were installing spectators' benches in prison courtyards—men on the right, women on the left—to display to them, as a gracious example of philanthropy, the spectacle of the aristocrats having their heads cut off.

Do not let us confuse, even for a moment, the imposing figure of Saint-Just with the sad spectacle of Marat—Rousseau's monkey, as Michelet rightly calls him. But the drama of Saint-Just lies in having at moments joined forces, for superior and much deeper reasons, with Marat. Factions join with factions, and minorities with minorities, and in the end it is not even sure that the scaffold functions in the service of the will of all. But at least Saint-Just will affirm, to the bitter end, that it functions in the service of the general will, since it functions in the service of virtue. "A revolution such as ours is not a trial, but a clap of thunder for the wicked." Good strikes like a thunderbolt, innocence is a flash of lightning—a flash of lightning that brings justice. Even the pleasure-seekers—in fact, they above all —are counterrevolutionaries. Saint-Just, who said that the idea of happiness was new to Europe (actually it was mainly new for Saint-Just, for whom history stopped at Brutus), remarks that some people have an "appalling idea of what happiness is and confuse it with pleasure." They, too, must be dealt with firmly. Finally, it is no longer a question of majority or minority. Paradise, lost and always coveted by universal innocence, disappears into the distance; on the unhappy earth, racked with the cries of civil and national wars, Saint-Just decrees, against his nature and against his principles, that when the whole country suffers, then all are guilty. The series of reports on the factions abroad, the law of the 22 Prairial, the speech of April 15, 1794 on the necessity of the police, mark the stages of this conversion. The man who with such nobility held that it was infamous to lay down one's arms while there remained, somewhere in the world, one master and one slave, is the same man who had to agree to suspend the Constitution of 1793 and to adopt arbitrary rule. In the speech that he made to defend Robespierre, he rejects fame and posterity and only refers himself to an abstract providence. At the same time, he recognized that virtue, of which he made a religion, has no other reward but history and the present, and that it must, at all costs, lay the foundations of its own reign. He did not like power which he called "cruel and wicked" and which, he said, "advanced toward repression, without any guiding principle." But the guiding principle was virtue and was derived from the people. When the people failed, the guiding principle became obscured and oppression increased. Therefore it was the people who were guilty and not power, which must remain, in principle, innocent. Such an extreme and outrageous contradiction could only be resolved by an even more extreme logic and by the final acceptance of principles in silence and in death. Saint-Just at least remained equal to this demand, and in this way was at last to find his greatness and that independent life in time and space of which he spoke with such emotion.

For a long time he had, in fact, had a presentiment that the demands he made implied a total and unreserved sacrifice on his part and had said himself that those who make revolutions in this world—"those who do good"— can sleep only in the tomb. Convinced that his principles, in order to triumph, must culminate in the virtue and happiness of his people, aware, perhaps, that he was asking the impossible, he cut off his own retreat in advance by declaring that he would stab himself in public on the day when he despaired of the people. Nevertheless, he despairs, since he has doubts about the Terror. "The revolution is frozen, every principle has been attenuated; all that remains are red caps worn by intriguers. The exercise of terror has blunted crime as strong drink blunts the palate." Even virtue "unites with crime in times of anarchy." He said that all crime sprang from tyranny, which was the greatest crime of all, and yet, confronted with the unflagging obstinacy of crime, the Revolution itself resorted to tyranny and became criminal. Thus crime cannot be obliterated, nor can factions, nor the despicable desire for enjoyment; the people must be despaired of and subjugated. But neither is it possible to govern innocently. Thus, evil must be either suffered or served, principles must be declared wrong or the people and mankind must be recognized as guilty. Then Saint-Just averts his mysterious and handsome face: "It would be leaving very little to leave a life in which one must be either the accomplice or the silent witness of evil." Brutus, who must kill himself if he does not kill others, begins by killing others. But the others are too many; they cannot all be killed. In that case he must die and demonstrate, yet again, that rebellion, when it gets out of hand, swings from the annihilation of others to the destruction of the self. This task, at any rate, is easy; once again it suffices to follow logic to the bitter end. In his speech in defense of Robespierre, shortly before his death, Saint-Just reaffirms the guiding principle of his actions, which is the very same principle that leads to his condemnation: "I belong to no faction, I shall fight against them all." He accepted then, and in advance, the decision of the general will—in other words, of the Assembly. He agreed to go to his death for love of principle and despite all the realities of the situation, since the opinion of the Assembly could only really be swayed by the eloquence and fanaticism of a faction. But that is beside the point! When principles fail, men have only one way to save them and to preserve their faith, which is to die for them. In the stifling heat of Paris in July, Saint-Just, ostensibly rejecting reality and the world, confesses that he stakes his life on the decision of principles. When this has been said, he seems to have a fleeting perception of another truth, and ends with a restrained denunciation of his colleagues Billaud-Varennes and Collot d'Herbois. "I want them to justify themselves and I want us to become wiser." The style and the guillotine are here suspended for a moment. But virtue, in that it has too much pride, is not wisdom. The guillotine is going to fall again on that head as cold and beautiful as morality itself. From the moment that the Assembly condemns him until the moment when he stretches his neck to the knife, Saint Just keeps silent. This long silence is more important than his death. He complained that silence reigned around thrones and that is why he wanted to speak so much and so well. But in the end, contemptuous of the tyranny and the enigma of a people who do not conform to pure reason, he resorts to silence himself. His principles do not allow him to accept things as they are; and, things not being what they should be, his principles are therefore fixed, silent, and alone. To abandon oneself to principles is really to die—and to die for an impossible love which is the contrary of love. Saint-Just dies, and, with him, all hope of a new religion.

"All the stones are cut to build the structure of freedom," said Saint-Just; "you can build a palace or a tomb of the same stones." The very principles of *The Social Contract* presided at the erection of the tomb that Napoleon Bonaparte came to seal. Rousseau, who was not wanting in common sense, understood very well that the society envisioned by *The Social Contract* was suitable only for gods. His successors took him at his word and tried to establish the divinity of man. The red flag—a symbol of martial law and therefore of the executive under the *ancien régime*—became the revolutionary symbol on August 10, 1792. A significant transfer about which Jaurès comments as follows: "It is we the people who are the law. . . . We are not rebels. The rebels are in the Tuileries." But it is not so easy as that to become God. Even the ancient gods did not die at the first blow, and the revolutions of the nineteenth century were intended to achieve the final liquidation of the principle of divinity. Paris rose to place the King under the rule of the people and to prevent him from restoring an authority of principle. The corpse which the rebels of 1830 dragged through the rooms of the Tuileries and installed on the throne in order to pay it derisory homage has no other significance. The king could still be, at that period, a respected minister, but his authority is now derived from the nation, and his guiding principle is the Charter. He is no longer Majesty. Now that the *ancien régime* had definitely disappeared in France, the new regime must again, after 1848, reaffirm itself, and the history of the nineteenth century up to 1914 is the history of the restoration of popular sovereignties against *ancien régime* monarchies; in other words, the history of the principle of nations. This principle finally triumphs in 1919, which witnesses the disappearance of all absolutist monarchies in Europe.[3] Everywhere, the sovereignty of the nation is substituted, in law and in fact,

[3] With the exception of the Spanish monarchy. But the German Empire collapsed, of which Wilhelm II said that it was "the proof that we Hohenzollerns derive our crown from heaven alone and that it is to heaven alone that we must give an accounting."

for the sovereign king. Only then can the consequences of the principles of 1789 be seen. We survivors are the first to be able to judge them clearly.

The Jacobins reinforced the eternal moral principles to the extent to which they suppressed the things which, up to then, had supported these principles. As preachers of a gospel, they wanted to base fraternity on the abstract law of the Romans. They substituted the law for divine commandments on the supposition that it must be recognized by all because it was the expression of the general will. The law found its justification in natural virtue and then proceeded to justify natural virtue. But immediately a single faction manifests itself, this reasoning collapses and we perceive that virtue has need of justification in order not to be abstract. In the same way, the bourgeois jurists of the eighteenth century, by burying under the weight of their principles the just and vital conquests of their people, prepared the way for the two contemporary forms of nihilism: individual nihilism and State nihilism.

Law can reign, in fact, in so far as it is the law of universal reason.[4] But it never is, and it loses its justification if man is not naturally good. A day comes when ideology conflicts with psychology. Then there is no more legitimate power. Thus the law evolves to the point of becoming confused with the legislator and with a new form of arbitrariness. Where turn then? The law has gone completely off its course; and, losing its precision, it becomes more and more inaccurate, to the point of making everything a crime. The law still reigns supreme, but it no longer has any fixed limits. Saint-Just had foreseen that this form of tyranny might be exercised in the name of a silent people. "Ingenious crime will be exalted into a kind of religion and criminals will be in the sacred hierarchy." But this is inevitable. If major principles have no foundation, if the law expresses nothing but a provisional inclination, it is only made in order to be broken or to be imposed. Sade or dictatorship, individual terrorism or State terrorism, both justified by the same absence of justification, are, from the moment that rebellion cuts itself off from its roots

[4] Hegel saw clearly that the philosophy of enlightenment wanted to deliver man from the irrational. Reason reunites mankind while the irrational destroys unity.

and abstains from any concrete morality, one of the alternatives of the twentieth century.

The revolutionary movement that was born in 1789 could not, however, stop there. God, for the Jacobins, is not completely dead, any more than He was dead for the romantics. They still preserve the Supreme Being. Reason, in a certain way, is still a mediator. It implies a pre-existent order. But God is at least dematerialized and reduced to the theoretical existence of a moral principle. The bourgeoisie succeeded in reigning during the entire nineteenth century only by referring itself to abstract principles. Less worthy than Saint-Just, it simply made use of this frame of reference as an alibi, while employing, on all occasions, the opposite values. By its essential corruption and disheartening hypocrisy, it helped to discredit, for good and all, the principles it proclaimed. Its culpability in this regard is infinite. From the moment that eternal principles are put in doubt simultaneously with formal virtue, and when every value is discredited, reason will start to act without reference to anything but its own successes. It would like to rule, denying everything that has been and affirming all that is to come. One day it will conquer. Russian Communism, by its violent criticism of every kind of formal virtue, puts the finishing touches to the revolutionary work of the nineteenth century by denying any superior principle. The regicides of the nineteenth century are succeeded by the deicides of the twentieth century, who draw the ultimate conclusions from the logic of rebellion and want to make the earth a kingdom where man is God. The reign of history begins and, identifying himself only with his history, man, unfaithful to his real rebellion, will henceforth devote himself to the nihilistic revolution of the twentieth century, which denies all forms of morality and desperately attempts to achieve the unity of the human race by means of a ruinous series of crimes and wars. The Jacobin Revolution, which tried to institute the religion of virtue in order to establish unity upon it, will be followed by the cynical revolutions, which can be either of the right or of the left and which will try to achieve the unity of the world so as to found, at last, the religion of man. All that was God's will henceforth be rendered to Cæsar.

The Deicides

✳

Justice, reason, truth still shone in the Jacobin heaven, performing the function of fixed stars, which could, at least, serve as guides. German nineteenth-century thinkers, particularly Hegel, wanted to continue the work of the French Revolution[1] while suppressing the causes of its failure. Hegel thought that he discerned the seeds of the Terror contained in the abstract principles of the Jacobins. According to him, absolute and abstract freedom must inevitably lead to terrorism; the rule of abstract law is identical with the rule of oppression. For example, Hegel remarks that the period between the time of Augustus and Alexander Severus (A.D. 235) is the period of the greatest legal proficiency but also the period of the most ruthless tyranny. To avoid this contradiction, it was therefore necessary to wish to construct a concrete society, invigorated by a principle that was not formal and in which freedom could be reconciled with necessity. German philosophy therefore finished by substituting, for the universal but abstract reason of Saint-Just and Rousseau, a less artificial but more ambiguous idea: concrete universal reason. Up to this point, reason had soared above the phenomena which were related to it. Now reason is, henceforth, incorporated in the stream of historical events, which it explains while deriving its substance from them.

It can certainly be said that Hegel rationalized to the point of being irrational. But, at the same time, he gave reason an unreasonable shock by endowing it with a lack of moderation, the results of which are now before our

[1] And of the Reformation—"the Germans' Revolution," according to Hegel.

eyes. Into the fixed ideas of this period, German thought suddenly introduced an irresistible urge to movement. Truth, reason, and justice were abruptly incarnated in the progress of the world. But by committing them to perpetual acceleration, German ideology confused their existence with their impulse and fixed the conclusion of this existence at the final stage of the historical future—if there was to be one. These values have ceased to be guides in order to become goals. As for the means of attaining these goals, specifically life and history, no pre-existent value can point the way. On the contrary, a large part of Hegelian demonstration is devoted to proving that moral conscience, by being so banal as to obey justice and truth, as though these values existed independently of the world, jeopardizes, precisely for this reason, the advent of these values. The rule of action has thus become action itself—which must be performed in darkness while awaiting the final illumination. Reason, annexed by this form of romanticism, is nothing more than an inflexible passion.

The ends have remained the same, only ambition has increased; thought has become dynamic, reason has embraced the future and aspired to conquest. Action is no more than a calculation based on results, not on principles. Consequently it confounds itself with perpetual movement. In the same way, all the disciplines that characterized eighteenth-century thought as rigid and addicted to classification were abandoned in the nineteenth century. Just as Darwin replaced Linnæus, the philosophers who supported the doctrine of an incessant dialectic replaced the harmonious and strict constructors of reason. From this moment dates the idea (hostile to every concept of ancient thought, which, on the contrary, reappeared to a certain extent in the mind of revolutionary France) that man has not been endowed with a definitive human nature, that he is not a finished creation but an experiment, of which he can be partly the creator. With Napoleon and the Napoleonic philosopher Hegel, the period of efficacy begins. Before Napoleon, men had discovered space and the universe; with Napoleon, they discovered time and the future in terms of this world; and by this discovery the spirit of rebellion is going to be profoundly transformed.

In any case, it is strange to find Hegel's philosophy at this new stage in the development of the spirit of rebellion. Actually, in one sense, his work exudes an absolute horror of dissidence: he wanted to be the very essence of reconciliation. But this is only one aspect of a system which, by its very method, is the most ambiguous in all philosophic literature. To the extent that, for him, what is real is rational, he justifies every ideological encroachment upon reality. What has been called Hegel's panlogism is a justification of the condition of fact. But his philosophy also exalts destruction for its own sake. Everything is reconciled, of course, in the dialectic, and one extreme cannot be stated without the other arising; there exists in Hegel, as in all great thinkers, the material for contradicting Hegel. Philosophers, however, are rarely read with the head alone, but often with the heart and all its passions, which can accept no kind of reconciliation.

Nevertheless, the revolutionaries of the twentieth century have borrowed from Hegel the weapons with which they definitively destroyed the formal principles of virtue. All that they have preserved is the vision of a history without any kind of transcendence, dedicated to perpetual strife and to the struggle of wills bent on seizing power. In its critical aspect, the revolutionary movement of our times is primarily a violent denunciation of the formal hypocrisy that presides over bourgeois society. The partially justified pretension of modern Communism, like the more frivolous claim of Fascism, is to denounce the mystification that undermines the principles and virtues of the bourgeois type of democracy. Divine transcendence, up to 1789, served to justify the arbitrary actions of the king. After the French Revolution, the transcendence of the formal principles of reason or justice serves to justify a rule that is neither just nor reasonable. This transcendence is therefore a mask that must be torn off. God is dead, but as Stirner predicted, the morality of principles in which the memory of God is still preserved must also be killed. The hatred of formal virtue—degraded witness to divinity and false witness in the service of injustice—has remained one of the principal themes of history today. Nothing is pure: that is the cry which convulses our period. Impurity, the equivalent of history, is going to become the rule, and the abandoned earth will be delivered to naked force, which will decide whether or not man is divine. Thus lies and violence are adopted in the same spirit in which a religion is adopted and on the same heartrending impulse.

But the first fundamental criticism of the good conscience—the denunciation of the beautiful soul and of ineffectual attitudes—we owe to Hegel, for whom the ideology of the good, the true, and the beautiful is the religion of those possessed of none of them. While the mere existence of factions surprises Saint-Just and contravenes the ideal order that he affirms, Hegel not only is not surprised, but even affirms that faction is the prelude to thought. For the Jacobin, everyone is virtuous. The movement which starts with Hegel, and which is triumphant today, presumes, on the contrary, that no one is virtuous, but that everyone will be. At the beginning, everything, according to Saint-Just, is an idyl; according to Hegel, everything is a tragedy. But in the end that amounts to the same thing. Those who destroy the idyl must be destroyed or destruction must be embarked on in order to create the idyl. Violence, in both cases, is the victor. The repudiation of the Terror, undertaken by Hegel, only leads to an extension of the Terror.

That is not all. Apparently the world today can no longer be anything other than a world of masters and slaves because contemporary ideologies, those that are changing the face of the earth, have learned from Hegel to conceive of history in terms of the dialectic of master and slave. If, on the first morning of the world, under the empty sky, there is only a master and a slave; even if there is only the bond of master and slave between a transcendent god and mankind, then there can be no other law in this world than the law of force. Only a god, or a principle above the master and the slave, could intervene and make men's history something more than a mere chronicle of their victories and defeats. First Hegel and then the Hegelians have tried, on the contrary, to destroy, more and more thoroughly, all idea of transcendence and any nostalgia for transcendence. Although there was infinitely more in Hegel than in the left-wing Hegelians who finally have triumphed over him, he nevertheless furnished, on the level of the dialectic of master and slave, the decisive justification of the spirit of power in the twentieth century. The conqueror is always right; that is one of the lessons which can be learned from the most important German philosophical system of the nineteenth century. Of course, there is to be found, in the prodigious Hegelian edifice, a means of partially contradicting those ideas. But twentieth-century ideology is not connected with what is improperly called the idealism of the master of Jena. Hegel's face, which reappears in Russian Communism, has been successively remodeled by David Strauss, Bruno Bauer, Feuerbach, Marx, and the entire Hegelian left wing. We are only interested in him here because he alone has any real bearing on the history of our time. If Nietzsche and Hegel serve as alibis to the masters of Dachau and Karaganda,[2] that does not condemn their entire philosophy. But it does lead to the suspicion that one aspect of their thought, or of their logic, can lead to these appalling conclusions.

Nietzschean nihilism is methodical. *The Phenomenology of the Mind* also has a didactic aspect. At the meeting-point of two centuries, it depicts, in its successive stages, the education of the mind as it pursues its way toward absolute truth. It is a metaphysical *Émile*.[3] Each stage is an error and is, moreover, accompanied by historic sanctions which are almost always fatal, either to the mind or to the civilization in which it is reflected. Hegel proposes to demonstrate the necessity of these painful stages. The *Phenomenology* is, in one aspect, a meditation on despair and death. The mission of despair is, simply, to be methodical in that it must be transfigured, at the end of history, into absolute satisfaction and absolute wisdom. The book has the defect, however, of only imagining highly intelligent pupils and it has been taken literally, while, literally, it only wanted to proclaim the spirit.

[2] They found less philosophic models in the Prussian, Napoleonic, and Czarist police and in the British concentration camps in South Africa.

[3] In one sense there is a ground of comparison between Hegel and Rousseau. The fortune of the *Phenomenology* has been, in its consequences, of the same kind as that of the *Social Contract*. It shaped the political thought of its time. Rousseau's theory of the general will, besides, recurs in the Hegelian system.

It is the same with the celebrated analysis of mastery and slavery.

Animals, according to Hegel, have an immediate knowledge of the exterior world, a perception of the self, but not the knowledge of self, which distinguishes man. The latter is only really born at the moment when he becomes aware of himself as a rational being. Therefore his essential characteristic is self-consciousness. Consciousness of self, to be affirmed, must distinguish itself from what it is not. Man is a creature who, to affirm his existence and his difference, denies. What distinguishes consciousness of self from the world of nature is not the simple act of contemplation by which it identifies itself with the exterior world and finds oblivion, but the desire it can feel with regard to the world. This desire re-establishes its identity when it demonstrates that the exterior world is something apart. In its desire, the exterior world consists of what it does not possess, but which nevertheless exists, and of what it would like to exist but which no longer does. Consciousness of self is therefore, of necessity, desire. But in order to exist it must be satisfied, and it can only be satisfied by the gratification of its desire. It therefore acts in order to gratify itself and, in so doing, it denies and suppresses its means of gratification. It is the epitome of negation. To act is to destroy in order to give birth to the spiritual reality of consciousness. But to destroy an object unconsciously, as meat is destroyed, for example, in the act of eating, is a purely animal activity. To consume is not yet to be conscious. Desire for consciousness must be directed toward something other than unconscious nature. The only thing in the world that is distinct from nature is, precisely, self-consciousness. Therefore desire must be centered upon another form of desire; self-consciousness must be gratified by another form of self-consciousness. In simple words, man is not recognized—and does not recognize himself—as a man as long as he limits himself to subsisting like an animal. He must be acknowledged by other men. All consciousness is, basically, the desire to be recognized and proclaimed as such by other consciousnesses. It is others who beget us. Only in association do we receive a human value, as distinct from an animal value.

In that the supreme value for the animal is the preservation of life, consciousness should raise itself above the level of that instinct in order to achieve human value. It should be capable of risking its life. To be recognized by another consciousness, man should be ready to risk his life and to accept the chance of death. Fundamental human relations are thus relations of pure prestige, a perpetual struggle, to the death, for recognition of one human being by another.

At the first stage of his dialectic, Hegel affirms that in so far as death is the common ground of man and animal, it is by accepting death and even by inviting it that the former differentiates himself from the latter. At the heart of this primordial struggle for recognition, man is thus identified with violent death. The mystic slogan "Die and become what you are" is taken up once more by Hegel. But "Become what you are" gives place to "Become what you so far are not." This primitive and passionate desire for recognition, which is confused with the will to exist, can be satisfied only by a recognition gradually extended until it embraces everyone. In that everyone wants equally much to be recognized by everyone, the fight for life will cease only with the recognition of all by all, which will mark the termination of history. The existence that Hegelian consciousness seeks to obtain is born in the hard-won glory of collective approval. It is not beside the point to note that, in the thought which will inspire our revolutions, the supreme good does not, in reality, coincide with existence, but with an arbitrary facsimile. The entire history of mankind is, in any case, nothing but a prolonged fight to the death for the conquest of universal prestige and absolute power. It is, in its essence, imperialist. We are far from the gentle savage of the eighteenth century and from the *Social Contract*. In the sound and fury of the passing centuries, each separate consciousness, to ensure its own existence, must henceforth desire the death of others. Moreover, this relentless tragedy is absurd, since, in the event of one consciousness being destroyed, the victorious consciousness is not recognized as such, in that it cannot be victorious in the eyes of something that no longer exists. In fact, it is here the philosophy of appearances reaches its limits.

No human reality would therefore have been engendered if, thanks to a propensity that can be considered fortunate for Hegel's system, there had not existed, from the beginning of time, two kinds of consciousness, one of which has not the courage to renounce life and is therefore willing to recognize the other kind of consciousness without being recognized itself in return. It consents, in short, to being considered as an object. This type of consciousness, which, to preserve its animal existence, renounces independent life, is the consciousness of a slave. The type of consciousness which by being recognized achieves independence is that of the master. They are distinguished one from the other at the moment when they clash and when one submits to the other. The dilemma at this stage is not to be free or to die, but to kill or to enslave. This dilemma will resound throughout the course of history, though at this moment its absurdity has not yet been resolved.

Undoubtedly the master enjoys total freedom first as regards the slave, since the latter recognizes him totally, and then as regards the natural world, since by his work the slave transforms it into objects of enjoyment which the master consumes in a perpetual affirmation of his own identity. However, this autonomy is not absolute. The master, to his misfortune, is recognized in his autonomy by a consciousness that he himself does not recognize as autonomous. Therefore he cannot be satisfied and his autonomy is only negative. Mastery is a blind alley. Since, moreover, he cannot renounce mastery and become a slave again, the eternal destiny of masters is to live unsatisfied or to be killed. The master serves no other purpose in history than to arouse servile consciousness, the only form of consciousness that really creates history. The slave, in fact, is not bound to his condition, but wants to change it. Thus, unlike his master, he can improve himself, and what is called history is nothing but the effects of his long efforts to obtain real freedom. Already, by work, by his transformation of the natural world into a technical world, he manages to escape from the nature which was the basis of his slavery in that he did not know how to raise himself above it by accepting death.[4] The very agony of death experienced in the humiliation of the entire being lifts the slave to the level of human totality. He knows, henceforth, that this totality exists; now it only remains for him to conquer it through a long series of struggles against nature and against the masters. History identifies itself, therefore, with the history of endeavor and rebellion. It is hardly astonishing that Marxism-Leninism derived from this dialectic the contemporary ideal of the soldier worker.

We shall leave aside the description of the various attitudes of the servile consciousness (stoicism, skepticism, guilty conscience) which then follows in the *Phenomenology*. But, thanks to its consequences, another aspect of this dialectic cannot be neglected: namely, the assimilation of the master-slave relationship to the relationship between man and God. One of Hegel's commentators[5] remarks that if the master really existed, he would be God. Hegel himself calls the Master of the world the real God. In his description of guilty conscience he shows how the Christian slave, wishing to deny everything that oppresses him, takes refuge in the world beyond and by doing so gives himself a new master in the person of God. Elsewhere Hegel identifies the supreme master with absolute death. And so the struggle begins again, on a higher level, between man in chains and the cruel God of Abraham. The solution to this new conflict between the universal God and the human entity will be furnished by Christ, who reconciles in Himself the universal and the unique. But, in one sense, Christ is a part of the palpable world. He is visible, He lived and He died. He is therefore only a stage on the road to the universal; He too must be denied dialectically. It is only necessary to recognize Him as the man-God to obtain a higher synthesis. Skipping the intermediary stages, it suffices to say that this synthesis, after being incarnated in the Church and in Reason, culminates in the absolute State, founded by the soldier workers,

[4] Actually, the ambiguity is profound, for the nature in question is not the same. Does the advent of the technical world suppress death or the fear of death in the natural world? That is the real question, which Hegel leaves in suspense.

[5] Jean Hyppolite.

where the spirit of the world will be finally reflected in the mutual recognition of each by all and in the universal reconciliation of everything that has ever existed under the sun. At this moment, "when the eyes of the spirit coincide with the eyes of the body," each individual consciousness will be nothing more than a mirror reflecting another mirror, itself reflected to infinity in infinitely recurring images. The City of God will coincide with the city of humanity; and universal history, sitting in judgment on the world, will pass its sentence by which good and evil will be justified. The State will play the part of Destiny and will proclaim its approval of every aspect of reality on "the sacred day of the Presence."

This sums up the essential ideas which in spite, or because, of the extreme ambiguity of their interpretation, have literally driven the revolutionary mind in apparently contradictory directions and which we are now learning to rediscover in the ideology of our times. Amorality, scientific materialism, and atheism have definitely replaced the antitheism of the rebels of former times and have made common cause, under Hegel's paradoxical influence, with a revolutionary movement which, until his time, was never really separated from its moral, evangelical, and idealistic origins. These tendencies, if they are sometimes very far from really originating with Hegel, found their source in the ambiguity of his thought and in his critique of transcendence. Hegel's undeniable originality lies in his definitive destruction of all vertical transcendence—particularly the transcendence of principles. There is no doubt that he restores the immanence of the spirit to the evolution of the world. But this immanence is not precisely defined and has nothing in common with the pantheism of the ancients. The spirit is and is not part of the world; it creates itself and will finally prevail. Values are thus only to be found at the end of history. Until then there is no suitable criterion on which to base a judgment of value. One must act and live in terms of the future. All morality becomes provisional. The nineteenth and twentieth centuries, in their most profound manifestations, are centuries that have tried to live without transcendence.

One of Hegel's commentators, Alexandre Kojève, of

left-wing tendencies it is true, but orthodox in his opinion on this particular point, notes Hegel's hostility to the moralists and remarks that his only axiom is to live according to the manners and customs of one's nation. A maxim of social conformity of which Hegel, in fact, gave the most cynical proofs. Kojève adds, however, that this conformity is legitimate only to the extent that the customs of the nation correspond to the spirit of the times—in other words, to the extent that they are solidly established and can resist revolutionary criticism and attacks. But who will determine their solidity and who will judge their validity? For a hundred years the capitalist regimes of the West have withstood violent assaults. Should they for that reason be considered legitimate? Inversely, should those who were faithful to the Weimar Republic have abandoned it and pledged themselves to Hitler in 1933 because the former collapsed when attacked by the latter? Should the Spanish Republic have been betrayed at the exact moment when General Franco's forces triumphed? These are conclusions that traditional reactionary thought would have justified within its own perspectives. The novelty, of which the consequences are incalculable, lies in the fact that revolutionary thought has assimilated them. The suppression of every moral value and of all principles and their replacement by fact, as provisional but actual king, could only lead, as we have plainly seen, to political cynicism, whether it be fact as envisioned by the individual or, more serious still, fact as envisioned by the State. The political movements, or ideologies, inspired by Hegel are all united in the ostensible abandonment of virtue.

Hegel could not, in fact, prevent those who had read him, with feelings of anguish which were far from methodical in a Europe that was already torn asunder by injustice, from finding themselves precipitated into a world without innocence and without principles—into the very world of which Hegel says that it is in itself a sin, since it is separated from the spirit. Hegel, of course, permits the forgiveness of sins at the end of history. Until then, however, every human activity is sinful. "Therefore only the absence of activity is innocent, the existence of a stone and not even the existence of a child." Thus even the innocence of stones is unknown to us. Without innocence there are no human relations and no reason. Without reason, there is nothing but naked force, the master and slave waiting for reason one day to prevail. Between master and slave, even suffering is solitary, joy is without foundation, and both are undeserved. Then how can one live, how endure life when friendship is reserved for the end of time? The only escape is to create order with the use of weapons. "Kill or enslave!"—those who have read Hegel with this single and terrible purpose have really considered only the first part of the dilemma. From it they have derived a philosophy of scorn and despair and have deemed themselves slaves and nothing but slaves, bound by death to the absolute Master and by the whip to their terrestrial masters. This philosophy of the guilty conscience has merely taught them that every slave is enslaved only by his own consent, and can be liberated only by an act of protest which coincides with death. Answering the challenge, the most courageous among them have completely identified themselves with this act of protest and have dedicated themselves to death. After all, to say that negation is in itself a positive act justified in advance every kind of negation and predicted the cry of Bakunin and Nechaiev: "Our mission is to destroy, not to construct." A nihilist for Hegel was only a skeptic who had no other escape but contradiction or philosophic suicide. But he himself gave birth to another type of nihilist, who, making boredom into a principle of action, identified suicide with philosophic murder.[6] It was at this point that the terrorists were born who decided that it was necessary to kill and die in order to exist, because mankind and history could achieve their creation only by sacrifice and murder. The magnificent idea that all idealism is chimerical if it is not paid for by risking one's life was to be developed to the fullest possible extent by young men who were not engaged in expounding the concept from the safe distance of a university chair before dying in their beds, but among the tumult of falling bombs and even

[6] This form of nihilism, despite appearances, is still nihilism in the Nietzschean sense, to the extent that it is a calumny of the present life to the advantage of a historical future in which one tries to believe.

on the gallows. By doing this and even by their errors they corrected their master and demonstrated, contrary to his teaching, that one kind of aristocracy, at least, is superior to the hideous aristocracy of success exalted by Hegel: the aristocracy of sacrifice.

Another sort of follower, who read Hegel more seriously, chose the second term of the dilemma and made the pronouncement that the slave could only free himself by enslaving in his turn. Post-Hegelian doctrines, unmindful of the mystic aspect or certain of the master's tendencies, have led his followers to absolute atheism and to scientific materialism. But this evolution is inconceivable without the absolute disappearance of every principle of transcendent explanation, and without the complete destruction of the Jacobin ideal. Immanence, of course, is not atheism. But immanence in the process of development is, if one can say so, provisional atheism.[7] The indefinite face of God which, with Hegel, is still reflected in the spirit of the world will not be difficult to efface. Hegel's successors will draw decisive conclusions from his ambiguous formula: "God without man is no more than man without God." David Strauss in his *Life of Jesus* isolates the theory of Christ considered as the God-man. Bruno Bauer (*The Critique of Evangelist History*) institutes a kind of materialist Christianity by insisting on the humanity of Jesus. Finally, Ludwig Feuerbach (whom Marx considered as a great mind and of whom he acknowledges himself the critical disciple), in his *Essence of Christianity*, replaces all theology by a religion of man and the species, which has converted a large part of contemporary thought. His task is to demonstrate that the distinction between human and divine is illusory, that it is nothing but the distinction between the essence of humanity—in other words, human nature—and the individual. "The mystery of God is only the mystery of the love of man for himself." The accents of a strange new prophecy ring out: "Individuality has replaced faith, reason the Bible, politics religion and the Church, the earth heaven, work

---

[7] In any event, the criticism of Kierkegaard is valid. To base divinity on history is, paradoxically, to base an absolute value on approximate knowledge. Something "eternally historic" is a contradiction in terms.

prayer, poverty hell, and man Christ." Thus there is only one hell and it is on this earth: and it is against this that the struggle must be waged. Politics is religion, and transcendent Christianity—that of the hereafter—establishes the masters of the earth by means of the slave's renunciation and creates one master more beneath the heavens. That is why atheism and the revolutionary spirit are only two aspects of the same movement of liberation. That is the answer to the question which is always being asked: why has the revolutionary movement identified itself with materialism rather than with idealism? Because to conquer God, to make Him a slave, amounts to abolishing the transcendence that kept the former masters in power and to preparing, with the ascendancy of the new tyrants, the advent of the man-king. When poverty is abolished, when the contradictions of history are resolved, "the real god, the human god, will be the State." Then *homo homini lupus* becomes *homo homini deus*. This concept is at the root of the contemporary world. With Feuerbach, we assist at the birth of a terrible form of optimism which we can still observe at work today and which seems to be the very antithesis of nihilist despair. But that is only in appearance. We must know Feuerbach's final conclusions in this *Theogony* to perceive the profoundly nihilist derivation of his inflamed imagination. In effect, Feuerbach affirms, in the face of Hegel, that man is only what he eats, and thus recapitulates his ideas and predicts the future in the following phrase: "The true philosophy is the negation of philosophy. No religion is my religion. No philosophy is my philosophy."

Cynicism, the deification of history and of matter, individual terror and State crime, these are the inordinate consequences that will now spring, armed to the teeth, from the equivocal conception of a world that entrusts to history alone the task of producing both values and truth. If nothing can be clearly understood before truth has been brought to light, at the end of time, then every action is arbitrary, and force will finally rule supreme. "If reality is inconceivable," Hegel exclaims, "then we must contrive inconceivable concepts." A concept that cannot be conceived must, perforce, like error, be contrived. But to be accepted it cannot rely on the persuasion innate in order and truth, but must finally be imposed. Hegel's attitude consists of saying: "This is truth, which appears to us, however, to be error, but which is true precisely because it happens to be error. As for proof, it is not I, but history, at its conclusion, that will furnish it." Such pretensions can only entail two attitudes: either the suspension of all affirmation until the production of proof, or the affirmation of everything, in history, which seems dedicated to success —force in particular. And both attitudes imply nihilism. Moreover, it is impossible to understand twentieth-century revolutionary thought if we overlook the fact that unfortunately it derived a large part of its inspiration from a philosophy of conformity and opportunism. True rebellion is not jeopardized on account of the distortion of these particular ideas.

Nevertheless, the basis of Hegel's claims is what renders them intellectually and forever suspect. He believed that history in 1807, with the advent of Napoleon and of himself, had come to an end, and that affirmation was possible and nihilism conquered. The *Phenomenology*, the Bible that was to have prophesied only the past, put a limit on time. In 1807 all sins were forgiven, and time had stopped. But history has continued. Other sins, since then, have been hurled in the face of the world and have revived the scandal of the former crimes, which the German philosopher had already forgiven forever. The deification of Hegel by himself, after the deification of Napoleon, who would henceforth be innocent since he had succeeded in stabilizing history, lasted only seven years. Instead of total affirmation, nihilism once more covered the face of the earth. Philosophy, even servile philosophy, has its Waterloos.

But nothing can discourage the appetite for divinity in the heart of man. Others have come and are still to come who, forgetting Waterloo, still claim to terminate history. The divinity of man is still on the march, and will be worthy of adoration only at the end of time. This apocalypse must be promoted and, despite the fact that there is no God, at least a Church must be built. After all, history, which has not yet come to an end, allows us a glimpse of a perspective that might even be that of the Hegelian system but for the simple reason that it is provisionally dragged along, if not led, by the spiritual heirs of Hegel. When cholera carries off the philosopher of the Battle of Jena at the height of his glory, everything is, in fact, in order for what is to follow. The sky is empty, the earth delivered into the hands of power without principles. Those who have chosen to kill and those who have chosen to enslave will successively occupy the front of the stage, in the name of a form of rebellion which has been diverted from the path of truth.

Individual Terrorism

∗

Pisarev, the theoretician of Russian nihilism, declares that the greatest fanatics are children and adolescents. That is also true of nations. Russia, at this period, is an adolescent nation, delivered with forceps, barely a century ago, by a Czar who was still ingenuous enough to cut off the heads of rebels himself. It is not astonishing that she should have pushed Germanic ideology to extremes of sacrifice and destruction which German professors had only been capable of theorizing about. Stendhal noticed an essential difference between Germans and other people in the fact that they are excited by meditation rather than soothed. That is true, but it is even more true of Russia. In that immature country, completely without philosophic tradition,[1] some very young people, akin to Lautréamont's tragic fellow students, enthusiastically embraced the concepts of German thought and incarnated the consequences in blood. A "proletariat of undergraduates"[2] then took the lead in the great movement of human emancipation and gave it its most violent aspect. Until the end of the nineteenth century these undergraduates never numbered more than a few thousand. Entirely on their own, however, and in defiance of the most integrated absolutism of the time, they aspired to liberate and provisionally did contribute to the liberation of forty million muzhiks. Almost all of them paid for this liberation by suicide, execution, prison, or madness. The entire history of Russian terrorism can be summed up in the struggle of a handful of intellectuals to

[1] Pisarev remarks that civilization, in its ideological aspects, has always been imported into Russia.

[2] Dostoievsky.

abolish tyranny, against a background of a silent populace. Their debilitated victory was finally betrayed. But by their sacrifice and even by their most extreme negations they gave substance to a new standard of values, a new virtue, which even today has not ceased to oppose tyranny and to give aid to the cause of true liberation.

The Germanization of nineteenth-century Russia is not an isolated phenomenon. The influence of German ideology at that moment was preponderant, and we are well aware, for example, that the nineteenth century in France, with Michelet and Quinet, is the century of Germanic thought. But in Russia this ideology did not encounter an already established system, while in France it had to contend and compromise with libertarian socialism. In Russia it was on conquered territory. The first Russian university, the University of Moscow, founded in 1750, is German. The slow colonization of Russia by German teachers, bureaucrats, and soldiers, which began under Peter the Great, was transformed at the instance of Nicholas I into systematic Germanization. The intelligentsia developed a passion for Schelling (simultaneously with their passion for French writers) in the 1830's, for Hegel in the 1840's, and in the second half of the century for German socialism derived from Hegel.[3] Russian youth then proceeded to pour into these abstract thoughts the inordinate violence of its passions and authentically experienced these already moribund ideas. The religion of man already formulated by its German pastors was still missing its apostles and martyrs. Russian Christians, led astray from their original vocation, played this role. For this reason they had to accept life without transcendence and without virtue.

The Renunciation of Virtue

In the 1820's among the first Russian revolutionaries, the Decembrists, virtue still existed. Jacobin idealism had not yet been uprooted from the hearts of these gentlemen. They even practiced conscious virtue: "Our fathers were

[3] *Das Kapital* was translated in 1872.

sybarites, we are Catos," said one of them, Peter Viazem-
sky. To this is only added the opinion, which will still be
found in Bakunin and the revolutionary socialists of 1905,
that suffering regenerates. The Decembrists remind us of
the French nobles who allied themselves with the third
estate and renounced their privileges. Patrician idealists,
they deliberately chose to sacrifice themselves for the
liberation of the people. Despite the fact that their leader,
Pestel, was a political and social theorist, their abortive
conspiracy had no fixed program; it is not even sure that
they believed in the possibility of success. "Yes, we shall
die," one of them said on the eve of the insurrection, "but
it will be a fine death." It was, in fact, a fine death. In
December 1825 the rebels, arranged in formation, were
mown down by cannon fire in the square in front of the
Senate at St. Petersburg. The survivors were deported, but
not before five had been hanged, and so clumsily that it
had to be done twice. It is easy to understand why these
ostensibly inefficacious victims have been venerated, with
feelings of exaltation and horror, by all of revolutionary
Russia. They were exemplary, if not efficacious. They indicated, at the beginning of this chapter of revolutionary
history, the ambitions and the greatness of what Hegel
ironically called the beautiful soul in relation to which
Russian revolutionary ideas were, nevertheless, to be defined.

In this atmosphere of exaltation, German thought
came to combat French influence and impose its prestige
on minds torn between their desire for vengeance and
justice and the realization of their own impotent isolation.
It was first received, extolled, and commented upon as
though it were revelation itself. The best minds were inflamed with a passion for philosophy. They even went so
far as to put Hegel's *Logic* into verse. For the most part,
Russian intellectuals at first inferred, from the Hegelian
system, the justification of a form of social quietism. To
be aware of the rationality of the world sufficed; the Spirit
would realize itself, in any case, at the end of time. That
is the first reaction of Stankevich,[4] Bakunin, and Bielinsky, for example. Then the Russian mind recoiled at this

[4] "The world is ordered by the spirit of reason, this re-
assures me about everything else."

factual, if not intentional, complicity with absolutism and, immediately, jumped to the opposite extreme.

Nothing is more revealing, in this respect, than the evolution of Bielinsky, one of the most remarkable and most influential minds of the 1830's and 40's. Beginning with a background of rather vague libertarian idealism, Bielinsky suddenly discovers Hegel. In his room, at midnight, under the shock of revelation, he bursts into tears like Pascal and suddenly becomes a new man. "Neither chance nor the absolute exists, I have made my adieux to the French." At the same time he is still a conservative and a partisan of social quietism. He writes to that effect without a single hesitation and defends his position, as he perceives it, courageously. But this essentially kindhearted man then sees himself allied with what is most detestable in this world: injustice. If everything is logical, then everything is justified. One must consent to the whip, to serfdom, to Siberia. To accept the world and its sufferings seemed to him, at one moment, the noble thing to do because he imagined that he would only have to bear his own sufferings and his own contradictions. But if it also implied consent to the sufferings of others, he suddenly discovered that he had not the heart to continue. He set out again in the opposite direction. If one cannot accept the suffering of others, then something in the world cannot be justified, and history, at one point at least, no longer coincides with reason. But history must be completely reasonable or it is not reasonable at all. This man's solitary protest, quieted for a moment by the idea that everything can be justified, bursts forth again in vehement terms. Bielinsky addresses Hegel himself: "With all the esteem due to your philistine philosophy, I have the honor to inform you that even if I had the opportunity of climbing to the very top of the ladder of evolution, I should still ask you to account for all the victims of life and history. I do not want happiness, even gratuitous happiness, if my mind is not at rest concerning all my blood brothers."

Bielinsky understood that what he wanted was not the absolute of reason but the fullness of life. He refuses to identify them. He wants the immortality of the entire man, clothed in his living body, not the abstract immortality of the species become Spirit. He argues with equal passion against new adversaries, and draws, from this fierce interior debate, conclusions that he owes to Hegel, but which he turns against him.

These are the conclusions of individualism in revolt. The individual cannot accept history as it is. He must destroy reality, not collaborate with it, in order to affirm his own existence. "Negation is my god, as reality formerly was. My heroes are the destroyers of the past: Luther, Voltaire, the Encyclopedists, the Terrorists, Byron in *Cain*." Thus we rediscover here, simultaneously, all the themes of metaphysical rebellion. Certainly, the French tradition of individualistic socialism always remained alive in Russia. Saint-Simon and Fourier, who were read in the 1830's, and Proudhon, who was imported in the forties, inspired the great concepts of Herzen, and, very much later, those of Pierre Lavrov. But this system, which remained attached to ethical values, finally succumbed, provisionally at any rate, during its great debate with cynical thought. On the other hand, Bielinsky rediscovers both with and against Hegel the same tendencies to social individualism, but under the aspect of negation, in the rejection of transcendental values. When he dies, in 1848, his thought will moreover be very close to that of Herzen. But when he confronts Hegel, he defines, with precision, an attitude that will be adopted by the nihilists, and at least in part by the terrorists. Thus he furnishes a type of transition between the idealist aristocrats of 1825 and the "nothingist" students of 1860.

Three of the Possessed

When Herzen, in making his apology for the nihilist movement—only to the extent, it is true, that he sees in it a still greater emancipation from ready-made ideas—writes: "The annihilation of the past is the procreation of the future," he is using the language of Bielinsky. Koteiarevsky, speaking of the so-called radicals of the period, defined them as apostles "who thought that the past must be completely renounced and the human personality must be constructed to quite another plan."

Stirner's claim reappears with the total rejection of history and the determination to construct the future, no longer with regard to the historical spirit, but so as to coincide with the man-king. But the man-king cannot raise himself to power unaided. He has need of others and therefore enters into a nihilist contradiction which Pisarev, Bakunin, and Nechaiev will try to resolve by slightly extending the area of destruction and negation, to the point where terrorism finally kills the contradiction itself, in a simultaneous act of sacrifice and murder.

The nihilism of the 1860's began, apparently, with the most radical negation imaginable: the rejection of any action that was not purely egoistic. We know that the very term *nihilism* was invented by Turgeniev in his novel *Fathers and Sons*, whose hero, Bazarov, was an exact portrayal of this type of man. Pisarev, when he wrote a criticism of this book, proclaimed that the nihilists recognized Bazarov as their model. "We have nothing," said Bazarov, "to boast about but the sterile knowledge of understanding, up to a certain point, the sterility of what exists." "Is that," he was asked, "what is called nihilism?" "Yes, that is what is called nihilism." Pisarev praises Bazarov's attitude, which for the sake of clarity he defines thus: "I am a stranger to the order of existing things, I have nothing to do with it." Thus the only value resides in rational egoism.

In denying everything that is not satisfaction of the self, Pisarev declares war on philosophy, on art, which he considers absurd, on erroneous ethics, on religion, and even on customs and on good manners. He constructs a theory of intellectual terrorism which makes one think of the present-day surrealists. Provocation is made into a doctrine, but on a level of which Raskolnikov provides the perfect example. At the height of this fine transport, Pisarev asks himself, without even laughing, whether he is justified in killing his own mother and answers: "And why not, if I want to do so, and if I find it useful?"

From that point on, it is surprising not to find the nihilists engaged in making a fortune or acquiring a title or in cynically taking advantage of every opportunity that offers itself. It is true that there were nihilists to be found in advantageous positions on all levels of society. But they did not construct a theory from their cynicism and preferred on all occasions to pay visible and quite inconsequential homage to virtue. As for those we are discussing, they contradicted themselves by the defiance they hurled in the face of society, which in itself was the affirmation of a value. They called themselves materialists; their bedside book was Buchner's *Force and Matter*. But one of them confessed: "Every one of us was ready to go to the scaffold and to give his head for Moleschott and Darwin," thus putting doctrine well ahead of matter. Doctrine, taken seriously to this degree, has an air of religion and fanaticism. For Pisarev, Lamarck was a traitor because Darwin was right. Whoever in this intellectual sphere began talking about the immortality of the soul was immediately excommunicated. Vladimir Veidle is therefore right when he defines nihilism as rationalist obscurantism. Reason among the nihilists, strangely enough, annexed the prejudices of faith; choosing the most popularized forms of science-worship for their prototype of reason was not the least of the contradictions accepted by these individualists. They denied everything but the most debatable of values, the values of Flaubert's Monsieur Homais.

However, it was by choosing to make reason, in its most limited aspect, into an act of faith that the nihilists provided their successors with a model. They believed in nothing but reason and self-interest. But instead of skepticism, they chose to propagate a doctrine and became socialists. Therein lies their basic contradiction. Like all adolescent minds they simultaneously experienced doubt and the need to believe. Their personal solution consists in endowing their negation with the intransigence and passion of faith. What, after all, is astonishing about that? Veidle quotes the scornful phrase used by Soloviev, the philosopher, in denouncing this contradiction: "Man is descended from monkeys, therefore let us love one another." Pisarev's truth, however, is to be found in this dilemma. If man is the image of God, then it does not matter that he is deprived of human love; the day will come when he will be satiated with it. But if he is a blind creature, wandering in the darkness of a cruel and circumscribed condition, he has need of his equals and of their ephemeral love. Where can charity take refuge, after all,

if not in the world without God? In the other, grace provides for all, even for the rich. Those who deny everything at least understand that negation is a calamity. They
can then open their hearts to the misery of others and
finally deny themselves. Pisarev did not shrink from the
idea of murdering his mother, and yet he managed to
find the exact words to describe injustice. He wanted to
enjoy life egoistically, but he suffered imprisonment and
finally went mad. Such an ostentatious display of cynicism
finally led him to an understanding of love, to be exiled
from it and to suffer from it to the point of suicide, thus
revealing, in place of the man-god he wanted to create,
the unhappy, suffering old man whose greatness illuminates the pages of history.

Bakunin embodies, but in a manner spectacular in a
different way, the very same contradictions. He died on
the eve of the terrorist epic, in 1876. Moreover, he rejected in advance individual outrages and denounced "the
Brutuses of the period." He had a certain respect for them,
however, since he reproached Herzen for having openly
criticized Karakosov for his abortive attempt to assassinate
Alexander II in 1866. This feeling of respect had its
reasons. Bakunin influenced the course of events in the
same manner as Bielinsky and the nihilists and directed
them into the channel of individual revolt. But he contributed something more: a germ of political cynicism,
which will congeal, with Nechaiev, into a doctrine and will
drive the revolutionary movement to extremes.

Bakunin had hardly emerged from adolescence when
he was overwhelmed and uprooted by Hegelian philosophy,
as if by a gigantic earthquake. He buries himself in it
day and night "to the point of madness," he says, and
adds: "I saw absolutely nothing but Hegel's categories."
When he emerges from this initiation, it is with the exaltation of a neophyte. "My personal self is dead forever, my
life is the true life. It is in some way identified with the
absolute life." He required very little time to see the
dangers of that comfortable position. He who has understood reality does not rebel against it, but rejoices in it;
in other words, he becomes a conformist. Nothing in
Bakunin's character predestined him to that watchdog
philosophy. It is possible, also, that his travels in Germany,

and the unfortunate opinion he formed of the Germans, may have ill-prepared him to agree with the aged Hegel that the Prussian State was the privileged depositary of the final fruits of the mind. More Russian than the Czar himself, despite his dreams of universality, he could in no event subscribe to the apology of Prussia when it was founded on a logic brash enough to assert: "The will of other peoples has no rights, for it is the people who represent the will [of the Spirit] who dominate the world." In the 1840's, moreover, Bakunin discovered French socialism and anarchism, from which he appropriated a few tendencies. Bakunin rejects, with a magnificent gesture, any part of German ideology. He approached the absolute in the same way as he approached total destruction, with the same passionate emotion, and with the blind enthusiasm for the "All or Nothing" which we again find in him in its purest form.

After having extolled absolute Unity, Bakunin enthusiastically embraces the most elementary form of Manichæism. What he wants, of course, is once and for all "the universal and authentically democratic Church of Freedom." That is his religion; he belongs to his times. It is not sure, however, that his faith on this point had been perfect. In his *Confession* to Czar Nicholas I, he seems to be sincere when he says that he has never been able to believe in the final revolution "except with a supernatural and painful effort to stifle forcibly the interior voice which whispered to me that my hopes were absurd." His theory of immorality, on the other hand, is much more firmly based and he is often to be seen plunging about in it with the ease and pleasure of a mettlesome horse. History is governed by only two principles: the State and social revolution, revolution and counterrevolution, which can never be reconciled, and which are engaged in a death struggle. The State is the incarnation of crime. "The smallest and most inoffensive State is still criminal in its dreams." Therefore revolution is the incarnation of good. This struggle, which surpasses politics, is also the struggle of Luciferian principles against the divine principle. Bakunin explicitly reintroduces into rebellious action one of the themes of romantic rebellion. Proudhon had already decreed that God is Evil and exclaimed: "Come, Satan,

victim of the calumnies of kings and of the petty-minded!"
Bakunin also gives a glimpse of the broader implications of
an apparently political rebellion: "Evil is satanic rebellion
against divine authority, a rebellion in which we see, nevertheless, the fruitful seed of every form of human emancipation." Like the Fraticelli of fourteenth-century Bo-
hemia, revolutionary socialists today use this phrase as a
password: "In the name of him to whom a great wrong has
been done."

The struggle against creation will therefore be without
mercy and without ethics, and the only salvation lies in
extermination. "The passion for destruction is a creative
passion." Bakunin's burning words on the subject of the
revolution of 1848 in his *Confession* vehemently proclaim
this pleasure in destruction. "A feast without beginning
and without end," he says. In fact, for him as for all who
are oppressed, the revolution is a feast, in the religious
sense of the word. Here we are reminded of the French
anarchist Cœurderoy, who, in his book *Hurrah, or the
Cossack Revolution*, summoned the hordes of the north
to lay waste to the whole world. He also wanted to "apply
the torch to my father's house" and proclaimed that the
only hope lay in the human deluge and in chaos. Rebellion
is grasped, throughout these manifestations, in its pure
state, in its biological truth. That is why Bakunin with
exceptional perspicacity was the only one of his period to
declare war on science, the idol of his contemporaries.
Against every abstract idea he pleaded the cause of the
complete man, completely identified with his rebellion. If
he glorifies the brigand leader of the peasant rising, if he
chooses to model himself on Stenka Razin and Pugachev,
it is because these men fought, without either doctrine or
principle, for an ideal of pure freedom. Bakunin introduces
into the midst of revolution the naked principle of rebellion. "The tempest and life, that is what we need. A new
world, without laws, and consequently free."

But is a world without laws a free world? That is the
question posed by every rebellion. If the question were to
be asked of Bakunin, the answer would not be in doubt.
Despite the fact that he was opposed in all circumstances,
and with the most extreme lucidity, to authoritarian so-

cialism, yet from the moment when he himself begins to define the society of the future, he does so—without being at all concerned about the contradiction—in terms of a dictatorship. The statutes of the International Fraternity (1864–7), which he edited himself, already establish the absolute subordination of the individual to the central committee, during the period of action. It is the same for the period that will follow the revolution. He hopes to see in liberated Russia "a strong dictatorial power . . . a power supported by partisans, enlightened by their advice, fortified by their free collaboration, but which would be limited by nothing and by no one." Bakunin contributed as much as his enemy Marx to Leninist doctrine. The dream of the revolutionary Slav empire, moreover, as Bakunin conjures it up before the Czar, is exactly the same, down to the last detail of its frontiers, as that realized by Stalin. Coming from a man who was wise enough to say that the essential driving-force of Czarist Russia was fear and who rejected the Marxist theory of party dictatorship, these conceptions may seem contradictory. But this contradiction demonstrates that the origins of authoritarian doctrines are partially nihilistic. Pisarev justifies Bakunin. Certainly, the latter wanted total freedom; but he hoped to realize it through total destruction. To destroy everything is to pledge oneself to building without foundations, and then to holding up the walls with one's hands. He who rejects the entire past, without keeping any part of it which could serve to breathe life into the revolution, condemns himself to finding justification only in the future and, in the meantime, to entrusting the police with the task of justifying the provisional state of affairs. Bakunin proclaims dictatorship, not despite his desire for destruction, but in accordance with it. Nothing, in fact, could turn him from this path since his ethical values had also been dissolved in the crucible of total negation. In his openly obsequious *Confession* to the Czar, which he wrote in order to gain his freedom, he spectacularly introduces the double game into revolutionary politics. With his *Catechism of a Revolutionary*, which he probably drafted in Switzerland, with the help of Nechaiev, he voices, even though he denies it later, the political cynicism that will never cease to weigh on the revolutionary movement and which Nechaiev himself has so provocatively illustrated.

A less well-known figure than Bakunin, still more mysterious, but more significant for our purpose, Nechaiev pushed nihilism to the farthest coherent point. His thought presents practically no contradiction. He appeared, about 1866, in revolutionary intellectual circles, and died, obscurely, in January 1882. In this short space of time he never ceased to suborn the students around him, Bakunin himself, the revolutionary refugees, and finally the guards in his prison, whom he succeeded in persuading to take part in a crazy conspiracy. When he first appears, he is already quite sure of what he thinks. If Bakunin was fascinated by him to the point of consenting to entrust him with imaginary authority, it is because he recognized in that implacable figure the type of human being that he recommended and what he himself, in a certain manner, would have been if he had been able to silence his heart. Nechaiev was not content with saying that one must unite with "the savage world of bandits, the true and unique revolutionary environment of Russia," nor with writing once more, like Bakunin, that henceforth politics would be religion and religion politics. He made himself the cruel high priest of a desperate revolution; his most recurrent dream was to found a homicidal order that would permit him to propagate and finally enthrone the sinister divinity that he had decided to serve.

He not only gave dissertations on universal destruction; his originality lay in coldly claiming, for those who dedicate themselves to the revolution, an "Everything is permitted" and in actually permitting himself everything. "The revolutionary is a man condemned in advance. He must have neither romantic relationships nor objects to engage his feelings. He should even cast off his own name. Every part of him should be concentrated in one single passion: the revolution." If history is, in fact, independent of all principles and composed only of a struggle between revolution and counterrevolution, there is no way out but to espouse wholeheartedly one of the two and either die or be resurrected. Nechaiev pursues this logic to the bitter end. With him, for the first time, revolution is going to be explicitly separated from love and friendship.

The consequences of arbitrary psychology set in motion by Hegel's method can be seen, for the first time, in Nechaiev. Hegel had allowed that the mutual recognition of minds could be accomplished in love.[5] He would not, however, give a place in the foreground of his analysis to this "phenomenon," which, according to him, he found "had not the strength, the patience, nor the application of the negative." He had chosen to demonstrate human minds in blind combat, dimly groping on the sands, like crabs that finally come to grips in a fight to the death, and voluntarily abandoned the equally legitimate image of beams of light painfully searching for one another in the night and finally focusing together in a blaze of illumination. Those who love, friends or lovers, know that love is not only a blinding flash, but also a long and painful struggle in the darkness for the realization of definitive recognition and reconciliation. After all, if virtue in the course of history is recognized by the extent to which it gives proof of patience, real love is as patient as hatred. Moreover, the demand for justice is not the only justification throughout the centuries for revolutionary passion, which is sustained by a painful insistence on universal friendship, even—and above all—in defiance of an inimical heaven. Those who die for justice, throughout history, have always been called "brothers." Violence, for every one of them, is directed only against the enemy, in the service of the community of the oppressed. But if the revolution is the only positive value, it has a right to claim everything—even the denunciation and therefore the sacrifice of the friend. Henceforth, violence will be directed against one and all, in the service of an abstract idea. The accession to power of the possessed had to take place so that it could be said, once and for all, that the revolution, in itself, was more important than the people it wanted to save, and that friendship, which until then had transformed defeats into the semblance of victories, must be

[5] It could also be brought about by the kind of admiration in which the word *master* assumes its fullest meaning: he who creates without destroying.

sacrificed and postponed until the still invisible day of victory.

Nechaiev's originality thus lies in justifying the violence done to one's brothers. He decided, with Bakunin, on the terms of the *Catechism*. But once the latter, in a fit of mental aberration, had given him the mission of representing in Russia a European Revolutionary Union, which existed only in his imagination, Nechaiev in effect came to Russia, founded his Society of the Ax, and himself defined its regulations. There we find again the secret central committee, necessary no doubt to any military or political action, to whom everyone must swear absolute allegiance. But Nechaiev does more than militarize the revolution from the moment when he admits that the leaders, in order to govern their subordinates, have the right to employ violence and lies. Nechaiev lies, to begin with, when he claims to be a delegate of a central committee that is still nonexistent and when, to enlist certain skeptics in the action that he proposes to undertake, he describes the committee as disposing of unlimited resources. He goes still farther by distinguishing between categories of revolutionaries, with those of the first category (by which he means the leaders) reserving the right to consider the rest as "expendable capital." All the leaders in history may have thought in these terms, but they never said so. Until Nechaiev, at any rate, no revolutionary leader had dared to make this the guiding principle of his conduct. Up to his time no revolution had put at the head of its table of laws the concept that man could be a chattel. Traditionally, recruiting relied on its appeal to courage and to the spirit of self-sacrifice. Nechaiev decided that the skeptics could be terrorized or blackmailed and the believers deceived. Even pseudo-revolutionaries could still be used, if they were urged on systematically to perform the most dangerous deeds. As for the oppressed, since they were going to be saved once and for all, they could be oppressed still more. What they would lose, the oppressed of the future would gain. Nechaiev states, in principle, that governments must be driven to take repressive measures, that the official representatives most hated by the population must never be touched, and that finally the secret society must employ all its resources to increase the suffering and misery of the masses.

Although these beautiful thoughts have realized their full meaning today, Nechaiev did not live to see the triumph of his principles. He tried to apply them, at all events, at the time of the student Ivanov's murder, which so struck the popular imagination of the time that Dostoievsky made it one of the themes of *The Possessed*. Ivanov, whose only fault seems to have been that he had doubts about the central committee of which Nechaiev claimed to be a delegate, was considered an enemy of the revolution because he was opposed to the man who was identified with the revolution. Therefore he must die. "What right have we to take a man's life?" asks Uspensky, one of Nechaiev's comrades.—"It is not a question of right, but of our duty to eliminate everything that may harm our cause." When revolution is the sole value, there are, in fact, no more rights, there are only duties. But by an immediate inversion, every right is assumed in the name of duty. For the sake of the cause, Nechaiev, who has never made an attempt on the life of any tyrant, ambushes and kills Ivanov. Then he leaves Russia and returns to Bakunin, who turns his back on him and condemns his "repugnant tactics." "He has gradually come," writes Bakunin, "to the conclusion that to found an indestructible society it must be based on the politics of Machiavelli and the methods of the Jesuits: for the body, only violence; for the soul, deception." That is well said. But in the name of what value is it possible to decide that this tactic is repugnant if the revolution, as Bakunin believed, is the only good? Nechaiev is really in the service of the revolution; it is not his own ends that he serves, but the cause. Extradited, he yields not an inch to his judges. Condemned to twenty-five years in jail, he still reigns over the prisons, organizes the jailers into a secret society, plans the assassination of the Czar, and is again brought up for trial. Death in the dungeon of a fortress, after twelve years' confinement, brings an end to the life of this rebel who is the first of the contemptuous aristocrats of the revolution.

At this period, in the bosom of the revolution, everything is really permitted and murder can be elevated into a principle. It was thought, however, with the renewal of Populism in 1870, that this revolutionary movement, sprung from the ethical and religious tendencies to be found in the Decembrists, and in the socialism of Lavrov and Herzen, would put a check on the evolution toward political cynicism that Nechaiev had illustrated. This movement appealed to "living souls," prompted them to turn to the people and educate them so that they would march forward to their own liberation. "Repentant noblemen" left their families, dressed like the poor, and went into the villages to preach to the peasants. But the peasants were suspicious and held their peace. When they did not hold their peace, they denounced the apostle to the police. This check to the noble souls had the result of throwing back the movement on the cynicism of a Nechaiev or, at any rate, on violence. In so far as the intelligentsia was unable to reclaim the allegiance of the people, it felt itself once more alone, face to face with autocracy; once more the world appeared to it in the aspect of master and slave. The group known as the People's Will was then to elevate individual terrorism into a principle and inaugurate the series of murders which continued until 1905 with the Socialist Revolutionary Party. This is the point at which the terrorists were born, disillusioned with love, united against the crimes of their masters, but alone in their despair, and face to face with their contradictions, which they could resolve only in the double sacrifice of their innocence and their life.

The Fastidious Assassins

In the year 1878 Russian terrorism was born. A very young girl, Vera Zassulich, on the day following the trial of one hundred and eighty-three Populists, the 24th of January, shot down General Trepov, the Governor of St. Petersburg. At her trial she was acquitted and then succeeded in escaping the police of the Czar. This revolver-shot unleashed a whole series of repressive actions and attempted assassinations, which kept pace with one another and which, it was already evident, could only be terminated by mutual exhaustion.

The same year a member of the People's Will Party, Kravchinsky, stated the principles of terror in his pamphlet *Death for Death*. Consequences always follow principles. In Europe, attempts were made on the lives of the Emperor of Germany, the King of Italy, and the King of Spain. Again in 1878 Alexander II created, in the shape of the Okhrana, the most efficient weapon of State terrorism the world has ever seen. From then on, the nineteenth century abounds in murders, both in Russia and in the West. In 1879 there is a new attack on the King of Spain and an abortive attempt on the life of the Czar. In 1881 the Czar is murdered by terrorist members of the People's Will. Sofia Perovskaia, Jeliabov, and their friends are hanged. In 1883 takes place the attempt on the life of the Emperor of Germany, whose assailant is beheaded with an ax. In 1887 there are the executions of the Chicago martyrs and the congress of Spanish anarchists at Valencia, where they issue the terrorist proclamation: "If society does not capitulate, vice and evil must perish, even if we must all perish with them." In France the 1890's mark the culminating-point of what is called propaganda by action. The exploits of Ravachol, Vaillant, and Henry are the prelude to Carnot's assassination. In the year 1892 alone there are more than a thousand dynamite outrages in Europe, and in America almost five hundred. In 1898 the Empress Elisabeth of Austria is murdered. In 1901 the President of the United States, McKinley, is assassinated. In Russia, where the series of attempts against the lives of minor representatives of the regime had not ceased, the Organization for Combat of the Socialist Revolutionary Party comes into being in 1903 and unites the most outstanding personalities of Russian terrorism. The murders of Plehve by Sazonov and of the Grand Duke Sergei by Kaliayev, in 1905, mark the culminating-point of the thirty years' apostolate of blood and terminate, for revolutionary religion, the age of martyrs.

Nihilism, intimately involved with a frustrated religious movement, thus culminates in terrorism. In the universe of total negation, these young disciples try, with bombs, and revolvers and also with the courage with which they walk to the gallows, to escape from contradiction and to create the values they lack. Until their time, men died for what they knew, or for what they thought they knew. From their time on, it became the rather more difficult habit to sacrifice oneself for something about which one knew nothing, except that it was necessary to die so that it might exist. Until then, those who had to die put themselves in the hand of God in defiance of the justice of man. But on reading the declarations of the condemned victims of that period, we are amazed to see that all, without exception, entrusted themselves, in defiance of their judges, to the justice of other men who were not yet born. These men of the future remained, in the absence of supreme values, their last recourse. The future is the only transcendental value for men without God. The terrorists no doubt wanted first of all to destroy—to make absolutism totter under the shock of exploding bombs. But by their death, at any rate, they aimed at re-creating a community founded on love and justice, and thus to resume a mission that the Church had betrayed. The terrorists' real mission is to create a Church from whence will one day spring the new God. But is that all? If their voluntary assumption of guilt and death gave rise to nothing but the promise of a value still to come, the history of the world today would justify us in saying, for the moment at any rate, that they have died in vain and that they never have ceased to be nihilists. A value to come is, moreover, a contradiction in terms, since it can neither explain an action nor furnish a principle of choice as long as it has not been formulated. But the men of 1905, tortured by contradictions, really did give birth, by their very negation and death, to a value that will henceforth be imperative, which they brought to light in the belief that they were only announcing its advent. They ostensibly placed, above themselves and their executioners, that supreme and painful good which we have already found at the origins of rebellion. Let us stop and consider this value, at the moment when the spirit of rebellion encounters, for the last time in our history, the spirit of compassion.

"How can we speak of terrorist activity without taking part in it?" exclaims the student Kaliayev. His companions, united ever since 1903, in the Organization for Combat of the Socialist Revolutionary Party, under the direction of Aze and later of Boris Savinkov, all live up to the standard of this admirable statement. They are men of the highest principles: the last, in the history of rebellion, to refuse no part of their condition or their drama. If their lives were dedicated to the terror, "if they had faith in it," as Pokotilov says, they never ceased to be torn asunder by it. History offers few examples of fanatics who have suffered from scruples, even in action. But the men of 1905 were always prey to doubts. The greatest homage we can pay them is to say that we would not be able, in 1950, to ask them one question that they themselves had not already asked and that, in their life or by their death, they had not partially answered.

They quickly passed into the realms of history, however. When Kaliayev, for example, in 1903, decided to take part with Savinkov in terrorist activity, he was twenty-six years old. Two years later the "Poet," as he was called, was hanged. It was a short career. But to anyone who examines with a little feeling the history of that period, Kaliayev, in his breathtaking career, displays the most significant aspect of terrorism. Sazonov, Schweitzer, Pokotilov, Voinarovsky, and most of the other anarchists likewise burst upon the scene of Russian history and poised there for a moment, dedicated to destruction, as the swift and unforgettable witnesses to an increasingly agonized protest.

Almost all are atheists. "I remember," wrote Boris Voinarovsky, who died in throwing a bomb at Admiral Dubassov, "that even before going to high school I preached atheism to one of my childhood friends. Only one question embarrassed me. Where did my ideas come from? For I had not the least conception of eternity." Kaliayev himself believed in God. A few moments before an attempted assassination, which failed, Savinkov saw him in the street, standing in front of an ikon, holding the bomb in one hand and making the sign of the cross with the other. But he repudiated religion. In his cell, before his execution, he refused its consolations.

The need for secrecy compelled them to live in solitude. They did not know, except perhaps in the abstract, the profound joy experienced by the man of action in contact with a large section of humanity. But the bond that united them replaced every other attachment in their minds. "Chivalry!" writes Sazonov, and comments on it thus: "Our chivalry was permeated with such a degree of feeling that the word *brother* in no way conveyed with sufficient clarity the essence of our relations with one another." From prison Sazonov writes to his friends: "For my part, the indispensable condition of happiness is to keep forever the knowledge of my perfect solidarity with you." As for Voinarovsky, he confesses that to a woman he loved who wished to detain him he made the following remark, which he recognizes as "slightly comic" but which, according to him, proves his state of mind: "I should curse you if I arrived late for my comrades."

This little group of men and women, lost among the Russian masses, bound only to one another, chose the role of executioner, to which they were in no way destined. They lived in the same paradox, combining in themselves respect for human life in general and contempt for their own lives—to the point of nostalgia for the supreme sacrifice. For Dora Brilliant, the anarchist program was of no importance; terrorist action was primarily embellished by the sacrifice it demanded from the terrorist. "But," says Savinkov, "terror weighed on her like a cross." Kaliayev himself is ready to sacrifice his life at any moment. "Even better than that, he passionately desired to make this sacrifice." During the preparations for the attempt on Plehve, he stated his intention of throwing himself under the horses' hoofs and perishing with the Minister. With Voinarovsky also the desire for sacrifice coincides with the attraction of death. After his arrest he writes to his parents: "How many times during my adolescence the idea came to me to kill myself! . . ."

At the same time, these executioners who risked their own lives so completely, made attempts on the lives of others only after the most scrupulous examination of conscience. The first attempt on the Grand Duke Sergei failed because Kaliayev, with the full approval of his comrades, refused to kill the children who were riding in the Grand Duke's carriage. Of Rachel Louriée, another terrorist, Savinkov writes: "She had faith in terrorist action, she considered it an honor and a duty to take part in it, but blood upset her no less than it did Dora." The same Savinkov was opposed to an attempt on Admiral Dubassov in the

Petersburg-Moscow express because "if there were the least mistake, the explosion could take place in the car and kill strangers." Later Savinkov, "in the name of terrorist conscience," will deny with indignation having made a child of sixteen take part in an attempted assassination. At the moment of escaping from a Czarist prison, he decides to shoot any officers who might attempt to prevent his flight, but to kill himself rather than turn his revolver on an ordinary soldier. It is the same with Voinarovsky, who does not hesitate to kill men, but who confesses that he has never hunted, "finding the occupation barbarous," and who declares in his turn: "If Dubassov is accompanied by his wife, I shall not throw the bomb."

Such a degree of self-abnegation, accompanied by such profound consideration for the lives of others, allows the supposition that these fastidious assassins lived out the rebel destiny in its most contradictory form. It is possible to believe that they too, while recognizing the inevitability of violence, nevertheless admitted to themselves that it is unjustifiable. Necessary and inexcusable—that is how murder appeared to them. Mediocre minds, confronted with this terrible problem, can take refuge by ignoring one of the terms of the dilemma. They are content, in the name of formal principles, to find all direct violence inexcusable and then to sanction that diffuse form of violence which takes place on the scale of world history. Or they will console themselves, in the name of history, with the thought that violence is necessary, and will add murder to murder, to the point of making of history nothing but a continuous violation of everything in man which protests against injustice. This defines the two aspects of contemporary nihilism, the bourgeois and the revolutionary.

But the extremists, with whom we are concerned, forgot nothing. From their earliest days they were incapable of justifying what they nevertheless found necessary, and conceived the idea of offering themselves as a justification and of replying by personal sacrifice to the question they asked themselves. For them, as for all rebels before them, murder is identified with suicide. A life is paid for by another life, and from these two sacrifices springs the promise of a value. Kaliayev, Voinarovsky, and the others believe in the equal value of human lives.

Therefore they do not value any idea above human life, though they kill for the sake of ideas. To be precise, they live on the plane of their idea. They justify it, finally, by incarnating it to the point of death. We are again confronted with a concept of rebellion which, if not religious, is at least metaphysical. Other men to come, consumed with the same devouring faith as these, will find their methods sentimental and refuse to admit that any one life is the equivalent of any other. They will then put an abstract idea above human life, even if they call it history, to which they themselves have submitted in advance and to which they will also decide, quite arbitrarily, to submit everyone else. The problem of rebellion will no longer be resolved by arithmetic, but by estimating probabilities. Confronted with the possibility that the idea may be realized in the future, human life can be everything or nothing. The greater the faith that the estimator places in this final realization, the less the value of human life. At the ultimate limit, it is no longer worth anything at all.

We shall have occasion to examine this limit—that is, the period of State terrorism and of the philosophical executioners. But meanwhile the rebels of 1905, at the frontier on which they stand united, teach us, to the sound of exploding bombs, that rebellion cannot lead, without ceasing to be rebellion, to consolation and to the comforts of dogma. Their only evident victory is to triumph at least over solitude and negation. In the midst of a world which they deny and which rejects them, they try, man after man, like all the great-hearted ones, to reconstruct a brotherhood of man. The love they bear for one another, which brings them happiness even in the desert of a prison, which extends to the great mass of their enslaved and silent fellow men, gives the measure of their distress and of their hopes. To serve this love, they must first kill; to inaugurate the reign of innocence, they must accept a certain culpability. This contradiction will be resolved for them only at the very last moment. Solitude and chivalry, renunciation and hope will only be surmounted by the willing acceptance of death. Already Jeliabov, who organized the attempt on Alexander II in

1881 and was arrested forty-eight hours before the murder, had asked to be executed at the same time as the real perpetrator of the attempt. "Only the cowardice of the government," he said, "could account for the erection of one gallows instead of two." Five were erected, one of which was for the woman he loved. But Jeliabov died smiling, while Ryssakov, who had broken down during his interrogations, was dragged to the scaffold, half-mad with fear.

Jeliabov did this because of a sort of guilt which he did not want to accept and from which he knew he would suffer, like Ryssakov, if he remained alone after having committed or been the cause of a murder. At the foot of the gallows, Sofia Perovskaia kissed the man she loved and her two other friends, but turned away from Ryssakov, who died solitary and damned by the new religion. For Jeliabov, death in the midst of his comrades coincided with his justification. He who kills is guilty only if he consents to go on living or if, to remain alive, he betrays his comrades. To die, on the other hand, cancels out both the guilt and the crime itself. Thus Charlotte Corday shouts at Fouquier-Tinville: "Oh, the monster, he takes me for an assassin!" It is the agonizing and fugitive discovery of a human value that stands halfway between innocence and guilt, between reason and irrationality, between history and eternity. At the moment of this discovery, but only then, these desperate people experience a strange feeling of peace, the peace of definitive victory. In his cell, Polivanov says that it would have been "easy and sweet" for him to die. Voinarovsky writes that he has conquered the fear of death. "Without a single muscle in my face twitching, without saying a word, I shall climb on the scaffold. . . . And this will not be an act of violence perpetrated on myself, it will be the perfectly natural result of all that I have lived through." Very much later Lieutenant Schmidt wlil write before being shot: "My death will consummate everything, and my cause, crowned by my death, will emerge irreproachable and perfect." Kaliayev, condemned to the gallows after having stood as prosecutor before the tribunal, declares firmly: "I consider my death as a supreme protest against a world of blood and tears," and again writes· "From the moment when I found myself behind bars, I never for one moment wanted to stay alive in any way whatsoever." His wish is granted. On May 10, at two o'clock in the morning, he walks toward the only justification he recognizes. Entirely dressed in black, without an overcoat, and wearing a felt hat, he climbs the scaffold. To Father Florinsky, who offers him the crucifix, the condemned man, turning from the figure of Christ, only answers: "I have already told you that I have finished with life and that I am prepared for death."

Yes, the ancient value lives once more, at the culmination of nihilism, at the very foot of the gallows. It is the reflection, historic on this occasion, of the "we are" which we found at the termination of our analysis of the rebel mind. It is privation and at the same time enlightened conviction. It is this that shone with such mortal radiance on the agonized countenance of Dora Brilliant at the thought of him who died for himself and for tireless friendship; it is this that drives Sazonov to suicide in prison as a protest and "to earn respect for his comrades"; and this, again, which exonerates even Nechaiev on the day when he is asked to denounce his comrades by a general, whom he knocks to the ground with a single blow. By means of this, the terrorists, while simultaneously affirming the world of men, place themselves above this world, thus demonstrating for the last time in our history that real rebellion is a creator of values.

Thanks to them, 1905 marks the highest peak of revolutionary momentum. But from then on, a decline sets in. Martyrs do not build Churches; they are the mortar, or the alibi. Then come the priests and the bigots. The revolutionaries who follow will not demand an exchange of lives. They accept the risk of death, but will also agree to preserve themselves as far as they can for the sake of serving the revolution. Thus they will accept complete culpability for themselves. Acquiescence in humiliation— that is the true characteristic of twentieth-century revolutionaries, who place the revolution and the Church of man above themselves. Kaliayev proves, on the contrary, that though the revolution is a necessary means, it is not a sufficient end. In this way he elevates man instead of degrading him. It is Kaliayev and his Russian and German comrades who, in the history of the world, really oppose Hegel,[6] who first recognizes universal recognition as necessary and then as insufficient. Appearances did not suffice for him. When the whole world would have been willing to recognize him, a doubt would still have remained in Kaliayev's mind: he needed his own form of acquiescence, and the approbation of the whole world would not have sufficed to silence the doubt that a hundred enthusiastic acclamations give rise to in the mind of any honest man. Kaliayev doubted to the end, but this doubt did not prevent him from acting; it is for that reason that he is the purest image of rebellion. He who accepts death, to pay for a life with a life, no matter what his negations may be, affirms, by doing so, a value that surpasses him in his aspect of an individual in the historical sense. Kaliayev dedicates himself to history until death and, at the moment of dying, places himself above history. In a certain way, it is true, he prefers himself to history. But what should his preference be? Himself, whom he kills without hesitation, or the value he incarnates and makes immortal? The answer is not difficult to guess. Kaliayev and his comrades triumphed over nihilism.

The Path of Chigalev

But this triumph is to be short-lived: it coincides with death. Nihilism, provisionally, survives its victors. In the very bosom of the Socialist Revolutionary Party, political cynicism continues to wend its way to victory. The party leader who sends Kaliayev to his death, Azev, plays a double game and denounces the revolutionaries to the Okhrana while planning the deaths of ministers and grand dukes. The concept of provocation reinstates the "Everything is permitted," and again identifies history and absolute values. This particular form of nihilism, after having influenced individualistic socialism, goes on to contaminate so-called scientific socialism, which appears in Russia dur-

[6] Two different species of men. One kills only once and pays with his life. The other justifies thousands of crimes and consents to be rewarded with honors.

ing the 1880's.[7] The joint legacy of Nechaiev and Marx will give birth to the totalitarian revolution of the twentieth century. While individual terrorism hunted down the last representatives of divine right, State terrorism was getting ready to destroy divine right definitively, at the very root of human society. The technique of the seizure of power for the realization of ultimate ends takes the first step toward the exemplary affirmation of these ends.

Lenin, in fact, borrows from Tkachev, a friend and spiritual brother of Nechaiev, a concept of the seizure of power that he found "majestic" and that he himself recapitulated thus: "absolute secrecy, meticulous care in the choice of members, creation of professional revolutionaries." Tkachev, who died insane, makes the transition from nihilism to military socialism. He claimed to have created a Russian Jacobinism and yet only borrowed from the Jacobins their technique of action, since he, too, denied every principle and every virtue. An enemy of art and ethics, he reconciles the rational and the irrational only in tactics. His aim is to achieve human equality by seizure of the power of the State. Secret organizations, revolutionary alliances, dictatorial powers for revolutionary leaders—these were the themes that defined the concept, if not the realization, of "the apparatus" which was to enjoy so great and efficacious a success. As for the method itself, it is possible to form a fair idea of it when one learns that Tkachev proposed to suppress and eliminate all Russians over the age of twenty-five as incapable of assimilating the new ideas. A really inspired method, and one that was to prevail in the techniques of the modern super-State, where the fanatical education of children is carried on in the midst of a terrorized adult population. Cæsarian socialism undoubtedly condemns individual terrorism to the extent that it revives values incompatible with the domination of historic reason. But it will restore terror on the level of the State—with the creation of an ultimately deified humanity as its sole justification.

We have come full circle here, and rebellion, cut off from its real roots, unfaithful to man in having surrendered to history, now contemplates the subjection of the entire

[7] The first Social Democratic group, Plekhanov's, began in 1883.

universe. It is at this point that the era of Chigalevism begins—proclaimed, in *The Possessed*, by Verkhovensky, the nihilist who claims the right to choose dishonor. His is an unhappy and implacable mind [8] and he chooses the will to power, which, in fact, alone is capable of reigning over a history that has no other significance but itself. Chigalev, the philanthropist, is his guarantor; love of mankind will henceforth justify the enslavement of man. Possessed by the idea of equality,[9] Chigalev, after long consideration, arrived at the despairing conclusion that only one system is possible even though it is a system of despair. "Beginning with the premise of unlimited freedom, I arrive at unlimited despotism." Complete freedom, which is the negation of everything, can only exist and justify itself by the creation of new values identified with the entire human race. If the creation of these values is postponed, humanity will tear itself to peices. The shortest route to these new standards passes by way of total dictatorship. "One tenth of humanity will have the right to individuality and will exercise unlimited authority over the other nine tenths. The latter will lose their individuality and will become like a flock of sheep; compelled to passive obedience, they will be led back to original innocence and, so to speak, to the primitive paradise, where, nevertheless, they must work." It is the government by philosophers of which the Utopians dream; philosophers of this type, quite simply, believe in nothing. The kingdom has come, but it negates real rebellion, and is only concerned with the reign of "the Christs of violence," to use the expression of an enthusiastic writer extolling the life and death of Ravachol. "The pope on high," says Verkhovensky bitterly, "with us around him, and beneath us Chigalevism."

The totalitarian theocrats of the twentieth century and State terrorism are thus announced. The new aristocracy and the grand inquisitors reign today, by making use of the rebellion of the oppressed, over one part of our history. Their reign is cruel, but they excuse their cruelty,

---

[8] "He represented himself as man after his fashion, and then he gave up his idea."

[9] "Slander and assassination in extreme cases, but especially equality."

like the Satan of the romantics, by claiming that it is hard
for them to bear. "We reserve desire and suffering for ourselves; for the slaves there is Chigalevism." A new and
somewhat hideous race of martyrs is now born. Their
martyrdom consists in consenting to inflict suffering on
others; they become the slaves of their own domination.
For man to become god, the victim must abase himself
to the point of becoming the executioner. That is why
both victim and executioner are equally despairing. Neither slavery nor power will any longer coincide with happiness; the masters will be morose and the slaves sullen.
Saint-Just was right: it is a terrible thing to torment the
people. But how can one avoid tormenting men if one has
decided to make them gods? Just as Kirilov, who kills himself in order to become God, accepts seeing his suicide
made use of by Verkhovensky's "conspiracy," so man's
deification by man breaks the bounds which rebellion,
nevertheless, reveals, and thereby irrevocably commits itself to the labyrinth of tactics and terror from which history has not yet emerged.

State Terrorism and Irrational Terror

✳

All modern revolutions have ended in a reinforcement of the power of the State. 1789 brings Napoleon; 1848, Napoleon III; 1917, Stalin; the Italian disturbances of the twenties, Mussolini; the Weimar Republic, Hitler. These revolutions, particularly after the First World War had liquidated the vestiges of divine right, still proposed, with increasing audacity, to build the city of humanity and of authentic freedom. The growing omnipotence of the State sanctioned this ambition on each occasion. It would be erroneous to say that this was bound to happen. But it is possible to examine how it did happen; and perhaps the lesson will follow.

Apart from a few explanations that are not the subject of this essay, the strange and terrifying growth of the modern State can be considered as the logical conclusion of inordinate technical and philosophical ambitions, foreign to the true spirit of rebellion, but which nevertheless gave birth to the revolutionary spirit of our time. The prophetic dream of Marx and the over-inspired predictions of Hegel or of Nietzsche ended by conjuring up, after the city of God had been razed to the ground, a rational or irrational State, which in both cases, however, was founded on terror.

In actual fact, the Fascist revolutions of the twentieth century do not merit the title of revolution. They lacked the ambition of universality. Mussolini and Hitler, of course, tried to build an empire, and the National Socialist ideologists were bent, explicitly, on world domination. But the difference between them and the classic revolutionary movement is that, of the nihilist inheritance, they chose to deify the irrational, and the irrational alone, instead of deifying reason. In this way they renounced their claim to universality. And yet Mussolini makes use of Hegel, and Hitler of Nietzsche; and both illustrate, historically, some of the prophecies of German ideology. In this respect they belong to the history of rebellion and of nihilism. They were the first to construct a State on the concept that everything is meaningless and that history is only written in terms of the hazards of force. The consequences were not long in appearing.

As early as 1914 Mussolini proclaimed the "holy religion of anarchy," and declared himself the enemy of every form of Christianity. As for Hitler, his professed religion unhesitatingly juxtaposed the God-Providence and Valhalla. Actually his god was a political argument and a manner of reaching an impressive climax at the end of his speeches. As long as he was successful, he chose to believe that he was inspired. In the hour of defeat, he considered himself betrayed by his people. Between the two nothing intervened to announce to the world that he would ever have been capable of thinking himself guilty in relation to any principle. The only man of superior culture who gave Nazism an appearance of being a philosophy, Ernst Junger, even went so far as to choose the actual formulas of nihilism: "The best answer to the betrayal of life by the spirit is the betrayal of the spirit by the spirit, and one of the great and cruel pleasures of our times is to participate in the work of destruction."

Men of action, when they are without faith, have never believed in anything but action. Hitler's untenable paradox lay precisely in wanting to found a stable order on perpetual change and no negation. Rauschning, in his *Revolution of Nihilism*, was right in saying that the Hitlerian revolution represented unadulterated dynamism. In Germany, shaken to its foundations by a calamitous war, by defeat, and by economic distress, values no longer existed. Although one must take into account what Goethe called "the German destiny of making everything difficult," the epidemic of suicides that swept through the entire country between the two wars indicates a great deal about the state of mental confusion. To those who despair of everything, not reason but only passion can provide a faith, and in this particular case it must be the same passion that lay at the root of the despair—namely, humiliation and hatred. There was no longer any standard of values, both common to and superior to all these men, in the name of which it would have been possible for them to judge one another. The Germany of 1933 thus agreed to adopt the degraded values of a mere handful of men and tried to impose them on an entire civilization. Deprived of the morality of Goethe, Germany chose, and submitted to, the ethics of the gang.

Gangster morality is an inexhaustible round of triumph and revenge, defeat and resentment. When Mussolini extolled "the elemental forces of the individual," he announced the exaltation of the dark powers of blood and instinct, the biological justification of all the worst things produced by the instinct of domination. At the Nuremberg trials, Frank emphasized "the hatred of form" which animated Hitler. It is true that this man was nothing but an elemental force in motion, directed and rendered more effective by calculated cunning and by a relentless tactical clairvoyance. Even his physical appearance, which was thoroughly mediocre and commonplace, was no limitation: it established him firmly with the masses. Action alone kept him alive. For him, to exist was to act. That is why Hitler and his regime could not dispense with enemies. They could only define themselves, psycopathic dandies[1] that they were, in relation to their enemies, and only assume their final form in the bloody battle that was to be their downfall. The Jews, the Freemasons, the plutocrats, the Anglo-Saxons, the bestial Slavs succeeded one another in their propaganda and their history as a means of propping up, each time a little higher, the blind force that was stumbling headlong toward its end. Perpetual strife demanded perpetual stimulants.

Hitler was history in its purest form. "Evolution," said Junger, "is far more important than living." Thus he preached complete identification with the stream of life, on the lowest level and in defiance of all superior reality. A regime which invented a biological foreign policy was obviously acting against its own best interests. But at

[1] It is well known that Göring sometimes entertained dressed as Nero and with his face made up.

least it obeyed its own particular logic. Rosenberg speaks pompously of life in the following terms: "Like a column on the march, and it is of little importance toward what destination and for what ends this column is marching." Though later the column will strew ruins over the pages of history and will devastate its own country, it will at least have had the gratification of living. The real logic of this dynamism was either total defeat or a progress from conquest to conquest and from enemy to enemy, until the eventual establishment of the empire of blood and action. It is very unlikely that Hitler ever had any conception, at least at the beginning, of this empire. Neither by culture nor even by instinct or tactical intelligence was he equal to his destiny. Germany collapsed as a result of having engaged in a struggle for empire with the concepts of provincial politics. But Junger had grasped the import of this logic and had formulated it in definite terms. He had a vision of "a technological world empire," of a "religion of anti-Christian technology," of which the faithful and the militants would have themselves been the priests because (and here Junger rejoins Marx), on account of his human form, the worker is universal. "The statutes of a new authoritarian regime take the place of a change in the social contract. The worker is removed from the sphere of negotiation, from pity, and from literature and elevated to the sphere of action. Legal obligations are transformed into military obligations." It can be seen that the empire is simultaneously the factory and the barracks of the world, where Hegel's soldier worker reigns as a slave. Hitler was halted relatively soon on the way to the realization of this empire. But even if he had gone still farther, we should only have witnessed the more and more extensive deployment of an irresistible dynamism and the increasingly violent enforcement of cynical principles which alone would be capable of serving this dynamism.

Speaking of such a revolution, Rauschning says that it has nothing to do with liberation, justice, and inspiration: it is "the death of freedom, the triumph of violence, and the enslavement of the mind." Fascism is an act of contempt, in fact. Inversely, every form of contempt, if it intervenes in politics, prepares the way for, or establishes, Fascism. It must be added that Fascism cannot be anything else but an expression of contempt without denying itself. Junger drew the conclusion, from his own principles, that it was better to be criminal than bourgeois. Hitler, who was endowed with less literary talent but, on this occasion, with more coherence, knew that to be either one or the other was a matter of complete indifference, from the moment that one ceased to believe in anything but success. Thus he authorized himself to be both at the same time. "Fact is all," said Mussolini. And Hitler added: "When the race is in danger of being oppressed . . . the question of legality plays only a secondary role." Moreover, in that the race must always be menaced in order to exist, there is never any legality. "I am ready to sign anything, to agree to anything. . . . As far as I am concerned, I am capable, in complete good faith, of signing treaties today and of dispassionately tearing them up tomorrow if the future of the German people is at stake." Before he declared war, moreover, Hitler made the statement to his generals that no one was going to ask the victor if he had told the truth or not. The leitmotiv of Göring's defense at the Nuremberg trials returned time and again to this theme: "The victor will always be the judge, and the vanquished will always be the accused." That is a point that can certainly be argued. But then it is hard to understand Rosenberg when he said during the Nuremberg trials that he had not foreseen that the Nazi myth would lead to murder. When the English prosecuting attorney observes that "from *Mein Kampf* the road led straight to the gas chambers at Maidenek," he touches on the real subject of the trial, that of the historic responsibilities of Western nihilism and the only one which, nevertheless, was not really discussed at Nuremberg, for reasons only too evident. A trial cannot be conducted by announcing the general culpability of a civilization. Only the actual deeds which, at least, stank in the nostrils of the entire world were brought to judgment.

Hitler, in any case, invented the perpetual motion of conquest, without which he would have been nothing at all. But the perpetual enemy is perpetual terror, this time on the level of the State. The State is identified with the "apparatus"; that is to say, with the sum total of mechanisms of conquest and repression. Conquest directed toward the interior of the country is called repression or propaganda ("the first step on the road to hell," according to Frank). Directed toward the exterior, it creates the army. All problems are thus militarized and posed in terms of power and efficiency. The supreme commander determines policy and also deals with all the main problems of administration. This principle, axiomatic as far as strategy is concerned, is applied to civil life in general. One leader, one people, signifies one master and millions of slaves. The political intermediaries who are, in all societies, the guarantors of freedom, disappear to make way for a booted and spurred Jehovah who rules over the silent masses or, which comes to the same thing, over masses who shout slogans at the top of their lungs. There is no organ of conciliation or mediation interposed between the leader and the people, nothing in fact but the apparatus—in other words, the party—which is the emanation of the leader and the tool of his will to oppress. In this way the first and sole principle of this degraded form of mysticism is born, the *Führerprinzip*, which restores idolatry and a debased deity to the world of nihilism.

Mussolini, the Latin lawyer, contented himself with reasons of State, which he transformed, with a great deal of rhetoric, into the absolute. "Nothing beyond the State, above the State, against the State. Everything to the State, for the State, in the State." The Germany of Hitler gave his false reasoning its real expression, which was that of a religion. "Our divine mission," says a Nazi newspaper during a party congress, "was to lead everyone back to his origins, back to the common Mother. It was truly a divine mission." These origins are thus to be found in primitive howls and shrieks. Who is the god in question? An official party declaration answers that: "All of us here below believe in Adolf Hitler, our Führer . . . and [we confess] that National Socialism is the only faith which can lead our people to salvation." The commandments of the leader, standing in the burning bush of spotlights, on a Sinai of planks and flags, therefore comprise both law and virtue. If the superhuman microphones give orders only once for a crime to be committed, then the crime is handed down from chief to subchief until it reaches the slave who receives orders without being able to pass them on to anybody. One of the Dachau executioners weeps in prison and says: "I only obeyed orders. The Führer and the Reichsführer alone planned all this, and then they ran away. Gluecks received orders from Kaltenbrunner and, finally, I received orders to carry out the shootings. I have been left holding the bag because I was only a little *Hauptscharführer* and because I couldn't hand it on any lower down the line. Now they say that I am the assassin." Göring during the trial proclaimed his loyalty to the Führer and said that "there was still a code of honor in that accursed life." Honor lay in obedience, which was often confused with crime. Military law punishes disobedience by death, and its honor is servitude. When all the world has become military, then crime consists in not killing if orders insist on it.

Orders, unfortunately, seldom insist on good deeds. Pure doctrinal dynamism cannot be directed toward good, but only toward efficacy. As long as enemies exist, terror will exist; and there will be enemies as long as dynamism exists to ensure that: "All the influences liable to undermine the sovereignty of the people, as exercised by the Führer with the assistance of the party . . . must be eliminated." Enemies are heretics and must be converted by preaching or propaganda, exterminated by inquisition or by the Gestapo. The result is that man, if he is a member of the party, is no more than a tool in the hands of the Führer, a cog in the apparatus, or, if he is the enemy of the Führer, a waste product of the machine. The impetus toward irrationality of this movement, born of rebellion, now even goes so far as to propose suppressing all that makes man more than a cog in the machine; in other words, rebellion itself. The romantic individualism of the German revolutions finally satiated in the world of inanimate objects. Irrational terror transforms men into objects, "planetary bacilli," according to Hitler's formula. It proposes the destruction, not only of the individual, but of the universal possibilities of the individual, of reflection, solidarity, and the urge to absolute love. Propaganda and torture are the direct means of bringing about disintegration; more destructive still are systematic degradation, identification with the cynical criminal, and forced complicity. The triumph of the man who kills or tortures is marred by only one shadow: he is unable to feel that he is innocent. Thus, he must create guilt in his victim so that, in a world that has no direction, universal guilt will authorize no other course of action than the use of force and give its blessing to nothing but success. When the concept of innocence disappears from the mind of the innocent victim himself, the value of power establishes a definitive rule over a world in despair. That is why an unworthy and cruel penitence reigns over this world where only the stones are innocent. The condemned are compelled to hang one another. Even the innocent cry of maternity is stifled, as in the case of the Greek mother who was forced by an officer to choose which of her three sons was to be shot. This is the final realization of freedom: the power to kill and degrade saves the servile soul from utter emptiness. The hymn of German freedom is sung, to the music of a prisoners' orchestra, in the camps of death.

The crimes of the Hitler regime, among them the massacre of the Jews, are without precedent in history because history gives no other example of a doctrine of such total destruction being able to seize the levers of command of a civilized nation. But above all, for the first time in history, the rulers of a country have used their immense power to establish a *mystique* beyond the bounds of any ethical considerations. This first attempt to found a Church on nihilism was paid for by complete annihilation. The destruction of Lidice demonstrates clearly that the systematic and scientific aspect of the Nazi movement really hides an irrational drive that can only be interpreted as a drive of despair and arrogance. Until then, there were supposedly only two possible attitudes for a conqueror toward a village that was considered rebellious. Either calculated repression and cold-blooded execution of hostages, or a savage and necessarily brief sack by enraged soldiers. Lidice was destroyed by both methods simultaneously. It illustrates the ravages of that irrational form of reason which is the only value that can be found in the whole story. Not only were all the houses burned to the ground, the hundred and seventy-four men of the village shot, the two hundred and three women deported, and the three hundred children transferred elsewhere to be educated in the religion of the Führer, but special teams spent months at work leveling the terrain with dynamite, destroying the very stones, filling in the village pond, and finally diverting the course of the river. After that, Lidice was really nothing more than a mere possibility, according to the logic of the movement. To make assurance doubly sure, the cemetery was emptied of its dead, who might have been a perpetual reminder that once something existed in this place.[2]

The nihilist revolution, which is expressed historically in the Hitlerian religion, thus only aroused an insensate passion for nothingness, which ended by turning against itself. Negation, this time at any rate, and despite Hegel, has not been creative. Hitler presents the example, perhaps unique in history, of a tyrant who left absolutely nothing to his credit. For himself, for his people, and for the world, he was nothing but the epitome of suicide and murder. Seven million Jews assassinated, seven million Europeans deported or killed, ten million war victims, are perhaps not sufficient to allow history to pass judgment: history is accustomed to murderers. But the very destruction of Hitler's final justification—that is, the German nation—henceforth makes this man, whose presence in history for years on end haunted the minds of millions of men, into an inconsistent and contemptible phantom. Speer's deposition at the Nuremberg trials showed that Hitler, though he could have stopped the war before the point of total disaster, really wanted universal suicide and the material and political destruction of the German nation. The only value for him remained, until the bitter end, success. Since Germany had lost the war, she was cowardly and treacherous and she deserved to die. "If the German people are incapable of victory, they are unworthy to live." Hitler therefore decided to drag them with him to the grave and to make their destruction an apotheosis, when the Russian cannon were already splitting apart the walls of his palace in Berlin. Hitler, Göring, who

[2] It is striking to note that atrocities reminiscent of these excesses were committed in colonies (India, 1857; Algeria, 1945; etc.) by European nations that in reality obeyed the same irrational prejudice of racial superiority.

wanted to see his bones placed in a marble tomb, Goebbels, Himmler, Ley, killed themselves in dugouts or in cells. But their deaths were deaths for nothing; they were like a bad dream, a puff of smoke that vanishes. Neither efficacious nor exemplary, they consecrate the bloodthirsty vanity of nihilism. "They thought they were free," Frank cries hysterically; "didn't they know that no one escapes from Hitlerism?" They did not know; nor did they know that the negation of everything is in itself a form of servitude and that real freedom is an inner submission to a value which defies history and its successes.

But the Fascist mystics, even though they aimed at gradually dominating the world, really never had pretensions to a universal empire. At the very most, Hitler, astonished at his own victories, was diverted from the provincial origins of his movement towards the indefinite dream of an empire of the Germans that had nothing to do with the universal City. Russian Communism, on the contrary, by its very origins, openly aspires to world empire. That is its strength, its deliberate significance, and its importance in our history. Despite appearances, the German revolution had no hope of a future. It was only a primitive impulse whose ravages have been greater than its real ambitions. Russian Communism, on the contrary, has appropriated the metaphysical ambition that this book describes, the erection, after the death of God, of a city of man finally deified. The name *revolution*, to which Hitler's adventure had no claim, was once deserved by Russian Communism, and although it apparently deserves it no longer, it claims that one day it will deserve it forever. For the first time in history, a doctrine and a movement based on an Empire in arms has as its purpose definitive revolution and the final unification of the world. It remains for us to examine this pretension in detail. Hitler, at the height of his madness, wanted to fix the course of history for a thousand years. He believed himself to be on the point of doing so, and the realist philosophers of the conquered nations were preparing to acknowledge this and to excuse it, when the Battle of Britain and Stalingrad threw him back on the path of death and set history once more on the march. But, as indefatigable as history itself, the claim of the human race to divinity is once more brought to life, with more seriousness, more efficiency, and more reason, under the auspices of the rational State as it is to be found in Russia.

State Terrorism and Rational Terror

∗

Marx, in nineteenth-century England, in the midst of the terrible sufferings caused by the transition from an agricultural economy to an industrial economy, had plenty of material for constructing a striking analysis of primitive capitalism. As for Socialism, apart from the lessons, which for the most part contradicted his doctrines, that he could draw from the French Revolution, he was obliged to speak in the future tense and in the abstract. Thus it is not astonishing that he could blend in his doctrine the most valid critical method with a Utopian Messianism of highly dubious value. The unfortunate thing is that his critical method, which, by definition, should have been adjusted to reality, has found itself farther and farther separated from facts to the exact extent that it wanted to remain faithful to the prophecy. It was thought, and this is already an indication of the future, that what was conceded to truth could be taken from Messianism. This contradiction is perceptible in Marx's lifetime. The doctrine of the *Communist Manifesto* is no longer strictly correct twenty years later, when *Das Kapital* appears. *Das Kapital*, nevertheless, remained incomplete, because Marx was influenced at the end of his life by a new and prodigious mass of social and economic facts to which the system had to be adapted anew. These facts concerned, in particular, Russia, which he had spurned until then. We now know that the Marx-Engels Institute in Moscow ceased, in 1935, the publication of the complete works of Marx while more than thirty volumes still remained unpublished; doubtless the content of these volumes was not "Marxist" enough.

Since Marx's death, in any case, only a minority of

disciples have remained faithful to his method. The Marxists who have made history have, on the contrary, appropriated the prophecy and the apocalyptic aspects of his doctrine in order to realize a Marxist revolution, in the exact circumstances under which Marx had foreseen that a revolution could not take place. It can be said of Marx that the greater part of his predictions came into conflict with facts as soon as his prophecies began to become an object of increasing faith. The reason is simple: the predictions were short-term and could be controlled. Prophecy functions on a very long-term basis and has as one of its properties a characteristic that is the very source of strength of all religions: the impossibility of proof. When the predictions failed to come true, the prophecies remained the only hope; with the result that they alone rule over our history. Marxism and its successors will be examined here from the angle of prophecy.

The Bourgeois Prophecy

Marx is simultaneously a bourgeois and a revolutionary prophet. The latter is better known than the former. But the former explains many things in the career of the latter. A Messianism of Christian and bourgeois origin, which was both historical and scientific, influenced his revolutionary Messianism, which sprang from German ideology and the French rebellions.

In contrast to the ancient world, the unity of the Christian and Marxist world is astonishing. The two doctrines have in common a vision of the world which completely separates them from the Greek attitude. Jaspers defines this very well: "It is a Christian way of thinking to consider that the history of man is strictly unique." The Christians were the first to consider human life and the course of events as a history that is unfolding from a fixed beginning toward a definite end, in the course of which man achieves his salvation or earns his punishment. The philosophy of history springs from a Christian representation, which is surprising to a Greek mind. The Greek idea of evolution has nothing in common with our idea of historical evolution. The difference between the two is the difference between a circle and a straight line. The Greeks imagined the history of the world as cyclical. Aristotle, to give a definite example, did not believe that the time in which he was living was subsequent to the Trojan War. Christianity was obliged, in order to penetrate the Mediterranean world, to Hellenize itself, and its doctrine then became more flexible. But its originality lay in introducing into the ancient world two ideas that had never before been associated: the idea of history and the idea of punishment. In its concept of mediation, Christianity is Greek. In its idea of history, Christianity is Judaic and will be found again in German ideology.

It is easier to understand this dissimilarity by underlining the hostility of historical methods of thought toward nature, which they considered as an object not for contemplation but for transformation. For the Christian, as for the Marxist, nature must be subdued. The Greeks are of the opinion that it is better to obey it. The love of the ancients for the cosmos was completely unknown to the first Christians, who, moreover, awaited with impatience an imminent end of the world. Hellenism, in association with Christianity, then produces the admirable efflorescence of the Albigensian heresy on the one hand, and on the other Saint Francis. But with the Inquisition and the destruction of the Albigensian heresy, the Church again parts company with the world and with beauty, and gives back to history its pre-eminence over nature. Jaspers is again right in saying: "It is the Christian attitude that gradually empties the world of its substance . . . since the substance resided in a conglomeration of symbols." These symbols are those of the drama of the divinity, which unfolds throughout time. Nature is only the setting for this drama. The delicate equilibrium between humanity and nature, man's consent to the world, which gives ancient thought its distinction and its refulgence, was first shattered for the benefit of history by Christianity. The entry into this history of the Nordic peoples, who have no tradition of friendship with the world, precipitated this trend. From the moment that the divinity of Christ is denied, or that, thanks to the efforts of German ideology, He only symbolizes the man-god, the concept of mediation disappears and a Judaic world reappears. The implacable god of war rules again; all beauty is insulated as the source of idle pleasures, nature itself is enslaved. Marx, from this point of view, is the Jeremiah of the god of history and the Saint Augustine of the revolution. That this explains the really reactionary aspects of his doctrine can be demonstrated by a simple comparison with his one contemporary who was an intelligent theorist of reaction.

Joseph de Maistre refutes Jacobinism and Calvinism, two doctrines which summed up for him "everything bad that has been thought for three centuries," in the name of a Christian philosophy of history. To counter schisms and heresies, he wanted to re-create "the robe without a seam" of a really catholic Church. His aim—and this can be seen at the period of his Masonic adventures—is the universal Christian city. Maistre dreams of the protoplastic Adam, or the Universal Man, of Fabre d'Olivet, who will be the rallying-point of individual souls, and of the Adam Kadmon of the cabalists, who preceded the Fall and who must now be brought to life again. When the Church has reclaimed the world, she will endow this first and last Adam with a body. In the *Soirées in St. Petersburg* there is a mass of formulas on this subject which bear a striking resemblance to the Messianic formulas of Hegel and Marx. In both the terrestrial and the celestial Jerusalem that Maistre imagines, "all the inhabitants pervaded by the same spirit will pervade one another and will reflect one another's happiness." Maistre does not go so far as to deny personal survival after death; he only dreams of a mysterious unity reconquered in which, "evil having been annihilated, there will be no more passion nor self-interest," and where "man will be reunited with himself when his double standard will be obliterated and his two centers unified."

In the city of absolute knowledge, where the eyes of the mind and the eyes of the body became as one, Hegel also reconciled contradictions. But Maistre's vision again coincides with that of Marx, who proclaims "the end of the quarrel between essence and existence, between freedom and necessity." Evil, for Maistre, is nothing but the destruction of unity. But humanity must rediscover its unity on earth and in heaven. By what means? Maistre, who is an *ancien régime* reactionary, is less explicit on this point than Marx. Meanwhile he was waiting for a great religious revolution of which 1789 was only the "appalling preface." He quotes Saint John, who asks that we *make* truth, which is exactly the program of the modern revolutionary mind, and Saint Paul, who announces that "the last enemy that shall be destroyed is death." Humanity marches, by way of crimes, violence, and death, toward this final consummation, which will justify everything. The earth for Maistre is nothing but "an immense altar on which all the living must be sacrificed, without end, without limit, without respite, until the end of time, until the extinction of evil, until the death of death." His fatalism, however, is active as well as passive. "Man must act as if he were capable of all things and resign himself as if he were capable of nothing." We find in Marx the same sort of creative fatalism. Maistre undoubtedly justifies the established order. But Marx justifies the order that is established in his time. The most eloquent eulogy of capitalism was made by its greatest enemy. Marx is only anti-capitalist in so far as capitalism is out of date. Another order must be established which will demand, in the name of history, a new conformity. As for the means, they are the same for Marx as for Maistre: political realism, discipline, force. When Maistre adopts Bossuet's bold idea that "the heretic is he who has personal ideas"—in other words, ideas that have no reference to either a social or a religious tradition—he provides the formula for the most ancient and the most modern of conformities. The attorney general, pessimistic choirmaster of the executioner, announcess our diplomatic prosecutors.

It goes without saying that these resemblances do not make Maistre a Marxist, nor Marx a traditional Christian. Marxist atheism is absolute. But nevertheless it does reinstate the supreme being on the level of humanity. "Criticism of religion leads to this doctrine that man is for man the supreme being. From this angle, socialism is therefore an enterprise for the deification of man and has assumed some of the characteristics of traditional religions.[1] This reconciliation, in any case, is instructive as

[1] Saint-Simon, who influences Marx, is, moreover, influenced himself by Maistre and Bonald.

concerns the Christian origins of all types of historic Messianism, even revolutionary Messianism. The only difference lies in a change of symbols. With Maistre, as with Marx, the end of time realizes Vigny's ambitious dream, the reconciliation of the wolf and the lamb, the procession of criminal and victim to the same altar, the reopening or opening of a terrestrial paradise. For Marx, the laws of history reflect material reality; for Maistre, they reflect divine reality. But for the former, matter is the substance; for the latter, the substance of his god is incarnate here below. Eternity separates them at the beginning, but the doctrines of history end by reuniting them in a realistic conclusion.

Maistre hated Greece (it also irked Marx, who found any form of beauty under the sun completely alien), of which he said that it had corrupted Europe by bequeathing it its spirit of division. It would have been more appropriate to say that Greek thought was the spirit of unity, precisely because it could not do without intermediaries, and because it was, on the contrary, quite unaware of the historical spirit of totality, which was invented by Christianity and which, cut off from its religious origins, threatens the life of Europe today. "Is there a fable, a form of madness, a vice which has not a Greek name, a Greek emblem, or a Greek mask?" We can ignore the outraged puritanism. This passionate denunciation expresses the spirit of modernity at variance with the ancient world and in direct continuity with authoritarian socialism, which is about to deconsecrate Christianity and incorporate it in a Church, bent on conquest.

Marx's scientific Messianism is itself of bourgeois origin. Progress, the future of science, the cult of technology and of production, are bourgeois myths, which in the nineteenth century became dogma. We note that the *Communist Manifesto* appeared in the same year as Renan's *Future of Science*. This profession of faith, which would cause considerable consternation to a contemporary reader, nevertheless gives the most accurate idea of the almost mystic hopes aroused in the nineteenth century by the expansion of industry and the surprising progress made by science. This hope is the hope of bourgeois society itself—the final beneficiary of technical progress.

The idea of progress is contemporary with the age of enlightenment and with the bourgeois revolution. Of course, certain sources of its inspiration can be found in the seventeenth century; the quarrel between the Ancients and the Moderns already introduced into European ideology the perfectly absurd conception of an artistic form of progress. In a more serious fashion, the idea of a science that steadily increases its conquests can also be derived from Cartesian philosophy. But Turgot, in 1750, is the first person to give a clear definition of the new faith. His treatise on the progress of the human mind basically recapitulates Bossuet's universal history. The idea of progress alone is substituted for the divine will. "The total mass of the human race, by alternating stages of calm and agitation, of good and evil, always marches, though with dragging footsteps, toward greater and greater perfection." This optimistic statement will furnish the basic ingredient of the rhetorical observations of Condorcet, the official theorist of progress, which he linked with the progress of the State and of which he was also the official victim in that the enlightened State forced him to poison himself. Sorel[2] was perfectly correct in saying that the philosophy of progress was exactly the philosophy to suit a society eager to enjoy the material prosperity derived from technical progress. When we are assured that tomorrow, in the natural order of events, will be better than today, we can enjoy ourselves in peace. Progress, paradoxically, can be used to justify conservatism. A draft drawn on confidence in the future, it allows the master to have a clear conscience. The slave and those whose present life is miserable and who can find no consolation in the heavens are assured that at least the future belongs to them. The future is the only kind of property that the masters willingly concede to the slaves.

These reflections are not, as we can see, out of date. But they are not out of date because the revolutionary spirit has resumed this ambiguous and convenient theme of progress. Of course, it is not the same kind of progress; Marx cannot pour enough scorn on bourgeois rational optimism. His concept of reason, as we shall see, is differ-

[2] *Les Illusions du progrès.*

ent. But arduous progress toward a future of reconciliation nevertheless defines Marx's thought. Hegel and Marxism destroyed the formal values that lighted for the Jacobins the straight road of this optimistic version of history. In this way they preserved the idea of the forward march of history, which was simply confounded by them with social progress and declared necessary. Thus they continued on the path of nineteenth-century bourgeois thought. Tocqueville, enthusiastically succeeded by Pecqueur (who influenced Marx), had solemnly proclaimed that: "The gradual and progressive development of equality is both the past and the future of the history of man." To obtain Marxism, substitute the term *level of production* for equality and imagine that in the final stage of production a transformation takes place and a reconciled society is achieved.

As for the necessity of evolution, Auguste Comte, with the law of three stages of man, which he formulates in 1822, gives the most systematic definition of it. Comte's conclusions are curiously like those finally accepted by scientific socialism.[3] Positivism demonstrates with considerable clarity the repercussions of the ideological revolution of the nineteenth century, of which Marx is one of the representatives, and which consisted in relegating to the end of history the Garden of Eden and the Revelation, which tradition had always placed at the beginning. The positivist era, which was bound to follow the metaphysical era and the theological era, was to mark the advent of a religion of humanity. Henri Gouhier gives an exact definition of Comte's enterprise when he says that his concern was to discover a man without any traces of God. Comte's primary aim, which was to substitute everywhere the relative for the absolute, was quickly transformed, by force of circumstances, into the deification of the relative and into preaching a religion that is both universal and without transcendence. Comte saw in the Jacobin cult of Reason an anticipation of positivism and considered himself, with perfect justification, as the real successor of the revolutionaries of 1789. He continued and enlarged the scope of this revolution by suppressing

[3] The last volume of *Cours de philosophie positive* appeared in the same year as Feuerbach's *Essence of Christianity*.

the transcendence of principles and by systematically founding the religion of the species. His formula: "Set aside God in the name of religion," meant nothing else but this. Inaugurating a mania that has since enjoyed a great vogue, he wanted to be the Saint Paul of this new religion and replace the Catholicism of Rome by the Catholicism of Paris. We know that he wanted to see in all the cathedrals "the statue of deified humanity on the former altar of God." He calculated with considerable accuracy that positivism would be preached in Notre-Dame before 1860. This calculation was not so ridiculous as it seems. Notre-Dame, in a state of siege, still resists: but the religion of humanity was effectively preached toward the end of the nineteenth century, and Marx, despite the fact that he had not read Comte, was one of its prophets. Marx only understood that a religion which did not embrace transcendence should properly be called politics. Comte knew it too, after all, or at least he understood that his religion was primarily a form of social idolatry and that it implied political realism,[4] the negation of individual rights, and the establishment of despotism. A society whose experts would be priests, two thousand bankers and technicians ruling over a Europe of one hundred and twenty million inhabitants where private life would be absolutely identified with public life, where absolute obedience "of action, of thought, and of feeling" would be given to the high priest who would reign over everything, such was Comte's Utopia, which announces what might be called the horizontal religions of our times. It is true that it is Utopian because, convinced of the enlightening powers of science, Comte forgot to provide a police force. Others will be more practical; the religion of humanity will be effectively founded on the blood and suffering of humanity.

Finally, if we add to these observations the remark that Marx owes to the bourgeois economists the idea, which he claims exclusively as his own, of the part played by industrial production in the development of humanity, and that he took the essentials of his theory of work-value from Ricardo, an economist of the bourgeois industrial

[4] "Everything that develops spontaneously is necessarily legitimate, for a certain time."

revolution, our right to say that his prophecy is bourgeois in content will doubtless be recognized. These comparisons only aim to show that Marx, instead of being, as the fanatical Marxists of our day would have it, the beginning and the end of the prophecy,[5] participates on the contrary in human nature: he is an heir before he is a pioneer. His doctrine, which he wanted to be a realist doctrine, actually was realistic during the period of the religion of science, of Darwinian evolutionism, of the steam engine and the textile industry. A hundred years later, science encounters relativity, uncertainty, and chance; the economy must take into account electricity, metallurgy, and atomic production. The inability of pure Marxism to assimilate these successive discoveries was shared by the bourgeois optimism of Marx's time. It renders ridiculous the Marxist pretension of maintaining that truths one hundred years old are unalterable without ceasing to be scientific. Nineteenth-century Messianism, whether it is revolutionary or bourgeois, has not resisted the successive developments of this science and this history, which to different degrees they have deified.

The Revolutionary Prophecy

Marx's prophecy is also revolutionary in principle. In that all human reality has its origins in the fruits of production, historical evolution is revolutionary because the economy is revolutionary. At each level of production the economy arouses the antagonisms that destroy, to the profit of a superior level of production, the corresponding society. Capitalism is the last of these stages of production because it produces the conditions in which every antagonism will be resolved and where there will be no more economy. On that day our history will become prehistory. This representation is the same as Hegel's, but in another perspective. The dialectic is considered from the

[5] According to Zhdanov, Marxism is "a philosophy that is qualitatively different from any previous system." This means, for example, either that Marxism is not Cartesianism, which no one would dream of denying, or that Marxism owes essentially nothing to Cartesianism, which is absurd.

angle of production and work instead of from the angle of the spirit. Marx, of course, never spoke himself about dialectical materialism. He left to his heirs the task of extolling this logical monstrosity. But he says, at the same time, that reality is dialectic and that it is economic. Reality is a perpetual process of evolution, propelled by the fertile impact of antagonisms which are resolved each time into a superior synthesis which, itself, creates its opposite and again causes history to advance. What Hegel affirmed concerning reality advancing toward the spirit, Marx affirms concerning economy on the march toward the classless society; everything is both itself and its opposite, and this contradiction compels it to become something else. Capitalism, because it is bourgeois, reveals itself as revolutionary and prepares the way for communism.

Marx's originality lies in affirming that history is simultaneously dialectic and economic. Hegel, more extreme, affirmed that it was both matter and spirit. Moreover, it could only be matter to the extent that it was spirit and vice versa. Marx denies the spirit as the definitive substance and affirms historical materialism. We can immediately remark, with Berdyaev, on the impossibility of reconciling the dialectic with materialism. There can be a dialectic only of the mind. But even materialism itself is an ambiguous idea. Only to form this word, it must be admitted that there is something more in the world than matter alone. For even stronger reasons, this criticism applies to historical materialism. History is distinguished from nature precisely by the fact that it transforms science and passion by means of will. Marx, then, is not a pure materialist, for the obvious reason that there is neither a pure nor an absolute materialism. So far is it from being pure or absolute that it recognizes that if weapons can secure the triumph of theory, theory can equally well give birth to weapons. Marx's position would be more properly called historical determinism. He does not deny thought; he imagines it absolutely determined by exterior reality. "For me, the process of thought is only the reflection of the process of reality transported and transposed to the mind of man." This particularly clumsy definition has no meaning. How and by what means can an exterior process be "transported to the mind," and this difficulty is as nothing compared to that of then defining "the transposition" of this process. But Marx used the abbreviated philosophy of his time. What he wishes to say can be defined on other planes.

For him, man is only history, and in particular the history of the means of production. Marx, in fact, remarks that man differs from animals in that he produces his own means of subsistence. If he does not first eat, if he does not clothe himself or take shelter, he does not exist. This *primum vivere* is his first determination. The little that he thinks at this moment is in direct relation to these inevitable necessities. Marx then demonstrates that his dependence is both invariable and inevitable. "The history of industry is the open book of man's essential faculties." His personal generalization consists in inferring from this affirmation, which is on the whole acceptable, that economic dependence is unique and suffices to explain everything, a concept that still remains to be demonstrated. We can admit that economic determination plays a highly important role in the genesis of human thoughts and actions without drawing the conclusion, as Marx does, that the German rebellion against Napoleon is explained only by the lack of sugar and coffee. Moreover, pure determinism is absurd in itself. If it were not, then one single affirmation would suffice to lead, from consequence to consequence, to the entire truth. If this is not so, then either we have never made a single true affirmation—not even the one stated by determinism—or we simply happen occasionally to say the truth, but without any consequences, and determinism is then false. Marx had his reasons, however, which are foreign to pure logic, for resorting to so arbitrary a simplification.

To put economic determination at the root of all human action is to sum man up in terms of his social relations. There is no such thing as a solitary man; that is the indisputable discovery of the nineteenth century. An arbitrary deduction then leads to the statement that man only feels solitary in society for social reasons. If, in fact, the solitary mind must be explained by something outside man, then man is on the road to some form of transcendence. On the other hand, society has only man as its source of origin; if, in addition, it can be affirmed that society is the creator of man, it would seem as though one had achieved the total explanation that would allow the final banishment of transcendence. Man would then be, as Marx wanted, "author and actor of his own history." Marx's prophecy is revolutionary because he completes the movement of negation begun by the philosophy of illumination. The Jacobins destroyed the transcendence of a personal god, but replaced it by the transcendence of principles. Marx institutes contemporary atheism by also destroying the transcendence of principles. Faith is replaced in 1789 by reason. But this reason itself, in its fixity, is transcendent. Marx destroys, even more radically than Hegel, the transcendence of reason and hurls it into the stream of history. Even before their time, history was a regulating principle; now it is triumphant. Marx goes farther than Hegel and pretends to consider him as an idealist (which he is not, at least no more than Marx is a materialist) to the precise extent that the reign of the mind restores in a certain way a supra-historical value. *Das Kapital* returns to the dialectic of mastery and servitude, but replaces a consciousness of self by economic autonomy and the final reign of the absolute Spirit through the advent of communism. "Atheism is humanism mediated by the suppression of religion, communism is humanism mediated by the suppression of private property." Religious alienation has the same origin as economic alienation. Religion can be disposed of only by achieving the absolute liberty of man in regard to his material determinations. The revolution is identified with atheism and with the reign of man.

That is why Marx is brought to the point of putting the emphasis on economic and social determination. His most profitable undertaking has been to reveal the reality that is hidden behind the formal values of which the bourgeois of his time made a great show. His theory of mystification is still valid, because it is in fact universally true, and is equally applicable to revolutionary mystifications. The freedom of which Monsieur Thiers dreamed was the freedom of privilege consolidated by the police; the family, extolled by the conservative newspapers, was supported by social conditions in which men and women were sent down into the mines, half-naked, attached to a communal rope; morality prospered on the prostitution of the working classes. That the demands of honesty and intelligence were put to egoistic ends by the hypocrisy of a mediocre and grasping society was a misfortune that Marx, the incomparable eye-opener, denounced with a vehemence quite unknown before him. This indignant denunciation brought other excesses in its train which require quite another denunciation. But, above all, we must recognize and state that the denunciation was born in the blood of the abortive Lyon rebellion of 1834 and in the despicable cruelty of the Versailles moralists in 1871. "The man who has nothing is nothing." If this affirmation is actually false, it was very nearly true in the optimist society of the nineteenth century. The extreme decadence brought about by the economy of prosperity was to compel Marx to give first place to social and economic relationships and to magnify still more his prophecy of the reign of man.

It is now easier to understand the purely economic explanation of history offered by Marx. If principles are deceptive, only the reality of poverty and work is true. If it is then possible to demonstrate that this suffices to explain the past and the future of mankind, then principles will be destroyed forever and with them the society that profits by them. This in fact is Marx's ambition.

Man is born into a world of production and social relations. The unequal opportunities of different lands, the more or less rapid improvements in the means of production, and the struggle for life have rapidly created social inequalities that have been crystallized into antagonisms between production and distribution; and consequently into class struggles. These struggles and antagonisms are the motive power of history. Slavery in ancient times and feudal bondage were stages on a long road that led to the artisanship of the classical centuries when the producer was master of the means of production. At this moment the opening of world trade routes and the discovery of new outlets demanded a less provincial form of production. The contradiction between the method of production and the new demands of distribution already announces the end of the regime of small-scale agricultural and industrial production. The industrial revolution, the invention of steam appliances, and competition for outlets inevitably led to the expropriation of the small proprietor and to the introduction of large-scale production. The means of production are then concentrated in the hands of those who are able to buy them; the real producers, the workers, now only dispose of the strength of their arms, which can be sold to the "man with the money." Thus bourgeois capitalism is defined by the separation of the producer from the means of production. From this conflict a series of inevitable consequences are going to spring which allow Marx to predicate the end of social antagonisms.

At first sight there is no reason why the firmly established principle of a dialectical class struggle should suddenly cease to be true. It is always true or it has never been true. Marx says plainly that there will be no more classes after the revolution than there were Estates after 1789. But Estates disappeared without classes disappearing, and there is nothing to prove that classes will not give way to some other form of social antagonism. The essential point of the Marxist prophecy lies, nevertheless, in this affirmation.

We know the Marxist scheme. Marx, following in the footsteps of Adam Smith and Ricardo, defines the value of all commodities in terms of the amount of work necessary to produce them. The amount of work is itself a commodity, sold by the proletarian to the capitalist, of which the value is defined by the quantity of work that produces it; in other words, by the value of the consumer's goods necessary for his subsistence. The capitalist, in buying this commodity, thereby undertakes to pay for it adequately so that he who sells it, the worker, may feed and perpetuate himself. But at the same time he acquires the right to make the latter work as long as he can. He can work for a long time, very much longer than is necessary to pay for his subsistence. In a twelve-hour day, if half the time suffices to produce a value equivalent to the value of the products of subsistence, the other six hours are hours not paid for, a plus-value, which constitutes the capitalist's own profit. Thus the capitalist's interest lies in prolonging to the maximum the hours of work or, when he can do so no longer, of increasing the worker's output to the maximum. The first type of coercion is a matter of oppression and cruelty. The second is a question of the organization of labor. It leads first to the division of labor, and then to the utilization of the machine, which dehumanizes the worker. Moreover, competition for foreign markets and the necessity for larger and larger investments in raw materials, produce phenomena of concentration and accumulation. First, small capitalists are absorbed by big capitalists who can maintain, for example, unprofitable prices for a longer period. A larger and larger part of the profits is finally invested in new machines and accumulated in the fixed assets of capital. This double movement first of all hastens the ruin of the middle classes, who are absorbed into the proletariat, and then proceeds to concentrate, in an increasingly small number of hands, the riches produced uniquely by the proletariat. Thus the proletariat increases in size in proportion to its increasing ruin. Capital is now concentrated in the hands of only a very few masters, whose growing power is based on robbery. Moreover, these masters are shaken to their foundations by successive crises, overwhelmed by the contradictions of the system, and can no longer assure even mere subsistence to their slaves, who then come to depend on private or public charity. A day comes, inevitably, when a huge army of oppressed slaves find themselves face to face with a handful of despicable masters. That day is the day of revolution. "The ruin of the bourgeoisie and the victory of the proletariat are equally inevitable."

This henceforth famous description does not yet give an account of the end of all antagonisms. After the victory of the proletariat, the struggle for life might well give birth to new antagonisms. Two ideas then intervene, one of which is economic, the identity of the development of production and the development of society, and the other, purely systematic, the mission of the proletariat. These two ideas reunite in what might be called Marx's activist fatalism.

The same economic evolution which in effect concentrates capital in a very few hands, makes the antagonism both more violent and, to a certain extent, unreal. It seems that, at the highest point of development of the productive forces, the slightest stimulus would lead to the proletariat finding itself alone in possession of the means of production, already snatched from the grasp of private ownership and concentrated in one enormous mass which, henceforth, would be held in common. When private property is concentrated in the hands of one single owner, it is only separated from collective ownership by the existence of one single man. The inevitable result of private capitalism is a kind of State capitalism which will then only have to be put to the service of the community to give birth to a society where capital and labor, henceforth indistinguishable, will produce, in one identical advance toward progress, both justice and abundance. It is in consideration of this happy outcome that Marx always extolled the revolutionary role played, unconsciously it is true, by the bourgeoisie. He spoke of the "historic rights" of capitalism, which he called a source both of progress and of misery. The historical mission and the justification of capitalism are, in his eyes, to prepare the conditions for a superior mode of production. This mode of production is not in itself revolutionary; it will only be the consummation of the revolution. Only the fundamental principles of bourgeois production are revolutionary. When Marx affirms that humanity only sets itself problems it can solve, he is simultaneously demonstrating that the germ of the solution of the revolutionary problem is to be found in the capitalist system itself. Therefore he recommends tolerating the bourgeois State, and even helping to build it, rather than returning to a less industrialized form of production. The proletariat "can and must accept the bourgeois revolution as a condition of the working-class revolution."

Thus Marx is the prophet of production and we are justified in thinking that on this precise point, and on no other, he ignored reality in favor of the system. He never ceased defending Ricardo, the economist of production in the manner of Manchester, against those who accused him of wanting production for production's sake ("He was absolutely right!" Marx exclaims) and of wanting it without any consideration for mankind. "That is precisely his merit," Marx replies, with the same airy indifference as Hegel. What in fact does the sacrifice of individual men matter as long as it contributes to the salvation of all mankind! Progress resembles "that horrible pagan god who wished to drink nectar only from the skulls of his fallen enemies." But at least it is progress, and it will cease to inflict torture after the industrial apocalypse when the day of reconciliation comes.

But if the proletariat cannot avoid this revolution nor avoid being put in possession of the means of production, will it at least know how to use them for the benefit of all? Where is the guarantee that, in the very bosom of the revolution, Estates, classes, and antagonisms will not arise? The guarantee lies in Hegel. The proletariat is forced to use its wealth for the universal good. It is not the proletariat, it is the universal in opposition to the particular— in other words, to capitalism. The antagonism between capital and the proletariat is the last phase of the struggle between the particular and the universal, the same struggle that animated the historical tragedy of master and slave. At the end of the visionary design constructed by Marx, the proletariat will unite all classes and discard only a handful of masters, perpetrators of "notorious crime," who will be justly destroyed by the revolution. What is more, capitalism, by driving the proletariat to the final point of degradation, gradually delivers it from every decision that might separate it from other men. It has nothing, neither property nor morality nor country. Therefore it clings to nothing but the species of which it is henceforth the naked and implacable representative. In affirming itself it affirms everything and everyone. Not because members of the proletariat are gods, but precisely because they have been reduced to the most abjectly inhuman condition. "Only the proletariat, totally excluded from this affirmation of their personality, are capable of realizing the complete affirmation of self."

That is the mission of the proletariat: to bring forth supreme dignity from supreme humiliation. Through its suffering and its struggles, it is Christ in human form redeeming the collective sin of alienation. It is, first of all, the multiform bearer of total negation and then the herald of definitive affirmation. "Philosophy cannot realize itself without the disappearance of the proletariat, the proletariat cannot liberate itself without the realization of philosophy," and again: "The proletariat can exist only on the basis of world history. . . . Communist action can exist only as historical reality on the planetary scale." But this Christ is, at the same time, an avenger. According to Marx, he carries out the sentence that private property passes on itself. "All the houses, in our times, are marked with a mysterious red cross. The judge is history, the executioner is the proletariat." Thus the fulfillment is inevitable. Crisis will succeed crisis,[6] the degradation of the proletariat will become more and more profound, it will increase in numbers until the time of the universal crisis when the world of change will vanish and when history, by a supreme act of violence, will cease to be violent any longer. The kingdom of ends will have come.

We can see that this fatalism could be driven (as happened to Hegelian thought) to a sort of political quietism by Marxists, like Kautsky, for whom it was as little within the power of the proletariat to create the revolution as within the power of the bourgeois to prevent it. Even Lenin, who was to choose the activist aspect of the doctrine, wrote in 1905, in the style of an act of excommunication: "It is a reactionary way of thinking to try to find salvation in the working class in any other way than in the top-heavy development of capitalism." It is not in the nature of economics, according to Marx, to make leaps in the dark and it must not be encouraged to gallop ahead. It is completely false to say that the socialist reformers remained faithful to Marx on this point. On the contrary, fatalism excludes all reforms, in that there would be a risk of mitigating the catastrophic aspect of the outcome and, consequently, delaying the inevitable result. The logic of such an attitude leads to the approval of everything that tends to increase working-class poverty. The worker must be given nothing so that one day he can have everything.

And yet Marx saw the danger of this particular form of quietism. Power cannot be looked forward to or else it is looked forward to indefinitely. A day comes when it must be seized, and it is the exact definition of this day that remains of doubtful clarity to all readers of Marx. On this point he never stops contradicting himself. He re-

[6] Every ten or eleven years, Marx predicted. But the period between the recurrence of the cycles "will gradually shorten."

marked that society was "historically compelled to pass through a period of dictatorship by the working classes." As for the nature of this dictatorship, his definitions are contradictory.[7] We are sure that he condemned the State in no uncertain terms, saying that its existence and the existence of servitude are inseparable. But he protested against Bakunin's nevertheless judicious observation of finding the idea of provisional dictatorship contrary to what is known as human nature. Marx thought, it is true, that the dialectical truths were superior to psychological truths. What does the dialectic say? That "the abolition of the State has no meaning except among communists, where it is an inevitable result of the suppression of classes, the disappearance of which necessarily leads to the disappearance of the need for a power organized by one class for the oppression of another." According to the sacred formula, the government of people was then to be replaced by the administration of affairs. The dialectic was therefore explicit and justified the existence of the proletarian State only for the period necessary for the destruction or integration of the bourgeois class. But, unfortunately, the prophecy and its attitude of fatalism allowed other interpretations. If it is certain that the kingdom will come, what does time matter? Suffering is never provisional for the man who does not believe in the future. But one hundred years of suffering are fleeting in the eyes of the man who prophesies, for the hundred and first year, the definitive city. In the perspective of the Marxist prophecy, nothing matters. In any event, when the bourgeois class has disappeared, the proletariat will establish the rule of the universal man at the summit of production, by the very logic of productive development. What does it matter that this should be accomplished by dictatorship and violence? In this New Jerusalem, echoing with the roar of miraculous machinery, who will still remember the cry of the victim?

The golden age, postponed until the end of history and coincident, to add to its attractions, with an apoc-

[7] Michel Collinet in *The Tragedy of Marxism* points out in Marx three forms of the seizure of power by the proletariat: Jacobin republic in the *Communist Manifesto*, authoritarian dictatorship in the *18 Brumaire*, and federal and libertarian government in the Civil War in France.

alypse, therefore justifies everything. The prodigious ambitions of Marxism must be considered and its inordinate doctrines evaluated, in order to understand that hope on such a scale leads to the inevitable neglect of problems that therefore appear to be secondary. "Communism in so far as it is the real appropriation of the human essence by man and for man, in so far as it is the return of man to himself as a social being—in other words, as a human being—a complete conscious return which preserves all the values of the inner movement, this communism, being absolute naturalism, coincides with humanism: it is the real end of the quarrel between man and nature, between man and man, between essence and existence, between externalization and the affirmation of self, between liberty and necessity, between the individual and the species. It solves the mystery of history and is aware of having solved it." It is only the language here that attempts to be scientific. Basically, where is the difference from Fourier, who announces "fertile deserts, sea water made drinkable and tasting of violets, eternal spring . . ."? The eternal springtime of mankind is foretold to us in the language of an encyclical. What can man without God want and hope for, if not the kingdom of man? This explains the exaltation of Marxist disciples. "In a society without anguish, it is easy to ignore death," says one of them. However, and this is the real condemnation of our society, the anguish of death is a luxury that is felt far more by the idler than by the worker, who is stifled by his own occupation. But every kind of socialism is Utopian, most of all scientific socialism. Utopia replaces God by the future. Then it proceeds to identify the future with ethics; the only values are those which serve this particular future. For that reason Utopias have almost always been coercive and authoritarian.[8] Marx, in so far as he is a Utopian, does not differ from his frightening predecessors, and one part of his teaching more than justifies his successors.

It has undoubtedly been correct to emphasize the ethical demands that form the basis of the Marxist dream. It must, in all fairness, be said, before examining the check to Marxism, that in them lies the real greatness of Marx.

[8] Morelly, Babeuf, and Godwin in reality describe societies based on an inquisition.

The very core of his theory was that work is profoundly dignified and unjustly despised. He rebelled against the degradation of work to the level of a commodity and of the worker to the level of an object. He reminded the privileged that their privileges were not divine and that property was not an eternal right. He gave a bad conscience to those who had no right to a clear conscience, and denounced with unparelleled profundity a class whose crime is not so much having had power as having used it to advance the ends of a mediocre society deprived of any real nobility. To him we owe the idea which is the despair of our times —but here despair is worth more than any hope—that when work is a degradation, it is not life, even though it occupies every moment of a life. Who, despite the pretensions of this society, can sleep in it in peace when they know that it derives its mediocre pleasures from the work of millions of dead souls? By demanding for the worker real riches, which are not the riches of money but of leisure and creation, he has reclaimed, despite all appearance to the contrary, the dignity of man. In doing so, and this can be said with conviction, he never wanted the additional degradation that has been imposed on man in his name. One of his phrases, which for once is clear and trenchant, forever withholds from his triumphant disciples the greatness and the humanity which once were his: "An end that requires unjust means is not a just end."

But Nietzsche's tragedy is found here once again. The aims, the prophecies are generous and universal, but the doctrine is restrictive, and the reduction of every value to historical terms leads to the direst consequences. Marx thought that the ends of history, at least, would prove to be moral and rational. That was his Utopia. But Utopia, at least in the form he knew it, is destined to serve cynicism, of which he wanted no part. Marx destroys all transcendence, then carries out, by himself, the transition from fact to duty. But his concept of duty has no other origin but fact. The demand for justice ends in injustice if it is not primarily based on an ethical justification of justice; without this, crime itself one day becomes a duty. When good and evil are reintegrated in time and confused with events, nothing is any longer good or bad, but only either premature or out of date. Who will decide on the opportunity, if not the opportunist? Later, say the disciples, you shall judge. But the victims will not be there to judge. For the victim, the present is the only value, rebellion the only action. Messianism, in order to exist, must construct a defense against the victims. It is possible that Marx did not want this, but in this lies his responsibility which must be examined, that he incurred by justifying, in the name of the revolution, the henceforth bloody struggle against all forms of rebellion.

The Failing of the Prophecy

Hegel haughtily brings history to an end in 1807; the disciples of Saint-Simon believe that the revolutionary convulsions of 1830 and 1848 are the last; Comte dies in 1857 preparing to climb into the pulpit and preach positivism to a humanity returned at last from the path of error. With the same blind romanticism, Marx, in his turn, prophesies the classless society and the solution of the historical mystery. Slightly more circumspect, however, he does not fix the date. Unfortunately, his prophecy also described the march of history up to the hour of fulfillment; it predicted the trend of events. The events and the facts, of course, have forgotten to arrange themselves according to the synthesis; and this already explains why it has been necessary to rally them by force. But above all, the prophecies, from the moment that they begin to betray the living hopes of millions of men, cannot with impunity remain indeterminate. A time comes when deception transforms patient hope into furious disillusionment and when the ends, affirmed with the mania of obstinacy, demanded with ever-increasing cruelty, make obligatory the search for other means.

The revolutionary movement at the end of the nineteenth century and beginning of the twentieth lived, like the early Christians, in the expectation of the end of the world and the advent of the proletarian Christ. We know how persistent this sentiment was among primitive Christian communities. Even at the end of the fourth century a bishop in proconsular Africa calculated that the world would only exist for another one hundred and one years.

At the end of this period would come the kingdom of heaven, which must be merited without further delay. This sentiment is prevalent in the first century[9] and explains the indifference of the early Christians toward purely theological questions. If the advent is near, everything must be consecrated to a burning faith rather than to works and to dogma. Until Clement and Tertullian, during more than a century, Christian literature ignored theological problems and did not elaborate on the subject of works. But from the moment the advent no longer seems imminent, man must live with his faith—in other words, compromise. Then piety and the catechism appear on the scene. The evangelical advent fades into the distance; Saint Paul has come to establish dogma. The Church has incorporated the faith that has only an ardent desire for the kingdom to come. Everything had to be organized in the period, even martyrdom, of which the temporal witnesses are the monastic orders, and even the preaching, which was to be found again in the guise of the Inquisition.

A similar movement was born of the check to the revolutionary advent. The passages from Marx already cited give a fair idea of the burning hope that inspired the revolutionary spirit of the time. Despite partial setbacks, this faith never ceased to increase up to the moment when it found itself, in 1917, face to face with the partial realization of its dreams. "We are fighting for the gates of heaven," cried Liebknecht. In 1917 the revolutionary world really believed that it had arrived before those gates. Rosa Luxemburg's prophecy was being realized. "The revolution will rise resoundingly tomorrow to its full height and, to your consternation, will announce with the sound of all its trumpets: I was, I am, I shall be." The Spartakus movement believed that it had achieved the definitive revolution because, according to Marx himself, the latter would come to pass after the Russian Revolution had been consummated by a Western revolution. After the revolution of 1917, a Soviet Germany would, in fact, have opened the gates of heaven. But the Spartakus movement is crushed, the French general strike of 1920 fails,

[9] On the imminence of this event, see Mark ix, 1; xiii, 30; Matthew x, 23; xvi, 27–8; xxiv, 34; Luke ix, 26–7; xxi, 22, etc.

the Italian revolutionary movement is strangled. Liebknecht then recognizes that the time is not ripe for revolution. "The period had not yet drawn to a close." But also, and now we grasp how defeat can excite vanquished faith to the point of religious ecstasy: "At the crash of economic collapse whose rumblings can already be heard, the sleeping soldiers of the proletariat will awake as at the fanfare of the Last Judgment, and the corpses of the victims of the struggle will arise and demand an accounting from those who are bowed down with curses." While awaiting these events, Liebknecht and Rosa Luxemburg are assassinated, and Germany rushes toward servitude. The Russian Revolution remains isolated, living in defiance of its own system, still far from the celestial gates, with an apocalypse to organize. The advent is again postponed. Faith is intact, but it totters beneath an enormous load of problems and discoveries which Marxism had not foreseen. The new religion is once more confronted with Galilee: to preserve its faith, it must deny the sun and humiliate free man.

What does Galilee say, in fact, at this moment? What are the errors, demonstrated by history itself, of the prophecy? We know that the economic evolution of the contemporary world refutes a certain number of the postulates of Marx. If the revolution is to occur at the end of two parallel movements, the unlimited shrinking of capital and the unlimited expansion of the proletariat, it will not occur or ought not to have occurred. Capital and proletariat have both been equally unfaithful to Marx. The tendency observed in industrial England of the nineteenth century has, in certain cases, changed its course, and in others become more complex. Economic crises, which should have occurred with increasing frequency, have, on the contrary, become more sporadic: capitalism has learned the secrets of planned production and has contributed on its own part to the growth of the Moloch State. Moreover, with the introduction of companies in which stock could be held, capital, instead of becoming increasingly concentrated, has given rise to a new category of smallholders whose very last desire would certainly be to encourage strikes. Small enterprises have been, in many cases, destroyed by competition as Marx foresaw. But the complexity of modern production has generated a multitude of small factories around great enterprises. In 1938 Ford was able to announce that five thousand two hundred independent workshops supplied him with their products. Of course large industries inevitably assimilated these enterprises to a certain extent. But the essential thing is that these small industrialists form an intermediary social layer which complicates the scheme that Marx imagined. Finally, the law of concentration has proved absolutely false in agricultural economy, which was treated with considerable frivolity by Marx. The hiatus is important here. In one of its aspects, the history of socialism in our times can be considered as the struggle between the proletarian movement and the peasant class. This struggle continues, on the historical plane, the nineteenth-century ideological struggle between authoritarian socialism and libertarian socialism, of which the peasant and artisan origins are quite evident. Thus Marx had, in the ideological material of his time, the elements for a study of the peasant problem. But his desire to systematize made him oversimplify everything. This particular simplification was to prove expensive for the kulaks who constituted more than five million historic exceptions to be brought, by death and deportation, within the Marxist pattern.

The same desire for simplification diverted Marx from the phenomenon of the nation in the very century of nationalism. He believed that through commerce and exchange, through the very victory of the proletariat, the barriers would fall. But it was national barriers that brought about the fall of the proletarian ideal. As a means of explaining history, the struggle between nations has been proved at least as important as the class struggle. But nations cannot be entirely explained by economics; therefore the system ignored them.

The proletariat, on its part, did not toe the line. First of all, Marx's fear is confirmed: reforms and trade unions brought about a rise in the standard of living and an amelioration in working conditions. These improvements are very far from constituting an equitable settlement of the social problem; but the miserable condition of the English textile workers in Marx's time, far from becoming general and even deteriorating, as he would have liked, has on the contrary been alleviated. Marx would not complain about this today, the equilibrium having been reestablished by another error in his predictions. It has, in fact, been possible to prove that the most efficacious revolutionary or trade-union asset has always been the existence of a working-class elite who have not been sterilized by hunger. Poverty and degeneration have never ceased to be what they were before Marx's time, and what he did not want to admit they were despite all his observations: factors contributing to servitude not to revolution. One third of working-class Germany was unemployed in 1933. Bourgeois society was then obliged to provide a means of livelihood for these unemployed, thus bringing about the situation that Marx said was essential for revolution. But it is not a good thing that future revolutionaries should be put in the situation of expecting to be fed by the State. This unnatural habit leads to others, which are even less good, and which Hitler made into doctrine.

Finally, the proletariat did not increase in numbers indefinitely. The very conditions of industrial production, which every Marxist is called upon to encourage, improved, to a considerable extent, the conditions of the middle class[1] and even created a new social stratum, the technicians. The ideal, so dear to Lenin, of a society in which the engineer would at the same time be a manual laborer is in conflict with the facts. The principal fact is that technology, like science, has reached such a degree of complication that it is not possible for a single man to understand the totality of its principles and applications. It is almost impossible, for instance, for a physicist today to have a complete understanding of the biological science of his times. Even within the realms of physics he cannot claim to be equally familiar with every branch of the subject. It is the same in technology. From the moment that productivity, which is considered by both bourgeois and Marxist as a benefit in itself, is developed to enormous proportions, the division of labor, which Marx thought could have been avoided, became inevitable. Every worker

---

[1] From 1920 to 1930, in a period of intense productivity, the number of metallurgical workers decreased in the United States, while the number of salesmen working for the same industry almost doubled.

has been brought to the point of performing a particular function without knowing the over-all plan into which his work will fit. Those who co-ordinate individual work have formed, by their very function, a class whose social importance is decisive.

It is only fair to point out that this era of technocracy announced by Burnham was described, about twenty years ago, by Simone Weil in a form that can be considered complete, without drawing Burnham's unacceptable conclusions. To the two traditional forms of oppression known to humanity—oppression by armed force and by wealth— Simone Weil adds a third—oppression by occupation. "One can abolish the opposition between the buyer and the seller of work," she wrote, "without abolishing the opposition between those who dispose of the machine and those of whom the machine disposes." The Marxist plan to abolish the degrading opposition of intellectual work to manual work has come into conflict with the demands of production, which elsewhere Marx exalted. Marx undoubtedly foresaw, in *Das Kapital*, the importance of the "manager" on the level of maximum concentration of capital. But he did not believe that this concentration of capital could survive the abolition of private property. Division of labor and private property, he said, are identical expressions. History has demonstrated the contrary. The ideal regime based on collective property could be defined, according to Lenin, as justice plus electricity. In the final analysis it is only electricity, without justice.

The idea of a mission of the proletariat has not, so far, been able to formulate itself in history: this sums up the failing of the Marxist prophecy. The failure of the Second International has proved that the proletariat was influenced by other things as well as its economic condition and that, contrary to the famous formula, it had a fatherland. The majority of the proletariat accepted or submitted to the war and collaborated, willy-nilly, in the nationalist excesses of the times. Marx intended that the working classes before they triumphed should have acquired legal and political acumen. His error lay only in believing that extreme poverty, and particularly industrial poverty, could lead to political maturity. Moreover, it is quite certain that the revolutionary capacity of the masses was curtailed by the decapitation of the libertarian revolution, during and after the Commune. After all, Marxism easily dominated the working-class movement from 1872 on, undoubtedly because of its own strength, but also because the only socialist tradition that could have opposed it had been drowned in blood; there were practically no Marxists among the insurgents of 1871. This automatic purification of revolution has been continued, thanks to the activities of police states, until our times. More and more, revolution has found itself delivered into the hands of its bureaucrats and doctrinaires on the one hand, and to enfeebled and bewildered masses on the other. When the revolutionary elite are guillotined and when Talleyrand is left alive, who will oppose Bonaparte? But to these historical reasons are added economic necessities. The passages by Simone Weil on the condition of the factory worker[2] must be read in order to realize to what degree of moral exhaustion and silent despair the rationalization of labor can lead. Simone Weil is right in saying that the worker's condition is doubly inhumane in that he is first deprived of money and then of dignity. Work in which one can have an interest, creative work, even though it is badly paid, does not degrade life. Industrial socialism has done nothing essential to alleviate the condition of the workers because it has not touched on the very principle of production and the organization of labor, which, on the contrary, it has extolled. It even went so far as to offer the worker a historic justification of his lot of much the same value as a promise of celestial joys to one who works himself to death; never did it attempt to give him the joy of creation. The political form of society is no longer in question at this level, but the beliefs of a technical civilization on which capitalism and socialism are equally dependent. Any ideas that do not advance the solution of this problem hardly touch on the misfortunes of the worker.

Only through the interplay of economic forces, so much admired by Marx, has the proletariat been able to reject the historical mission with which Marx had rightly charged it. His error can be excused because, confronted with the debasement of the ruling classes, a man who has the future of civilization at heart instinctively looks for

[2] *La Condition ouvrière* (Paris: Gallimard).

an elite as a replacement. But this instinctive search is not, in itself alone, creative. The revolutionary bourgeoisie seized power in 1789 because they already had it. At this period legality, as Jules Monnerot says, was lagging behind the facts. The facts were that the bourgeoisie were already in possession of the posts of command and of the new power: money. The proletariat were not at all in the same position, having only their poverty and their hopes and being kept in their condition of misery by the bourgeoisie. The bourgeois class debased itself by a mania for production and material power, while the very organization of this mania made the creation of an elite impossible.[3] But criticism of this organization and the development of rebel conscience could, on the contrary, forge a reserve elite. Only revolutionary trade unionism, with Pelloutier and Sorel, embarked on this course and wanted to create, by professional and cultural education, new cadres for which a world without honor was calling and still calls. But that could not be accomplished in a day and the new masters were already on the scene, interested in making immediate use of human unhappiness for the sake of happiness in the distant future, rather than in relieving as much and as soon as possible the suffering of millions of men. The authoritarian socialists deemed that history was going too slowly and that it was necessary, in order to hurry it on, to entrust the mission of the proletariat to a handful of doctrinaires. For that very reason they have been the first to deny this mission. Nevertheless it exists, not in the exclusive sense that Marx gives it, but in the sense that a mission exists for any human group which knows how to derive pride and fecundity from its labors and its sufferings. So that it can manifest itself, however, a risk must be taken and confidence put in working-class freedom and spontaneity. Authoritarian socialism, on the contrary, has confiscated this living freedom for the

[3] Lenin was the first to record this truth, but without any apparent bitterness. If his words are terrible for revolutionary hopes, they are no less so for Lenin himself. He dared to say, in fact, that the masses would more easily accept bureaucratic and dictatorial centralism because "discipline and organization are assimilated more easily by the proletariat, thanks to the hard school of the factory."

benefit of an ideal freedom, which is yet to come. In so doing, whether it wished to or not, it reinforced the attempt at enslavement begun by industrial capitalism. By the combined action of these two factors and during a hundred and fifty years, except in the Paris of the Commune, which was the last refuge of rebel revolution, the proletariat has had no other historical mission but to be betrayed. The workers fought and died to give power to the military or to intellectuals who dreamed of becoming military and who would enslave them in their turn. This struggle, however, has been the source of their dignity, a fact that is recognized by all who have chosen to share their aspirations and their misfortunes. But this dignity has been acquired in opposition to the whole clan of old and new masters. At the very moment when they dare to make use of it, it denies them. In one sense, it announces their eclipse.

The economic predictions of Marx have, therefore, been at least called in question by reality. What remains true in his vision of the economic world is the establishment of a society more and more defined by the rhythm of production. But he shared this concept, in the enthusiasm of his period, with bourgeois ideology. The bourgeois illusions concerning science and technical progress, shared by the authoritarian socialists, gave birth to the civilization of the machine-tamers, which can, through the stresses of competition and the desire for domination, be separated into enemy blocs, but which on the economic plane is subject to identical laws: the accumulation of capital and rationalized and continually increasing production. The political difference, which concerns the degree of omnipotence of the State, is appreciable, but can be reduced by economic evolution. Only the difference in ethical concepts —formal virtue as opposed to historical cynicism—seems substantial. But the imperative of production dominates both universes and makes them, on the economic plane, one world.[4]

In any event, if the economic imperative can no longer

[4] It is worth specifying that productivity is only injurious when it is considered as an end, not as a means, in which case it could have a liberating effect.

be denied,[5] its consequences are not what Marx imagined. Economically speaking, capitalism becomes oppressive through the phenomenon of accumulation. It is oppressive through being what it is, it accumulates in order to increase what it is, to exploit it all the more, and accordingly to accumulate still more. At that moment accumulation would be necessary only to a very small extent in order to guarantee social benefits. But the revolution, in its turn, becomes industrialized and realizes that, when accumulation is an attribute of technology itself, and not of capitalism, the machine finally conjures up the machine. Every form of collectivity, fighting for survival, is forced to accumulate instead of distributing its revenues. It accumulates in order to increase in size and so to increase in power. Whether bourgeois or socialist, it postpones justice for a later date, in the interests of power alone. But power opposes other forms of power. It arms and rearms because others are arming and rearming. It does not stop accumulating and will never cease to do so until the day when perhaps it will reign alone on earth. Moreover, for that to happen, it must pass through a war. Until that day the proletariat will receive only the bare minimum for its subsistence. The revolution compels itself to construct, at a great expenditure in human lives, the industrial and capitalist intermediary that its own system demands. Revenue is replaced by human labor. Slavery then becomes the general condition, and the gates of heaven remain locked. Such is the economic law governing a world that lives by the cult of production, and the reality is even more bloody than the law. Revolution, in the dilemma into which it has been led by its bourgeois opponents and its nihilist supporters, is nothing but slavery. Unless it changes its principles and its path, it can have no other final result than servile rebellions, obliterated in blood or the hideous

[5] Although it was deniable—until the eighteenth century—during all the period in which Marx thought he had discovered it. Historical examples in which the conflict between forms of civilization did not end in progress in methods of production: destruction of the Mycenæan civilization, invasion of Rome by the barbarians, expulsion of the Moors from Spain, extermination of the Albigenses.

prospect of atomic suicide. The will to power, the nihilist struggle for domination and authority, have done considerably more than sweep away the Marxist Utopia. This has become in its turn a historic fact destined to be put to use like all the other historic facts. This idea, which was supposed to dominate history, has become lost in history; the concept of abolishing means has been reduced to a means in itself and cynically manipulated for the most banal and bloody ends. The uninterrupted development of production has not ruined the capitalist regime to the benefit of the revolution. It has equally been the ruin of both bourgeois and revolutionary society to the benefit of an idol that has the snout of power.

How could a so-called scientific socialism conflict to such a point with facts? The answer is easy: it was not scientific. On the contrary, its defeat resulted from a method ambiguous enough to wish to be simultaneously determinist and prophetic, dialectic and dogmatic. If the mind is only the reflection of events, it cannot anticipate their progress, except by hypothesis. If Marxist theory is determined by economics, it can describe the past history of production, not its future, which remains in the realms of probability. The task of historical materialism can only be to establish a method of criticism of contemporary society; it is only capable of making suppositions, unless it abandons its scientific attitude, about the society of the future. Moreover, is it not for this reason that its most important work is called *Capital* and not *Revolution?* Marx and the Marxists allowed themselves to prophesy the future and the triumph of communism to the detriment of their postulates and of scientific method.

Then predictions could be scientific, on the contrary, only by ceasing to prophesy definitively. Marxism is not scientific; at the best, it has scientific prejudices. It brought out into the open the profound difference between scientific reasoning, that fruitful instrument of research, of thought, and even of rebellion, and historical reasoning, which German ideology invented by its negation of all principles. Historical reasoning is not a type of reasoning that, within the framework of its own functions, can pass judgment on the world. While pretending to judge it, it really tries to determine its course. Essentially a part of events, it directs them and is simultaneously pedagogic and all-conquering. Moreover, its most abstruse descriptions conceal the most simple truths. If man is reduced to being nothing but a character in history, he has no other choice but to subside into the sound and fury of a completely irrational history or to endow history with the form of human reason. Therefore the history of contemporary nihilism is nothing but a prolonged endeavor to give order, by human forces alone and simply by force, to a history no longer endowed with order. The pseudo-reasoning ends by identifying itself with cunning and strategy, while waiting to culminate in the ideological Empire. What part could science play in this concept? Nothing is less determined on conquest than reason. History is not made with scientific scruples; we are even condemned to not making history from the moment when we claim to act with scientific objectivity. Reason does not preach, or if it does, it is no longer reason. That is why historical reason is an irrational and romantic form of reason, which sometimes recalls the false logic of the insane and at other times the mystic affirmation of the word.

The only really scientific aspect of Marxism is to be found in its preliminary rejection of myths and in its exposure of the crudest kind of interests. But in this respect Marx is not more scientific in his attitude than La Rochefoucauld; and that is just the attitude that he abandons when he embarks on prophecy. Therefore it is not surprising that, to make Marxism scientific and to preserve this fiction, which is very useful in this century of science, it has been a necessary first step to render science Marxist through terror. The progress of science, since Marx, has roughly consisted in replacing determinism and the rather crude mechanism of its period by a doctrine of provisional probability. Marx wrote to Engels that the Darwinian theory constituted the very foundation of their method. For Marxism to remain infallible, it has therefore been necessary to deny all biological discoveries made since Darwin. As it happens that all discoveries since the unexpected mutations established by De Vries have consisted in introducing, contrary to the doctrines of determinism, the idea of chance into biology, it has been necessary to entrust

Lyssenko with the task of disciplining chromosomes and of demonstrating once again the truth of the most elementary determinism. That is ridiculous: but put a police force under Flaubert's Monsieur Homais and he would no longer be ridiculous, and there we have the twentieth century. As far as that is concerned, the twentieth century has also witnessed the denial of the principle of indeterminism in science, of limited relativity, of the quantum theory,[6] and, finally, of every general tendency of contemporary science. Marxism is only scientific today in defiance of Heisenberg, Bohr, Einstein, and all the greatest minds of our time. After all, there is really nothing mysterious about the principle that consists in using scientific reasoning to the advantage of a prophecy. This has already been named the principle of authority, and it is this that guides the Churches when they wish to subject living reason to dead faith and freedom of the intellect to the maintenance of temporal power.

Finally, there remains of Marx's prophecy—henceforth in conflict with its two principles, economy and science—only the passionate annunciation of an event that will take place in the very far future. The only recourse of the Marxists consists in saying that the delays are simply longer than was imagined and that one day, far away in the future, the end will justify all. In other words, we are in purgatory and we are promised that there will be no hell. And so the problem that is posed is of another order. If the struggle waged by one or two generations throughout a period of economic evolution which is, perforce, beneficial suffices to bring about a classless society, then the necessary sacrifice becomes comprehensible to the man with a militant turn of mind; the future for him has a concrete aspect—the aspect of his child, for instance. But if, when the sacrifice of several generations has proved insufficient, we must then embark on an infinite period of universal strife one thousand times more destructive than before, then the conviction of faith is needed in order to accept the necessity of killing and

[6] Roger Caillois, in *Critique du Marxisme* (Paris: Gallimard), remarks that Stalinism objects to the quantum theory, but makes use of atomic science, which is derived from it.

dying. This new faith is no more founded on pure reason than were the ancient faiths.

In what terms is it possible to imagine this end of history? Marx did not fall back on Hegel's terms. He said, rather obscurely, that communism was only a necessary aspect of the future of humanity, and did not comprise the entire future. But either communism does not terminate the history of contradictions and suffering, and then it is no longer possible to see how one can justify so much effort and sacrifice; or it does terminate it, and it is no longer possible to imagine the continuation of history except as an advance toward this perfected form of society. Thus a mystic idea is arbitrarily introduced into a description that claims to be scientific. The final disappearance of political economy—the favorite theme of Marx and Engels—signifies the end of all suffering. Economics, in fact, coincides with pain and suffering in history, which disappear with the disappearance of history. We arrive at last in the Garden of Eden.

We come no nearer to solving the problem by declaring that it is not a question of the end of history, but of a leap into the midst of a different history. We can only imagine this other history in terms of our own history; for man they are both one and the same thing. Moreover, this other history poses the same dilemma. Either it is not the solution of all contradictions and we suffer, die, and kill for almost nothing, or it is the solution of contradictions and therefore, to all intents and purposes, terminates our history. Marxism, at this stage, is only justified by the definitive city.

Can it be said, therefore, that this city of ends has a meaning? It has, in terms of the sacred universe, once the religious postulate has been admitted. The world was created, it will have an end; Adam left Eden, humanity must return there. It has no meaning, in the historical universe, if the dialectical postulate is admitted. The dialectic correctly applied cannot and must not come to an end.[7] The antagonistic terms of a historical situation can negate one another and then be surmounted in a new synthesis.

[7] See the excellent discussion by Jules Mounerot in *Sociologie du communisme*, Part III.

But there is no reason why this new synthesis should be better than the original. Or rather there is only a reason for this supposition, if one arbitrarily imposes an end to the dialectic, and if one then applies a judgment based on outside values. If the classless society is going to terminate history, then capitalist society is, in effect, superior to feudal society to the extent that it brings the advent of this classless society still nearer. But if the dialectic postulate is admitted at all, it must be admitted entirely. Just as aristocratic society has been succeeded by a society without an aristocracy but with classes, it must be concluded that the society of classes will be succeeded by a classless society, but animated by a new antagonism still to be defined. A movement that is refused a beginning cannot have an end. "If socialism," says an anarchist essayist,[8] "is an eternal evolution, its means are its end." More precisely, it has no ends; it has only means which are guaranteed by nothing unless by a value foreign to evolution. In this sense, it is correct to remark that the dialectic is not and cannot be revolutionary. From our point of view, it is only nihilism—pure movement that aims at denying everything which is not itself.

There is in this universe no reason, therefore, to imagine the end of history. That is the only justification, however, for the sacrifices demanded of humanity in the name of Marxism. But it has no other reasonable basis but a *petitio principii*, which introduces into history—a kingdom that was meant to be unique and self-sufficient—a value foreign to history. Since that value is, at the same time, foreign to ethics, it is not, properly speaking, a value on which one can base one's conduct; it is a dogma without foundation that can be adopted only as the desperate effort to escape of a mind which is being stifled by solitude or by nihilism, or a value which is going to be imposed by those whom dogma profits. The end of history is not an exemplary or a perfectionist value; it is an arbitrary and terroristic principle.

Marx recognized that all revolutions before his time had failed. But he claimed that the revolution announced by him must succeed definitively. Up to now, the workers' movement has lived on this affirmation which has been

[8] Ernestan: *Socialism and Freedom.*

continually belied by facts and of which it is high time that the falsehood should be dispassionately denounced. In proportion as the prophecy was postponed, the affirmation of the coming of the final kingdom, which could only find the most feeble support in reason, became an article of faith. The sole value of the Marxist world henceforth resides, despite Marx, in a dogma imposed on an entire ideological empire. The kingdom of ends is used, like the ethics of eternity and the kingdom of heaven, for purposes of social mystification. Élie Halévy declared himself unqualified to say if socialism was going to lead to the universalization of the Swiss Republic or to European Cæsarism. Nowadays we are better informed. The prophecies of Nietzsche, on this point at least, are justified. Marxism is henceforth to win fame, in defiance of its own teachings and, by an inevitable process of logic, by intellectual Cæsarism, which we must now finally describe. The last representative of the struggle of justice against grace, it takes over, without having wanted to do so, the struggle of justice against truth. How to live without grace—that is the question that dominates the nineteenth century. "By justice," answered all those who did not want to accept absolute nihilism. To the people who despaired of the kingdom of heaven, they promised the kingdom of men. The preaching of the City of Humanity increased in fervor up to the end of the nineteenth century, when it became really visionary in tone and placed scientific certainties in the service of Utopia. But the kingdom has retreated into the distance, gigantic wars have ravaged the oldest countries of Europe, the blood of rebels has bespattered walls, and total justice has approached not a step nearer. The question of the twentieth century—for which the terrorists of 1905 died and which tortures the contemporary world—has gradually been specified: how to live without grace and without justice?

Only nihilism, and not rebellion, has answered that question. Up to now, only nihilism has spoken, returning once more to the theme of the romantic rebels: "Frenzy." Frenzy in terms of history is called power. The will to power came to take the place of the will to justice, pretending at first to be identified with it and then relegating it to a place somewhere at the end of history, waiting until such time as nothing remains on earth to dominate. Thus the ideological consequence has triumphed over the economic consequence: the history of Russian Communism gives the lie to every one of its principles. Once more we find, at the end of this long journey, metaphysical rebellion, which, this time, advances to the clash of arms and the whispering of passwords, but forgetful of its real principles, burying its solitude in the bosom of armed masses, covering the emptiness of its negations with obstinate scholasticism, still directed toward the future, which it has made its only god, but separated from it by a multitude of nations that must be overthrown and continents that must be dominated. With action as its unique principle, and with the kingdom of man as an alibi, it has already begun, in the east of Europe, to construct its own armed camp, face to face with other armed camps.

The Kingdom of Ends

Marx never dreamed of such a terrifying apotheosis. Nor, indeed, did Lenin though he took a decisive step toward establishing a military Empire. As good a strategist as he was a mediocre philosopher, he first of all posed himself the problem of the seizure of power. Let us note immediately that it is absolutely false to talk, as is often done, of Lenin's Jacobinism. Only his idea of units of agitators and revolutionaries is Jacobin. The Jacobins believed in principles and in virtue; they died because they had to deny them. Lenin believes only in the revolution and in the virtue of expediency. "One must be prepared for every sacrifice, to use if necessary every stratagem, ruse, illegal method, to be determined to conceal the truth, for the sole purpose of penetrating the labor unions . . . and of accomplishing, despite everything, the Communist task." The struggle against formal morality, inaugurated by Hegel and Marx, is found again in Lenin with his criticism of inefficacious revolutionary attitudes. Complete dominion was the aim of this movement.

If we examine the two works written at the beginning[9] and at the end[1] of his career as an agitator, one is

[9] *What to Do?* (1902).
[1] *The State and the Revolution* (1917).

struck by the fact that he never ceased to fight mercilessly against the sentimental forms of revolutionary action. He wanted to abolish the morality of revolutionary action because he believed, correctly, that revolutionary power could not be established while still respecting the Ten Commandments. When he appears, after his first experiments on the stage of history, where he was to play such an important role, to see him take the world so freely and so naturally as it had been shaped by the ideology and the economy of the preceding century, one would imagine him to be the first man of a new era. Completely impervious to anxiety, to nostalgia, to ethics, he takes command, looks for the best method of making the machine run, and decides that certain virtues are suitable for the driver of history's chariot and that others are not. He gropes a little at first and hesitates as to whether Russia should first pass through the capitalist and industrial phase. But this comes to the same as doubting whether the revolution can take place in Russia. He himself is Russian and his task is to make the Russian Revolution. He jettisons economic fatalism and embarks on action. He roundly declares, from 1902 on, that the workers will never elaborate an independent ideology by themselves. He denies the spontaneity of the masses. Socialist doctrine supposes a scientific basis that only the intellectuals can give it. When he says that all distinctions between workers and intellectuals must be effaced, what he really means is that it is possible not to be proletarian and know better than the proletariat what its interests are. He then congratulates Lassalle for having carried on a tenacious struggle against the spontaneity of the masses. "Theory," he says, "should subordinate spontaneity." [2] In plain language, that means that revolution needs leaders and theorists.

He attacks both reformism, which he considers guilty of dissipating revolutionary strength, and terrorism,[3] which he thinks an exemplary and inefficacious attitude. The revolution, before being either economic or sentimental,

---

[2] Marx said much the same: "What certain proletarians, or even the entire proletariat, imagine to be their goal is of no importance."

[3] We know that his elder brother, who had chosen terrorism, was hanged.

is military. Until the day that the revolution breaks out, revolutionary action is identified with strategy. Autocracy is its enemy, whose main source of strength is the police force, which is nothing but a corps of professional political soldiers. The conclusion is simple: "The struggle against the political police demands special qualities, demands professional revolutionaries." The revolution will have its professional army as well as the masses, which can be conscripted when needed. This corps of agitators must be organized before the mass is organized. A network of agents is the expression that Lenin uses, thus announcing the reign of the secret society and of the realist monks of the revolution: "We are the Young Turks of the revolution," he said, "with something of the Jesuit added." From that moment the proletariat no longer has a mission. It is only one powerful means, among others, in the hands of the revolutionary ascetics.[4]

The problem of the seizure of power brings in its train the problem of the State. *The State and the Revolution* (1917), which deals with this subject, is the strangest and most contradictory of pamphlets. Lenin employs in it his favorite method, which is the method of authority. With the help of Marx and Engels, he begins by taking a stand against any kind of reformism which would claim to utilize the bourgeois State—that organism of domination of one class over another. The bourgeois State owes its survival to the police and to the army because it is primarily an instrument of oppression. It reflects both the irreconcilable antagonism of the classes and the forcible subjugation of this antagonism. This authority of fact is only worthy of contempt. "Even the head of the military power of a civilized State must envy the head of the clan whom patriarchal society surrounded with voluntary respect, not with respect imposed by the club." Moreover, Engels has firmly established that the concept of the State and the concept of a free society are irreconcilable. "Classes will disappear as ineluctably as they appeared. With the disappearance of classes, the State will inevitably disappear. The society that reorganizes production on the basis of the free and equal association of the producers will

[4] Heine already called the socialists "the new puritans." Puritanism and revolution go, historically, together.

relegate the machine of State to the place it deserves: to the museum of antiquities, side by side with the spinning-wheel and the bronze ax."

Doubtless this explains why inattentive readers have ascribed the reason for writing *The State and the Revolution* to Lenin's anarchistic tendencies and have regretted the peculiar posterity of a doctrine so severe about the army, the police, the club, and bureaucracy. But Lenin's points of view, in order to be understood, must always be considered in terms of strategy. If he defends so very energetically Engels's thesis about the disappearance of the bourgeois State, it is because he wants, on the one hand, to put an obstacle in the way of the pure "economism" of Plekhanov and Kautsky and, on the other, to demonstrate that Kerensky's government is a bourgeois government, which must be destroyed. One month later, moreover, he destroys it.

It was also necessary to answer those who objected to the fact that the revolution itself had need of an administrative and repressive apparatus. There again Marx and Engels are largely used to prove, authoritatively, that the proletarian State is not a State organized on the lines of other states, but a State which, by definition, is in the process of withering away. "As soon as there is no longer a social class which must be kept oppressed . . . a State ceases to be necessary. The first act by which the [proletarian] State really establishes itself as the representative of an entire society—the seizure of the society's means of production—is, at the same time, the last real act of the State. For the government of people is substituted the administration of things. . . . The State is not abolished, it perishes." The bourgeois State is first suppressed by the proletariat. Then, but only then, the proletarian State fades away. The dictatorship of the proletariat is necessary —first, to crush or suppress what remains of the bourgeois class; secondly, to bring about the socialization of the means of production. Once these two tasks are accomplished, it immediately begins to wither away.

Lenin, therefore, begins from the firm and definite principle that the State dies as soon as the socialization of the means of production is achieved and the exploiting class has consequently been suppressed. Yet, in the same

pamphlet, he ends by justifying the preservation, even after
the socialization of the means of production and, without
any predictable end, of the dictatorship of a revolutionary
faction over the rest of the people. The pamphlet, which
makes continual reference to the experiences of the Commune, flatly contradicts the contemporary federalist and
anti-authoritarian ideas that produced the Commune; and
it is equally opposed to the optimistic forecasts of Marx
and Engels. The reason for this is clear; Lenin had not forgotten that the Commune failed. As for the means of such
a surprising demonstration, they were even more simple:
with each new difficulty encountered by the revolution, the
State as described by Marx is endowed with a supplementary prerogative. Ten pages farther on, without any
kind of transition, Lenin in effect affirms that power is
necessary to crush the resistance of the exploiters "and
also to direct the great mass of the population, peasantry,
lower middle classes, and semi-proletariat, in the management of the socialist economy." The shift here is undeniable; the provisional State of Marx and Engels is
charged with a new mission, which risks prolonging its
life indefinitely. Already we can perceive the contradiction
of the Stalinist regime in conflict with its official philosophy. Either this regime has realized the classless socialist
society, and the maintenance of a formidable apparatus
of repression is not justified in Marxist terms, or it has
not realized the classless society and has therefore proved
that Marxist doctrine is erroneous and, in particular, that
the socialization of the means of production does not mean
the disappearance of classes. Confronted with its official
doctrine, the regime is forced to choose: the doctrine is
false, or the regime has betrayed it. In fact, together with
Nechaiev and Tkachev, it is Lassalle, the inventor of State
socialism, whom Lenin has caused to triumph in Russia,
to the detriment of Marx. From this moment on, the history of the interior struggles of the party, from Lenin to
Stalin, is summed up in the struggle between the workers'
democracy and military and bureaucratic dictatorship; in
other words, between justice and expediency.

There is a moment's doubt about whether Lenin is
not going to find a kind of means of conciliation when we
hear him praising the measures adopted by the Commune:

elected, revocable functionaries, remunerated like workers, and replacement of industrial bureaucracy by direct workers' management. We even catch a glimpse of a federalist Lenin who praises the institution and representation of the communes. But it becomes rapidly clear that this federalism is only extolled to the extent that it signifies the abolition of parliamentarianism. Lenin, in defiance of every historical truth, calls it centralism and immediately puts the accent on the idea of the dictatorship of the proletariat, while reproaching the anarchists for their intransigence concerning the State. At this point a new affirmation, based on Engels, is introduced which justifies the continuation of the dictatorship of the proletariat after socialization, after the disappearance of the bourgeois class, and even after control by the masses has finally been achieved. The preservation of authority will now have as limits those that are prescribed for it by the very conditions of production. For example, the final withering away of the State will coincide with the moment when accommodation can be provided for all, free of charge. It is the higher phase of Communism: "To each according to his needs." Until then, the State will continue.

How rapid will be the development toward this higher phase of Communism when each shall receive according to his needs? "That, we do not and cannot know. . . . We have no data that allow us to solve these questions." "For the sake of greater clarity," Lenin affirms with his customary arbitrariness, "it has never been vouchsafed to any socialist to guarantee the advent of the higher phase of Communism." It can be said that at this point freedom definitely dies. From the rule of the masses and the concept of the proletarian revolution we first pass on to the idea of a revolution made and directed by professional agents. The relentless criticism of the State is then reconciled with the necessary, but provisional, dictatorship of the proletariat, embodied in its leaders. Finally, it is announced that the end of this provisional condition cannot be foreseen and that, what is more, no one has ever presumed to promise that there will be an end. After that it is logical that the autonomy of the soviets should be contested, Makhno betrayed, and the sailors of Kronstadt crushed by the party.

Undoubtedly, many of the affirmations of Lenin, who was a passionate lover of justice, can still be opposed to the Stalinist regime; mainly, the notion of the withering away of the State. Even if it is admitted that the proletarian State cannot disappear before many years have passed, it is still necessary, according to Marxist doctrine, that it should tend to disappear and become less and less restrictive in order that it should be able to call itself proletarian. It is certain that Lenin believed this trend to be inevitable and that, in this particular sense, he has been ignored. For more than thirty years the proletarian State has shown no signs of progressive anemia. On the contrary, it seems to be enjoying increasing prosperity. Meanwhile, in a lecture at the Sverdlov University two years later, under the pressure of outside events and interior realities, Lenin spoke with a precision which left little doubt about the indefinite continuation of the proletarian super-State. "With this machine, or rather this weapon [the State], we shall crush every form of exploitation, and when there are no longer any possibilities of exploitation left on earth, no more people owning land or factories, no more people gorging themselves under the eyes of others who are starving, when such things become impossible, then and only then shall we cast this machine aside. Then there will be neither State nor exploitation." Therefore as long as there exists on earth, and no longer in a specific society, one single oppressed person and one proprietor, so long the State will continue to exist. It also will be obliged to increase in strength during this period so as to vanquish one by one the injustices, the governments responsible for injustice, the obstinately bourgeois nations, and the people who are blind to their own interests. And when, on an earth that has finally been subdued and purged of enemies, the final iniquity shall have been drowned in the blood of the just and the unjust, then the State, which has reached the limit of all power, a monstrous idol covering the entire earth, will be discreetly absorbed into the silent city of Justice.

Under the easily predictable pressure of adverse imperialism, the imperialism of justice was born, in reality, with Lenin. But imperialism, even the imperialism of justice, has no other end but defeat or world empire. Until then it has no other means but injustice. From now on, the doctrine is definitively identified with the prophecy. For the sake of justice in the far-away future, it authorizes injustice throughout the entire course of history and becomes the type of mystification which Lenin detested more than anything else in the world. It contrives the acceptance of injustice, crime, and falsehood by the promise of a miracle. Still greater production, still more power, uninterrupted labor, incessant suffering, permanent war, and then a moment will come when universal bondage in the totalitarian empire will be miraculously changed into its opposite: free leisure in a universal republic. Pseudo-revolutionary mystification has now acquired a formula: all freedom must be crushed in order to conquer the empire, and one day the empire will be the equivalent of freedom. And so the way to unity passes through totality.

Totality and Trials

Totality is, in effect, nothing other than the ancient dream of unity common to both believers and rebels, but projected horizontally onto an earth deprived of God. To renounce every value, therefore, amounts to renouncing rebellion in order to accept the Empire and slavery. Criticism of formal values cannot pass over the concept of freedom. Once the impossibility has been recognized of creating, by means of the forces of rebellion alone, the free individual of whom the romantics dreamed, freedom itself has also been incorporated in the movement of history. It has become freedom fighting for existence, which, in order to exist, must create itself. Identified with the dynamism of history, it cannot play its proper role until history comes to a stop, in the realization of the Universal City. Until then, every one of its victories will lead to an antithesis that will render it pointless. The German nation frees itself from its oppressors, but at the price of the freedom of every German. The individuals under a totalitarian regime are not free, even though man in the collective sense is free. Finally, when the Empire delivers the entire human species, freedom will reign over herds of slaves, who at least will be free in relation to God and, in general, in relation to every kind of transcendence. The dialectic miracle, the transformation of quantity into quality, is explained here: it is the decision to call total servitude freedom. Moreover, as in all the examples cited by Hegel and Marx, there is no objective transformation, but only a subjective change of denomination. In other words, there is no miracle. If the only hope of nihilism lies in thinking that millions of slaves can one day constitute a humanity which will be freed forever, then history is nothing but a desperate dream. Historical thought was to deliver man from subjection to a divinity; but this liberation demanded of him the most absolute subjection to historical evolution. Then man takes refuge in the permanence of the party in the same way that he formerly prostrated himself before the altar. That is why the era which dares to claim that it is the most rebellious that has ever existed only offers a choice of various types of conformity. The real passion of the twentieth century is servitude.

But total freedom is no more easy to conquer than individual freedom. To ensure man's empire over the world, it is necessary to suppress in the world and in man everything that escapes the Empire, everything that does not come under the reign of quantity: and this is an endless undertaking. The Empire must embrace time, space, and people, which compose the three dimensions of history. It is simultaneously war, obscurantism, and tyranny, desperately affirming that one day it will be liberty, fraternity, and truth; the logic of its postulates obliges it to do so. There is undoubtedly in Russia today, even in its Communist doctrines, a truth that denies Stalinist ideology. But this ideology has its logic, which must be isolated and exposed if we wish the revolutionary spirit to escape final disgrace.

The cynical intervention of the armies of the Western powers against the Soviet Revolution demonstrated, among other things, to the Russian revolutionaries that war and nationalism were realities in the same category as the class struggle. Without an international solidarity of the working classes, a solidarity that would come into play automatically, no interior revolution could be considered likely to survive unless an international order were created.

From then on, it was necessary to admit that the Universal City could only be built on two conditions: either by almost simultaneous revolutions in every big country, or by the liquidation, through war, of the bourgeois nations; permanent revolution or permanent war. We know that the first point of view almost triumphed. The revolutionary movements in Germany, Italy, and France marked the high point in revolutionary hopes and aspirations. But the crushing of these revolutions and the ensuing reinforcement of capitalist regimes have made war the reality of the revolution. Thus the philosophy of enlightenment finally led to the Europe of the black-out. By the logic of history and of doctrine, the Universal City, which was to have been realized by the spontaneous insurrection of the oppressed, has been little by little replaced by the Empire, imposed by means of power. Engels, with the approval of Marx, dispassionately accepted this prospect when he wrote in answer to Bakunin's *Appeal to the Slavs:* "The next world war will cause the disappearance from the surface of the globe, not only of reactionary classes and dynasties, but of whole races of reactionaries. That also is part of progress." That particular form of progress, in Engels's mind, was destined to eliminate the Russia of the czars. Today the Russian nation has reversed the direction of progress. War, cold and lukewarm, is the slavery imposed by world Empire. But now that it has become imperialist, the revolution is in an impasse. If it does not renounce its false principles in order to return to the origins of rebellion, it only means the continuation, for several generations and until capitalism spontaneously decomposes, of a total dictatorship over hundreds of millions of men; or, if it wants to precipitate the advent of the Universal City, it only signifies the atomic war, which it does not want and after which any city whatsoever will only be able to contemplate complete destruction. World revolution, by the very laws of the history it so imprudently deified, is condemned to the police or to the bomb. At the same time, it finds itself confronted with yet another contradiction. The sacrifice of ethics and virtue, the acceptance of all the means that it constantly justified by the end it pursued, can only be accepted, if absolutely necessary, in terms of an end that is reasonably likely to be realized. The cold war supposes, by the indefinite prolongation of dictatorship, the indefinite negation of this end. The danger of war, moreover, makes this end highly unlikely. The extension of the Empire over the face of the earth is an inevitable necessity for twentieth-century revolution. But this necessity confronts it with a final dilemma: to construct new principles for itself or to renounce justice and peace, whose definitive reign it always wanted.

While waiting to dominate space, the Empire sees itself also compelled to reign over time. In denying every stable truth, it is compelled to go to the point of denying the very lowest form of truth—the truth of history. It has transported revolution, which is still impossible on a worldwide scale, back into a past that it is determined to deny. Even that, too, is logical. Any kind of coherence that is not purely economic between the past and the future of humanity supposes a constant which, in its turn, can lead to a belief in a human nature. The profound coherence that Marx, who was a man of culture, had perceived as existing between all civilizations, threatened to swamp his thesis and to bring to light a natural continuity, far broader in scope than economic continuity. Little by little, Russian Communism has been forced to burn its bridges, to introduce a solution of continuity into the problem of historical evolution. The negation of every genius who proves to be a heretic (and almost all of them do), the denial of the benefits of civilization, of art—to the infinite degree in which it escapes from history—and the renunciation of vital traditions, have gradually forced contemporary Marxism within narrower and narrower limits. It has not sufficed for Marxism to deny or to silence the things in the history of the world which cannot be assimilated by its doctrine, or to reject the discoveries of modern science. It has also had to rewrite history, even the most recent and the best-known, even the history of the party and of the Revolution. Year by year, sometimes month by month, *Pravda* corrects itself, and rewritten editions of the official history books follow one another off the presses. Lenin is censored, Marx is not published. At this point comparison with religious obscurantism is no longer even fair. The Church never went so far as to decide that the divine manifestation was embodied in two, then in four, or in three, and then again in two, persons. The acceleration of events that is part of our times also affects the fabrication of truth, which, accomplished at this speed, becomes pure fantasy. As in the fairy story, in which all the looms of an entire town wove the empty air to provide clothes for the king, thousands of men, whose strange profession it is, rewrite a presumptuous version of history, which is destroyed the same evening while waiting for the calm voice of a child to proclaim suddenly that the king is naked. This small voice, the voice of rebellion, will then be saying, what all the world can already see, that a revolution which, in order to last, is condemned to deny its universal vocation, or to renounce itself in order to be universal, is living by false principles.

Meanwhile, these principles continue to dominate the lives of millions of men. The dream of Empire, held in check by the realities of time and space, gratifies its desires on humanity. People are not only hostile to the Empire as individuals: in that case the traditional methods of terror would suffice. They are hostile to it in so far as human nature, to date, has never been able to live by history alone and has always escaped from it by some means. The Empire supposes a negation and a certainty: the certainty of the infinite malleability of man and the negation of human nature. Propaganda techniques serve to measure the degree of this malleability and try to make reflection and conditioned reflex coincide. Propaganda makes it possible to sign a pact with those who for years have been designated as the mortal enemy. Even more, it allows the psychological effect thus obtained to be reversed and the people, once again, to be aligned against this same enemy. The experiment has not yet been brought to an end, but its principle is logical. If there is no human nature, then the malleability of man is, in fact, infinite. Political realism, on this level, is nothing but unbridled romanticism, a romanticism of expediency.

In this way it is possible to explain why Russian Marxism rejects, in its entirety and even though it knows very well how to make use of it, the world of the irrational. The irrational can serve the Empire as well as refute it. The irrational escapes calculation, and calculation alone must reign in the Empire. Man is only an interplay of forces that can be rationally influenced. A few inconsiderate Marxists were rash enough to imagine that they could reconcile their doctrine with Freud's, for example. Their eyes were opened for them quickly enough. Freud is a heretic thinker and a "petit bourgeois" because he brought to light the unconscious and bestowed on it at least as much reality as on the super or social ego. This unconscious mind can therefore define the originality of a human nature opposed to the historic ego. Man, on the contrary, must be explained in terms of the social and rational ego and as an object of calculation. Therefore it has been necessary to enslave not only each individual life, but also the most irrational and the most solitary event of all, the expectancy of which accompanies man throughout his entire life. The Empire, in its convulsive effort to found a definitive kingdom, strives to integrate death.

A living man can be enslaved and reduced to the historic condition of an object. But if he dies in refusing to be enslaved, he reaffirms the existence of another kind of human nature which refuses to be classified as an object. That is why the accused is never produced and killed before the eyes of the world unless he consents to say that his death is just and unless he conforms to the Empire of objects. One must die dishonored or no longer exist—neither in life nor in death. In the latter event, the victim does not die, he disappears. If he is punished, his punishment would be a silent protest and might cause a fissure in the totality. But the culprit is not punished, he is simply replaced in the totality and thus helps to construct the machine of Empire. He is transformed into a cog in the machinery of production, so indispensable that in the long run he will not be used in production because he is guilty, but considered guilty because production has need of him. The concentration-camp system of the Russians has, in fact, accomplished the dialectical transition from the government of people to the administration of objects, but by identifying people with objects.

Even the enemy must collaborate in the common endeavor. Beyond the confines of the Empire there is no salvation. This is, or will be, the Empire of friendship.

But this friendship is the befriending of objects, for the friend cannot be preferred to the Empire. The friendship of people—and there is no other definition of it—is specific solidarity, to the point of death, against everything that is not part of the kingdom of friendship. The friendship of objects is friendship in general, friendship with everything, which supposes—when it is a question of self-preservation—mutual denunciation. He who loves his friend loves him in the present, and the revolution wants to love only a man who has not yet appeared. To love is, in a certain way, to kill the perfect man who is going to be born of the revolution. In order that one day he may live, he should from now on be preferred to anyone else. In the kingdom of humanity, men are bound by ties of affection; in the Empire of objects, men are united by mutual accusation. The city that planned to be the city of fraternity becomes an ant-heap of solitary men.

On another plane, only a brute in a state of irrational fury can imagine that men should be sadistically tortured in order to obtain their consent. Such an act only accomplishes the subjugation of one man by another, in an outrageous relationship between persons. The representative of rational totality is content, on the contrary, to allow the object to subdue the person in the soul of man. The highest mind is first of all reduced to the level of the lowest by the police technique of joint accusation. Then five, ten, twenty nights of insomnia will culminate an illusory conviction and will bring yet another dead soul into the world. From this point of view, the only psychological revolution known to our times since Freud's has been brought about by the NKVD and the political police in general. Guided by a determinist hypothesis that calculates the weak points and the degree of elasticity of the soul, these new techniques have once again thrust aside one of man's limits and have attempted to demonstrate that no individual psychology is original and that the common measure of all human character is matter. They have literally created the physics of the soul.

From that point on, traditional human relations have been transformed. These progressive transformations characterize the world of rational terror in which, in different degrees, Europe lives. Dialogue and personal relations have been replaced by propaganda or polemic, which are two kinds of monologue. Abstraction, which belongs to the world of power and calculation, has replaced the real passions, which are in the domain of the flesh and of the irrational. The ration coupon substituted for bread; love and friendship submitted to a doctrine, and destiny to a plan; punishment considered the norm, and production substituted for living creation, quite satisfactorily describe this disembodied Europe, peopled with positive or negative symbols of power. "How miserable," Marx exclaims, "is a society that knows no better means of defense than the executioner!" But in Marx's day the executioner had not yet become a philosopher and at least made no pretense of universal philanthropy.

The ultimate contradiction of the greatest revolution that history ever knew does not, after all, lie entirely in the fact that it lays claim to justice despite an uninterrupted procession of violence and injustice. This is an evil common to all times and a product of servitude or mystification. The tragedy of this revolution is the tragedy of nihilism—it confounds itself with the drama of contemporary intelligence, which, while claiming to be universal, is only responsible for a series of mutilations to men's minds. Totality is not unity. The state of siege, even when it is extended to the very boundaries of the earth, is not reconciliation. The claim to a universal city is supported in this revolution only by rejecting two thirds of the world and the magnificent heritage of the centuries, and by denying, to the advantage of history, both nature and beauty and by depriving man of the power of passion, doubt, happiness, and imaginative invention—in a word, of his greatness. The principles that men give to themselves end by overwhelming their noblest intentions. By dint of argument, incessant struggle, polemics, excommunications, persecutions conducted and suffered, the universal city of free and fraternal man is slowly diverted and gives way to the only universe in which history and expediency can in fact be elevated to the position of supreme judges: the universe of the trial.

Every religion revolves around the concepts of innocence and guilt. Prometheus, the first rebel, however, denies the right to punish. Zeus himself, Zeus above all, is not innocent enough to exercise this right. Thus rebellion, in its very first manifestation, refuses to recognize punishment as legitimate. But in his last incarnation, at the end of his exhausting journey, the rebel once more adopts the religious concept of punishment and places it at the center of his universe. The supreme judge is no longer in the heavens; history itself acts as an implacable divinity. History, in one sense, is nothing but a protracted punishment, for the real reward will be reaped only at the end of time. We are far, it would seem, from Marxism and from Hegel, and even farther from the first rebels. Nevertheless, all purely historical thought leads to the brink of this abyss. To the extent to which Marx predicted the inevitable establishment of the classless city and to the extent to which he thus established the good will of history, every check to the advance toward freedom must be imputed to the ill will of mankind. Marx reintroduced crime and punishment into the unchristian world, but only in relation to history. Marxism in one of its aspects is a doctrine of culpability on man's part and innocence on history's. His interpretation of history is that when it is deprived of power, it expresses itself in revolutionary violence; at the height of its power it risked becoming legal violence—in other words, terror and trial.

In the universe of religion, moreover, the final judgment is postponed; it is not necessary for crime to be punished without delay or for innocence to be rewarded. In the new universe, on the other hand, the judgment pronounced by history must be pronounced immediately, for culpability coincides with the check to progress and with punishment. History has judged Bukarin in that it condemned him to death. It proclaims the innocence of Stalin: he is the most powerful man on earth. It is the same with Tito, about whom we do not know, so we are told, whether he is guilty or not. He is on trial, as was Trotsky, whose guilt only became clear to the philosophers of historical crime at the moment when the murderer's ax cracked his skull. Tito has been denounced, but not yet struck down. When he has been struck down, his guilt will be certain. Besides, Trotsky's and Tito's provisional innocence depended and depends to a large extent on geography; they were far removed from the arm of secular power.

That is why those who can be reached by that arm must be judged without delay. The definitive judgment of history depends on an infinite number of judgments which will have been pronounced between now and then and which will finally be confirmed or invalidated. Thus there is the promise of mysterious rehabilitations on the day when the tribunal of the world will be established by the world itself. Some, who will proclaim themselves contemptible traitors, will enter the Pantheon of mankind; others who maintain their innocence will be condemned to the hell of history. But who, then, will be the judge? Man himself, finally fulfilled in his divinity. Meanwhile, those who conceived the prophecy, and who alone are capable of reading in history the meaning with which they previously endowed it, will pronounce sentence—definitive for the guilty, provisional sentences for the judges. But it sometimes happens that those who judge, like Rajk, are judged in their turn. Must we believe that he no longer interpreted history correctly? His defeat and death in fact prove it. Then who guarantees that those who judge him today will not be traitors tomorrow, hurled down from the height of their judgment seat to the concrete caves where history's damned are dying? The guarantee lies in their infallible clairvoyance. What proof is there of that? Their uninterrupted success. The world of trial is a spherical world in which success and innocence authenticate each other and where every mirror reflects the same mystification.

Thus there will be a historic grace,[5] whose power alone can interpret events and which favors or excommunicates the subject of the Empire. To guard against its caprices, the latter has only faith at his disposal—faith as defined in the *Spiritual Exercises* of Saint Ignatius: "We should always be prepared, so as never to err, to believe that what I see as white is black, if the hierarchic Church defines it thus." Only this active faith held by the representatives of truth can save the subject from the mysterious ravages of history. He is not yet free of the universe of trial to which he is bound by the historic sentiment of fear. But without this faith he runs a perpetual

[5] "The ruse of reason," in the historical universe, presents the problem of evil in a new form.

risk of becoming, without having wished to do so and with the best intentions in the world, an objective criminal.

The universe of trial finally culminates in this concept, at which point we have come full circle. At the end of this long insurrection in the name of human innocence, there arises, by an inevitable perversion of fact, the affirmation of general culpability. Every man is a criminal who is unaware of being so. The objective criminal is, precisely, he who believed himself innocent. His actions he considered subjectively inoffensive, or even advantageous for the future of justice. But it is demonstrated to him that objectively his actions have been harmful to that future. Are we dealing with scientific objectivity? No, but with historical objectivity. How is it possible to know, for example, if the future of justice is compromised by the unconsidered denunciation of present injustice? Real objectivity would consist in judging by those results which can be scientifically observed and by facts and their general tendencies. But the concept of objective culpability proves that this curious kind of objectivity is only based on results and facts which will only become accessible to science in the year 2000, at the very earliest. Meanwhile, it is embodied in an interminable subjectivity which is imposed on others as objectivity: and that is the philosophic definition of terror. This type of objectivity has no definable meaning, but power will give it a content by decreeing that everything of which it does not approve is guilty. It will consent to say, or allow to be said, to philosophers who live outside the Empire, that in this way it is taking a risk in regard to history, just as the objective culprit took a risk, though without knowing it. When victim and executioner have disappeared, the matter will be judged. But this consolation is of any value only to the executioner, who has really no need of it. Meanwhile, the faithful are regularly bidden to attend strange feasts where, according to scrupulous rites, victims overwhelmed with contrition are offered as sacrifice to the god of history.

The express object of this idea is to prevent indifference in matters of faith. It is compulsory evangelization. The law, whose function it is to pursue suspects, fabricates them. By fabricating them, it converts them. In bourgeois society, for example, every citizen is supposed to approve the law. In objective society every citizen will be presumed to disapprove of it. Or at least he should always be ready to prove that he does not disapprove of it. Culpability no longer has any factual basis; it simply consists of absence of faith, which explains the apparent contradiction of the objective system. Under a capitalist regime, the man who says he is neutral is considered objectively to be favorable to the regime. Under the regime of the Empire, the man who is neutral is considered hostile objectively to the regime. There is nothing astonishing about that. If a subject of the Empire does not believe in the Empire, he is, of his own choice, nothing, historically speaking; therefore he takes sides against history and is, in other words, a blasphemer. Even lip service paid to faith will not suffice; it must be lived and acted upon in order to be served properly and the citizen must be always on the alert to consent in time to the changes in dogma. At the slightest error potential culpability becomes in its turn objective culpability. Consummating its history in this manner, the revolution is not content with killing all rebellion. It insists on holding every man, even the most servile, responsible for the fact that rebellion ever existed and still exists under the sun. In the universe of the trial, conquered and completed at last, a race of culprits will endlessly shuffle toward an impossible innocence, under the grim regard of the grand inquisitors. In the twentieth century power wears the mask of tragedy.

Here ends Prometheus' surprising itinerary. Proclaiming his hatred of the gods and his love of mankind, he turns away from Zeus with scorn and approaches mortal men in order to lead them in an assault against the heavens. But men are weak and cowardly; they must be organized. They love pleasure and immediate happiness; they must be taught to refuse, in order to grow up, immediate rewards. Thus Prometheus, in his turn, becomes a master who first teaches and then commands. Men doubt that they can safely attack the city of light and are even uncertain whether the city exists. They must be saved from themselves. The hero then tells them that he, and he alone, knows the city. Those who doubt his word will be thrown into the desert, chained to a rock, offered to the vultures. The others will march henceforth in darkness, behind the pensive and solitary master. Prometheus alone has become god and reigns over the solitude of men. But from Zeus he has gained only solitude and cruelty; he is no longer Prometheus, he is Cæsar. The real, the eternal Prometheus has now assumed the aspect of one of his victims. The same cry, springing from the depths of the past, rings forever through the Scythian desert.

✳

The revolution based on principles kills God in the person of His representative on earth. The revolution of the twentieth century kills what remains of God in the principles themselves and consecrates historical nihilism. Whatever paths nihilism may proceed to take, from the moment that it decides to be the creative force of its period and ignores every moral precept, it begins to build the temple of Cæsar. To choose history, and history alone, is to choose nihilism, in defiance of the teachings of rebellion itself. Those who rush blindly to history in the name of the irrational, proclaiming that it is meaningless, encounter servitude and terror and finally emerge into the universe of concentration camps. Those who launch themselves into it preaching its absolute rationality encounter servitude and terror and emerge into the universe of the concentration camps. Fascism wants to establish the advent of the Nietzschean superman. It immediately discovers that God, if He exists, may well be this or that, but He is primarily the master of death. If man wants to become God, he arrogates to himself the power of life or death over others. Manufacturer of corpses and of submen, he is a sub-man himself and not God, but the ignoble servant of death. The rational revolution, on its part, wants to realize the total man described by Marx. The logic of history, from the moment that it is totally accepted, gradually leads it, against its most passionate convictions, to mutilate man more and more and to transform itself into objective crime. It is not legitimate to identify the ends of Fascism with the ends of Russian Communism. The first represents the exaltation of the executioner by the executioner; the second, more dramatic in concept, the exaltation of the executioner by the victims. The former never dreamed of liberating all men, but only of liberating a few by subjugating the rest. The latter, in its most profound principle, aims at liberating all men by provisionally enslaving them all. It must be granted the grandeur of its intentions. But, on the other hand, it is legitimate to identify the means employed by both with the political cynicism that they have drawn from the same source, moral nihilism. Everything has taken place as though the descendants of Stirner and of Nechaiev were making use of the descendants of Kaliayev and Proudhon. The nihilists today are seated on thrones. Methods of thought which claim to give the lead to our world in the name of revolution have become, in reality, ideologies of consent and not of rebellion. That is why our period is the period of private and public techniques of annihilation.

The revolution, obedient to the dictates of nihilism, has in fact turned against its rebel origins. Man, who hated death and the god of death, who despaired of personal survival, wanted to free himself in the immortality of the species. But as long as the group does not dominate the world, as long as the species does not reign, it is still necessary to die. Time is pressing, therefore; persuasion demands leisure, and friendship a structure that will never be completed; thus terror remains the shortest route to immortality. But these extremes simultaneously proclaim a longing for the primitive values of rebellion. The contemporary revolution that claims to deny every value is already, in itself, a standard for judging values. Man wants to reign supreme through the revolution. But why reign supreme if nothing has any meaning? Why wish for immortality if the aspect of life is so hideous? There is no method of thought which is absolutely nihilist except, perhaps, the method that leads to suicide, any more than there is absolute materialism. The destruction of man once more affirms man. Terror and concentration camps are the drastic means used by man to escape solitude. The thirst for unity must be assuaged, even in the common grave. If men kill one another, it is because they reject mortality and desire immortality for all men. Therefore, in one sense, they commit suicide. But they prove, at the same time, that they cannot dispense with mankind; they satisfy a terrible hunger for fraternity. "The human being needs happiness, and when he is unhappy, he needs another human being." Those who reject the agony of living and dying wish to dominate. "Solitude is power," says Sade. Power, today, because for thousands of solitary people it signifies the suffering of others, bears witness to the need for others. Terror is the homage that the malignant recluse finally pays to the brotherhood of man.

But nihilism, if it does not exist, tries to do so; and that is enough to make the world a desert. This particular form of madness is what has given our times their forbidding aspect. The land of humanism has become the Europe of today, the land of inhumanity. But the times are ours and how can we disown them? If our history is our hell, still we cannot avert our faces. This horror cannot be escaped, but is assumed in order to be ignored, by the very people who accepted it with lucidity and not by those who, having provoked it, think that they have a right to pronounce judgment. Such a plant could, in fact, thrive only in the fertile soil of accumulated iniquities. In the last throes of a death struggle in which men are indiscriminately involved by the insanity of the times, the enemy remains the fraternal enemy. Even when he has been denounced for his errors, he can be neither despised nor hated; misfortune is today the common fatherland, and the only earthly kingdom that has fulfilled the promise.

The longing for rest and peace must itself be thrust aside; it coincides with the acceptance of iniquity. Those who weep for the happy periods they encounter in history acknowledge what they want: not the alleviation but the silencing of misery. But let us, on the contrary, sing the praises of the times when misery cries aloud and disturbs the sleep of the surfeited rich! Maistre has already spoken of the "terrible sermon that the revolution preached to kings." It preaches the same sermon today, and in a still more urgent fashion, to the dishonoured elite of the times. This sermon must be heard. In every word and in every act, even though it be criminal, lies the promise of a value that we must seek out and bring to light. The future cannot be foreseen and it may be that the renaissance is impossible. Even though the historical dialectic is false and criminal, the world, after all, can very well realize itself in crime and in pursuit of a false concept. This kind of resignation is, quite simply, rejected here: we must stake everything on the renaissance.

Nothing remains for us, moreover, but to be reborn or to die. If we are at the moment in history when rebellion has reached the point of its most extreme contradiction by denying itself, then it must either perish with the world it has created or find a new object of faith and a new impetus. Before going any farther, this contradiction must at least be stated in plain language. It is not a clear definition to say like the existentialists, for example (who are also subjected for the moment to the cult of history and its contradictions),[1] that there is progress in the transition from rebellion to revolution and that the rebel is nothing if he is not revolutionary. The contradiction is, in reality, considerably more restricted. The revolutionary is simultaneously a rebel or he is not a revolutionary, but a policeman and a bureaucrat who turns against rebellion. But if he is a rebel, he ends by taking sides against the revolution. So much so that there is absolutely no progress from one attitude to the other, but coexistence and endlessly increasing contradiction. Every revolutionary ends by becoming either an oppressor or a heretic. In the purely historical universe that they have chosen, rebellion and revolution end in the same dilemma: either police rule or insanity.

On this level, therefore, history alone offers no hope. It is not a source of values, but is still a source of nihilism. Can one, at least, create values in defiance of history, on the single level of a philosophy based on eternity? That comes to the same as ratifying historical injustice and the sufferings of man. To slander the world leads to the nihilism defined by Nietzsche. Thought that is derived from history alone, like thought that rejects history completely, deprives man of the means and the reason for living. The former drives him to the extreme decadence of "why live?" the latter to "how live?" History, necessary but not

[1] Atheist existentialism at least wishes to create a morality. This morality is still to be defined. But the real difficulty lies in creating it without reintroducing into historical existence a value foreign to history.

sufficient, is therefore only an occasional cause. It is not absence of values, nor values themselves, nor even the source of values. It is one occasion, among others, for man to prove the still confused existence of a value that allows him to judge history. Rebellion itself makes us the promise of such a value.

Absolute revolution, in fact, supposes the absolute malleability of human nature and its possible reduction to the condition of a historical force. But rebellion, in man, is the refusal to be treated as an object and to be reduced to simple historical terms. It is the affirmation of a nature common to all men, which eludes the world of power. History, undoubtedly, is one of the limits of man's experience; in this sense the revolutionaries are right. But man, by rebelling, imposes in his turn a limit to history, and at this limit the promise of a value is born. It is the birth of this value that the Cæsarian revolution implacably combats today because it presages its final defeat and the obligation to renounce its principles. The fate of the world is not being played out at present, as it seemed it would be, in the struggle between bourgeois production and revolutionary production; their end results will be the same. It is being played out between the forces of rebellion and those of the Cæsarian revolution. The triumphant revolution must prove by means of its police, its trials, and its excommunications that there is no such thing as human nature. Humiliated rebellion, by its contradictions, its sufferings, its continuous defeats, and its inexhaustible pride, must give its content of hope and suffering to this nature.

"I rebel, therefore we exist," said the slave. Metaphysical rebellion then added: "we are alone," by which we still live today. But if we are alone beneath the empty heavens, if we must die forever, how can we really exist? Metaphysical rebellion, then, tried to construct existence with appearances. After which purely historical thought came to say that to be was to act. We did not exist, but we should exist by every possible means. Our revolution is an attempt to conquer a new existence, by action that recognizes no moral strictures. That is why it is condemned to live only for history and in a reign of terror. Man is nothing, according to the revolution, if he does not obtain from history, willingly or by force, unanimous approval.

At this exact point the limit is exceeded, rebellion is first betrayed and then logically assassinated, for it has never affirmed, in its purest form, anything but the existence of a limit and the divided existence that we represent: it is not, originally, the total negation of all existence. Quite the contrary, it says yes and no simultaneously. It is the rejection of one part of existence in the name of another part, which it exalts. The more profound the exaltation, the more implacable is the rejection. Then, when rebellion, in rage or intoxication, adopts the attitude of "all or nothing" and the negation of all existence and all human nature, it is at this point that it denies itself. Only total negation justifies the concept of a totality that must be conquered. But the affirmation of a limit, a dignity, and a beauty common to all men only entails the necessity of extending this value to embrace everything and everyone and of advancing toward unity without denying the origins of rebellion. In this sense rebellion, in its original authenticity, does not justify any purely historical concept. Rebellion's demand is unity; historical revolution's demand is totality. The former starts from a negative supported by an affirmative, the latter from absolute negation and is condemned to every aspect of slavery in order to fabricate an affirmative that is dismissed until the end of time. One is creative, the other nihilist. The first is dedicated to creation so as to exist more and more completely; the second is forced to produce results in order to negate more and more completely. The historical revolution is always obliged to act in the hope, which is invariably disappointed, of one day really existing. Even unanimous consent will not suffice to create its existence. "Obey," said Frederick the Great to his subjects; but when he died, his words were: "I am tired of ruling slaves." To escape this absurd destiny, the revolution is and will be condemned to renounce, not only its own principles, but nihilism as well as purely historical values in order to rediscover the creative source of rebellion. Revolution, in order to be creative, cannot do without either a moral or metaphysical rule to balance the insanity of history. Undoubtedly, it has nothing but scorn for the formal and mystifying morality to be found in bourgeois society. But its folly has been to extend this scorn to every moral demand. At the very

sources of its inspiration and in its most profound trans-
ports is to be found a rule that is not formal but that
nevertheless can serve as a guide. Rebellion, in fact, says—
and will say more and more explicitly—that revolution
must try to act, not in order to come into existence at
some future date in the eyes of a world reduced to acquiescence, but in terms of the obscure existence that is already made manifest in the act of insurrection. This rule
is neither formal nor subject to history, it is what can be
best described by examining it in its pure state—in artistic creation. Before doing so, let us only note that to the
"I rebel, therefore we exist" and the "We are alone" of
metaphysical rebellion, rebellion at grips with history adds
that instead of killing and dying in order to produce the
being that we are not, we have to live and let live in order
to create what we are.

Part Four

Rebellion and Art

*

Art is the activity that exalts and denies simultaneously. "No artist tolerates reality," says Nietzsche. That is true, but no artist can get along without reality. Artistic creation is a demand for unity and a rejection of the world. But it rejects the world on account of what it lacks and in the name of what it sometimes is. Rebellion can be observed here in its pure state and in its original complexities. Thus art should give us a final perspective on the content of rebellion.

The hostility to art shown by all revolutionary reformers must, however, be pointed out. Plato is moderately reasonable. He only calls in question the deceptive function of language and exiles only poets from his republic. Apart from that, he considers beauty more important than the world. But the revolutionary movement of modern times coincides with an artistic process that is not yet completed. The Reformation chooses morality and exiles beauty. Rousseau denounces in art a corruption of nature by society. Saint-Just inveighs against the theater, and in the elaborate program he composes for the "Feast of Reason" he states that he would like Reason to be impersonated by someone "virtuous rather than beautiful." The French Revolution gave birth to no artists, but only to a great journalist, Desmoulins, and to a clandestine writer, Sade. It guillotines the only poet of the times.[1] The only great prose-writer[2] took refuge in London and pleaded the cause of Christianity and legitimacy. A little later the followers of Saint-Simon demanded a "socially useful form

[1] André Chénier. (ED.)
[2] François René Chateaubriand. (ED.)

of art. "Art for progress" was a commonplace of the whole
period, and one that Hugo revived, without succeeding in
making it sound convincing. Vallès alone brings to his
malediction of art a tone of imprecation that gives it
authenticity.

This tone is also employed by the Russian nihilists.
Pisarev proclaims the deposition of æsthetic values, in
favor of pragmatic values. "I would rather be a Russian
shoemaker than a Russian Raphael." A pair of shoes, in
his eyes, is more useful than Shakespeare. The nihilist
Nekrassov, a great and moving poet, nevertheless affirms
that he prefers a piece of cheese to all of Pushkin. Finally,
we are familiar with the excommunication of art pronounced by Tolstoy. Revolutionary Russia finally even
turned its back on the marble statues of Venus and Apollo,
still gilded by the Italian sun, that Peter the Great had
had brought to his summer garden in St. Petersburg. Suffering, sometimes, turns away from too painful expressions
of happiness.

German ideology is no less severe in its accusations.
According to the revolutionary interpreters of Hegel's
Phenomenology, there will be no art in reconciled society.
Beauty will be lived and no longer only imagined. Reality,
become entirely rational, will satisfy, completely by itself,
every appetite. The criticism of formal conscience and of
escapist values naturally extends itself to embrace art. Art
does not belong to all times; it is determined, on the contrary, by its period, and expresses, says Marx, the privileged
values of the ruling classes. Thus there is only one revolutionary form of art, which is, precisely, art dedicated to the
service of the revolution. Moreover, by creating beauty outside the course of history, art impedes the only rational
activity: the transformation of history itself into absolute
beauty. The Russian shoemaker, once he is aware of his
revolutionary role, is the real creator of definitive beauty.
As for Raphael, he created only a transitory beauty, which
will be quite incomprehensible to the new man.

Marx asks himself, it is true, how the beauty created
by the Greeks can still be beautiful for us. His answer is
that this beauty is the expression of the naïve childhood
of this world and that we have, in the midst of our adult
struggles, a nostalgia for this childhood. But how can the

masterpieces of the Italian Renaissance, how can Rembrandt, how can Chinese art still be beautiful in our eyes? What does it matter! The trial of art has been opened definitively and is continuing today with the embarrassed complicity of artists and intellectuals dedicated to calumniating both their art and their intelligence. We notice, in fact, that in the contest between Shakespeare and the shoemaker, it is not the shoemaker who maligns Shakespeare or beauty but, on the contrary, the man who continues to read Shakespeare and who does not choose to make shoes—which he could never make, if it comes to that. The artists of our time resemble the repentant noblemen of nineteenth-century Russia; their bad conscience is their excuse. But the last emotion that an artist can experience, confronted with his art, is repentance. It is going far beyond simple and necessary humility to pretend to dismiss beauty, too, until the end of time, and meanwhile, to deprive all the world, including the shoemaker, of this additional bread of which one has taken advantage oneself.

This form of ascetic insanity, nevertheless, has its reasons, which at least are of interest to us. They express on the æsthetic level the struggle, already described, of revolution and rebellion. In every rebellion is to be found the metaphysical demand for unity, the impossibility of capturing it, and the construction of a substitute universe. Rebellion, from this point of view, is a fabricator of universes. This also defines art. The demands of rebellion are really, in part, æsthetic demands. All rebel thought, as we have seen, is expressed either in rhetoric or in a closed universe. The rhetoric of ramparts in Lucretius, the convents and isolated castles of Sade, the island or the lonely rock of the romantics, the solitary heights of Nietzsche, the primeval seas of Lautréamont, the parapets of Rimbaud, the terrifying castles of the surrealists, which spring up in a storm of flowers, the prison, the nation behind barbed wire, the concentration camps, the empire of free slaves, all illustrate, after their own fashion, the same need for coherence and unity. In these sealed worlds, man can reign and have knowledge at last.

This tendency is common to all the arts. The artist reconstructs the world to his plan. The symphonies of nature know no rests. The world is never quiet; even its silence eternally resounds with the same notes, in vibrations that escape our ears. As for those that we perceive, they carry sounds to us, occasionally a chord, never a melody. Music exists, however, in which symphonies are completed, where melody gives its form to sounds that by themselves have none, and where, finally, a particular arrangement of notes extracts from natural disorder a unity that is satisfying to the mind and the heart.

"I believe more and more," writes Van Gogh, "that God must not be judged on this earth. It is one of His sketches that has turned out badly." Every artist tries to reconstruct this sketch and to give it the style it lacks. The greatest and most ambitious of all the arts, sculpture, is bent on capturing, in three dimensions, the fugitive figure of man, and on restoring the unity of great style to the general disorder of gestures. Sculpture does not reject resemblance, of which, indeed, it has need. But resemblance is not its first aim. What it is looking for, in its periods of greatness, is the gesture, the expression, or the empty stare which will sum up all the gestures and all the stares in the world. Its purpose is not to imitate, but to stylize and to imprison in one significant expression the fleeting ecstasy of the body or the infinite variety of human attitudes. Then, and only then, does it erect, on the pediments of teeming cities, the model, the type, the motionless perfection that will cool, for one moment, the fevered brow of man. The frustrated lover of love can finally gaze at the Greek caryatides and grasp what it is that triumphs, in the body and face of the woman, over every degradation.

The principle of painting is also to make a choice. "Even genius," writes Delacroix, ruminating on his art, "is only the gift of generalizing and choosing." The painter isolates his subject, which is the first way of unifying it. Landscapes flee, vanish from the memory, or destroy one another. That is why the landscape painter or the painter of still life isolates in space and time things that normally change with the light, get lost in an infinite perspective, or disappear under the impact of other values. The first thing that a landscape painter does is to square off his canvas. He eliminates as much as he includes.

Similarly, subject-painting isolates, in both time and space, an action that normally would become lost in another action. Thus the painter arrives at a point of stabilization. The really great creative artists are those who, like Piero della Francesca, give the impression that the stabilization has only just taken place, that the projection machine has suddenly stopped dead. All their subjects give the impression that, by some miracle of art, they continue to live, while ceasing to be mortal. Long after his death, Rembrandt's philosopher still meditates, between light and shade, on the same problem.

"How vain a thing is painting that beguiles us by the resemblance to objects that do not please us at all." Delacroix, who quotes Pascal's celebrated remark, is correct in writing "strange" instead of "vain." These objects do not please us at all because we do not see them; they are obscured and negated by a perpetual process of change. Who looked at the hands of the executioner during the Flagellation, and the olive trees on the way to the Cross? But here we see them represented, transfigured by the incessant movement of the Passion; and the agony of Christ, imprisoned in images of violence and beauty, cries out again each day in the cold rooms of museums. A painter's style lies in this blending of nature and history, in this stability imposed on incessant change. Art realizes, without apparent effort, the reconciliation of the unique with the universal of which Hegel dreamed. Perhaps that is why periods, such as ours, which are bent on unity to the point of madness, turn to primitive arts, in which stylization is the most intense and unity the most provocative. The most extreme stylization is always found at the beginning and end of artistic movements; it demonstrates the intensity of negation and transposition which has given modern painting its disorderly impetus toward interpreting unity and existence. Van Gogh's admirable complaint is the arrogant and desperate cry of all artists. "I can very well, in life and in painting, too, do without God. But I cannot, suffering as I do, do without something that is greater than I am, that is my life—the power to create."

But the artist's rebellion against reality, which is automatically suspect to the totalitarian revolution, contains the same affirmation as the spontaneous rebellion of the oppressed. The revolutionary spirit, born of total negation, instinctively felt that, as well as refusal, there was also consent to be found in art; that there was a risk of contemplation counterbalancing action, beauty, and injustice, and that in certain cases beauty itself was a form of injustice from which there was no appeal. Equally well, no form of art can survive on total denial alone. Just as all thought, and primarily that of non-signification, signifies something, so there is no art that has no signification. Man can allow himself to denounce the total injustice of the world and then demand a total justice that he alone will create. But he cannot affirm the total hideousness of the world. To create beauty, he must simultaneously reject reality and exalt certain of its aspects. Art disputes reality, but does not hide from it. Nietzsche could deny any form of transcendence, whether moral or divine, by saying that transcendence drove one to slander this world and this life. But perhaps there is a living transcendence, of which beauty carries the promise, which can make this mortal and limited world preferable to and more appealing than any other. Art thus leads us back to the origins of rebellion, to the extent that it tries to give its form to an elusive value which the future perpetually promises, but of which the artist has a presentiment and wishes to snatch from the grasp of history. We shall understand this better in considering the art form whose precise aim is to become part of the process of evolution in order to give it the style that it lacks; in other words, the novel.

Rebellion and the Novel

It is possible to separate the literature of consent, which coincides, by and large, with ancient history and the classical period, from the literature of rebellion, which begins in modern times. We note the scarcity of fiction in the former. When it exists, with very few exceptions, it is not concerned with a story but with fantasy (*Theagenes and Charicleia* or *Astræa*). These are fairy tales, not novels. In the latter period, on the contrary, the novel form is really developed—a form that has not ceased to thrive and extend its field of activity up to the present day, simultaneously with the critical and revolutionary movement. The novel is born at the same time as the spirit of rebellion and expresses, on the æsthetic plane, the same ambition.

"A make-believe story, written in prose," says Littré about the novel. Is it only that? In any case, a Catholic critic, Stanislas Fumet, has written: "Art, whatever its aims, is always in sinful competition with God." Actually, it is more correct to talk about competition with God, in connection with the novel, than of competition with man's civil status. Thibaudet expresses a similar idea when he says of Balzac: "The *Comédie humaine* is the *Imitation* of God the Father." The aim of great literature seems to be to create a closed universe or a perfect type. The West, in its great creative works, does not limit itself to retracing the steps of its daily life. It consistently presents magnificent images which inflame its imagination and sets off, hotfoot, in pursuit of them.

After all, writing or even reading a novel is an unusual activity. To construct a story by a new arrangement of actual facts has nothing inevitable or even necessary about it. Even if the ordinary explanation of the mutual pleasure of reader and writer were true, it would still be necessary to ask why it was incumbent on a large part of humanity to take pleasure and an interest in make-believe stories. Revolutionary criticism condemns the novel in its pure form as being simply a means of escape for an idle imagination. In everyday speech we find the term *romance* used to describe an exaggerated description or lying account of some event. Not so very long ago it was a commonplace that young girls, despite all appearance to the contrary, were "romantic," by which was meant that these idealized creatures took no account of everyday realities. In general, it has always been considered that the romantic was quite separate from life and that it enhanced it while, at the same time, betraying it. The simplest and most common way of envisaging romantic expression is to see it as an escapist exercise. Common sense joins hands with revolutionary criticism.

But from what are we escaping by means of the

novel? From a reality we consider too overwhelming? Happy people read novels, too, and it is an established fact that extreme suffering takes away the taste for reading. From another angle, the romantic universe of the novel certainly has less substance than the other universe where people of flesh and blood harass us without respite. However, by what magic does Adolphe, for instance, seem so much more familiar to us than Benjamin Constant, and Count Mosca than our professional moralists? Balzac once terminated a long conversation about politics and the fate of the world by saying: "And now let us get back to serious matters," meaning that he wanted to talk about his novels. The incontestable importance of the world of the novel, our insistence, in fact, on taking seriously the innumerable myths with which we have been provided for the last two centuries by the genius of writers, is not fully explained by the desire to escape. Romantic activities undoubtedly imply a rejection of reality. But this rejection is not a mere escapist flight, and might be interpreted as the retreat of the soul which, according to Hegel, creates for itself, in its disappointment, a fictitious world in which ethics reigns alone. The edifying novel, however, is far from being great literature; and the best of all romantic novels, *Paul et Virginie*, a really heartbreaking book, makes no concessions to consolation.

The contradiction is this: man rejects the world as it is, without accepting the necessity of escaping it. In fact, men cling to the world and by far the majority do not want to abandon it. Far from always wanting to forget it, they suffer, on the contrary, from not being able to possess it completely enough, estranged citizens of the world, exiled from their own country. Except for vivid moments of fulfillment, all reality for them is incomplete. Their actions escape them in the form of other actions, return in unexpected guises to judge them, and disappear like the water Tantalus longed to drink, into some still undiscovered orifice. To know the whereabouts of the orifice, to control the course of the river, to understand life, at last, as destiny—these are their true aspirations. But this vision which, in the realm of consciousness at least, will reconcile them with themselves, can only appear, if it ever does appear, at the fugitive moment that is death, in which everything is consummated. In order to exist just once in the world, it is necessary never again to exist.

At this point is born the fatal envy which so many men feel of the lives of others. Seen from a distance, these existences seem to possess a coherence and a unity which they cannot have in reality, but which seem evident to the spectator. He sees only the salient points of these lives without taking into account the details of corrosion. Thus we make these lives into works of art. In an elementary fashion we turn them into novels. In this sense, everyone tries to make his life a work of art. We want love to last and we know that it does not last; even if, by some miracle, it were to last a whole lifetime, it would still be incomplete. Perhaps, in this insatiable need for perpetuation, we should better understand human suffering if we knew that it was eternal. It appears that great minds are sometimes less horrified by suffering than by the fact that it does not endure. In default of inexhaustible happiness, eternal suffering would at least give us a destiny. But we do not even have that consolation, and our worst agonies come to an end one day. One morning, after many dark nights of despair, an irrepressible longing to live will announce to us the fact that all is finished and that suffering has no more meaning than happiness.

The desire for possession is only another form of the desire to endure; it is this that comprises the impotent delirium of love. No human being, even the most passionately loved and passionately loving, is ever in our possession. On the pitiless earth where lovers are often separated in death and are always born divided, the total possession of another human being and absolute communion throughout an entire lifetime are impossible dreams. The desire for possession is insatiable, to such a point that it can survive even love itself. To love, therefore, is to sterilize the person one loves. The shamefaced suffering of the abandoned lover is not so much due to being no longer loved as to knowing that the other partner can and must love again. In the final analysis, every man devoured by the overpowering desire to endure and possess wishes that those whom he has loved were either sterile or dead. This is real rebellion. Those who have not insisted, at least once, on the absolute virginity of human beings and of the world, who have not trembled with longing and impotence at the fact that it is impossible, and have then not been destroyed by trying to love halfheartedly, perpetually forced back upon their longing for the absolute, cannot understand the realities of rebellion and its ravening desire for destruction. But the lives of others always escape us, and we escape them too; they have no firm outline. Life from this point of view is without style. It is only an impulse that endlessly pursues its form without ever finding it. Man, tortured by this, tries in vain to find the form that will impose certain limits between which he can be king. If only one single living thing had definite form, he would be reconciled!

There is not one human being who, above a certain elementary level of consciousness, does not exhaust himself in trying to find formulas or attitudes that will give his existence the unity it lacks. Appearance and action, the dandy and the revolutionary, all demand unity in order to exist, and in order to exist on this earth. As in those moving and unhappy relationships which sometimes survive for a very long time because one of the partners is waiting to find the right word, action, gesture, or situation which will bring his adventure to an end on exactly the right note, so everyone proposes and creates for himself the final word. It is not sufficient to live, there must be a destiny that does not have to wait for death. It is therefore justifiable to say that man has an idea of a better world than this. But better does not mean different, it means unified. This passion which lifts the mind above the commonplaces of a dispersed world, from which it nevertheless cannot free itself, is the passion for unity. It does not result in mediocre efforts to escape, however, but in the most obstinate demands. Religion or crime, every human endeavor in fact, finally obeys this unreasonable desire and claims to give life a form it does not have. The same impulse, which can lead to the adoration of the heavens or the destruction of man, also leads to creative literature, which derives its serious content from this source.

What, in fact, is a novel but a universe in which action is endowed with form, where final words are pronounced, where people possess one another completely, and where life assumes the aspect of destiny? [3] The world of the novel is only a rectification of the world we live in, in pursuance of man's deepest wishes. For the world is undoubtedly the same one we know. The suffering, the illusion, the love are the same. The heroes speak our language, have our weaknesses and our strength. Their universe is neither more beautiful nor more enlightening than ours. But they, at least, pursue their destinies to the bitter end and there are no more fascinating heroes than those who indulge their passions to the fullest, Kirilov and Stavrogin, Mme Graslin, Julien Sorel, or the Prince de Clèves. It is here that we can no longer keep pace with them, for they complete things that we can never consummate.

Mme de La Fayette derived the *Princesse de Clèves* from the most harrowing experiences. Undoubtedly she is Mme de Clèves and yet she is not. Where lies the difference? The difference is that Mme de La Fayette did not go into a convent and that no one around her died of despair. No doubt she knew moments, at least, of agony in her extraordinary passion. But there was no culminating-point; she survived her love and prolonged it by ceasing to live it, and finally no one, not even herself, would have known its pattern if she had not given it the perfect delineation of faultless prose.

Nor is there any story more romantic and beautiful than that of Sophie Tonska and Casimir in Gobineau's *Pléiades*. Sophie, a sensitive and beautiful woman, who makes one understand Stendahl's confession that "only women of great character can make me happy," forces Casimir to confess his love for her. Accustomed to being loved, she becomes impatient with Casimir, who sees her every day and yet never departs from an attitude of irritating detachment. Casimir confesses his love, but in the tone of one stating a legal case. He has studied it, knows it as well as he knows himself, and is convinced that this love, without which he cannot live, has no future. He has therefore decided to tell her of his love and at the same

---

[3] Even if the novel describes only nostalgia, despair, frustration, it still creates a form of salvation. To talk of despair is to conquer it. Despairing literature is a contradiction in terms.

time to acknowledge that it is vain and to make over his fortune to her—she is rich, and this gesture is of no importance—on condition that she give him a very modest pension which will allow him to install himself in the suburb of a town chosen at random (it will be Vilna) and there await death in poverty. Casimir recognizes, moreover, that the idea of receiving from Sophie the necessary money on which to live represents a concession to human weakness, the only one he will permit himself, with, at long intervals, the dispatch of a blank sheet of paper in an envelope on which he will write Sophie's name. After being first indignant, then perturbed, and then melancholy, Sophie accepts; and everything happens as Casimir foresaw. He dies, in Vilna, of a broken heart. Romanticism thus has its logic. A story is never really moving and successful without the imperturbable continuity which is never part of real life, but which is to be found on the borderland between reality and reverie. If Gobineau himself had gone to Vilna he would have got bored and come back, or would have settled down comfortably. But Casimir never experienced any desire to change nor did he ever wake cured of his love. He went to the bitter end, like Heathcliff, who wanted to go beyond death in order to reach the very depths of hell.

Here we have an imaginary world, therefore, which is created by the rectification of the actual world—a world where suffering can, if it wishes, continue until death, where passions are never distracted, where people are prey to obsessions and are always present to one another. Man is finally able to give himself the alleviating form and limits which he pursues in vain in his own life. The novel creates destiny to suit any eventuality. In this way it competes with creation and, provisionally, conquers death. A detailed analysis of the most famous novels would show, in different perspectives each time, that the essence of the novel lies in this perpetual alteration, always directed toward the same ends, that the artist makes in his own experience. Far from being moral or even purely formal, this alteration aims, primarily, at unity and thereby expresses a metaphysical need. The novel, on this level, is primarily an exercise of the intelligence in the service of nostalgic or rebellious sensibilities. It would be possible to study this quest for unity in the French analytical novel and in Melville, Balzac, Dostoievsky, or Tolstoy. But a brief comparison between two attempts that stand at different poles of the world of the novel—the works of Proust and American fiction of the last few years—will suffice for our purpose.

The American novel [4] claims to find its unity in reducing man either to elementals or to his external reactions and to his behavior. It does not choose feelings or passions to give a detailed description of, such as we find in classic French novels. It rejects analysis and the search for a fundamental psychological motive that could explain and recapitulate the behavior of a character. This is why the unity of this novel form is only the unity of the flash of recognition. Its technique consists in describing men by their outside appearances, in their most casual actions, of reproducing, without comment, everything they say down to their repetitions,[5] and finally by acting as if men were entirely defined by their daily automatisms. On this mechanical level men, in fact, seem exactly alike, which explains this peculiar universe in which all the characters appear interchangeable, even down to their physical peculiarities. This technique is called realistic only owing to a misapprehension. In addition to the fact that realism in art is, as we shall see, an incomprehensible idea, it is perfectly obvious that this fictitious world is not attempting a reproduction, pure and simple, of reality, but the most arbitrary form of stylization. It is born of a mutilation, and of a voluntary mutilation, performed on reality. The unity thus obtained is a degraded unity, a leveling off of human beings and of the world. It would seem that for these writers it is the inner life that deprives human actions of unity and that tears people away from one another. This is a partially legitimate suspicion. But rebellion, which is one of the sources of the art of fiction, can find satisfaction only in constructing unity on the basis of affirming this interior reality and not of denying it. To

---

[4] I am referring, of course, to the "tough" novel of the thirties and forties and not to the admirable American efflorescence of the nineteenth century.

[5] Even in Faulkner, a great writer of this generation, the interior monologue only reproduces the outer husk of thought.

deny it totally is to refer oneself to an imaginary man. Novels of violence are also love stories, of which they have the formal conceits—in their own way, they edify.[6] The life of the body, reduced to its essentials, paradoxically produces an abstract and gratuitous universe, continuously denied, in its turn, by reality. This type of novel, purged of interior life, in which men seem to be observed behind a pane of glass, logically ends, with its emphasis on the pathological, by giving itself as its unique subject the supposedly average man. In this way it is possible to explain the extraordinary number of "innocents" who appear in this universe. The simpleton is the ideal subject for such an enterprise since he can only be defined—and completely defined—by his behavior. He is the symbol of the despairing world in which wretched automatons live in a machine-ridden universe, which American novelists have presented as a heart-rending but sterile protest.

As for Proust, his contribution has been to create, from an obstinate contemplation of reality, a closed world that belonged only to him and that indicated his victory over the transitoriness of things and over death. But he uses absolutely the opposite means. He upholds, above everything, by a deliberate choice, a careful selection of unique experience, which the writer chooses from the most secret recesses of his past. Immense empty spaces are thus discarded from life because they have left no trace in the memory. If the American novel is the novel of men without memory, the world of Proust is nothing but memory. It is concerned only with the most difficult and most exacting of memories, the memory that rejects the dispersion of the actual world and derives, from the trace of a lingering perfume, the secret of a new and ancient universe. Proust chooses the interior life and, of the interior life, that which is more interior than life itself in preference to what is forgotten in the world of reality— in other words, the purely mechanical and blind aspects of the world. But by his rejection of reality he does not deny reality. He does not commit the error, which would counterbalance the error of American fiction, of suppressing

[6] Bernardin de Saint-Pierre and the Marquis de Sade, with different indications of it, are the creators of the propagandist novel.

the mechanical. He unites, on the contrary, into a superior form of unity, the memory of the past and the immediate sensation, the twisted foot and the happy days of times past.

It is difficult to return to the places of one's early happiness. The young girls in the flower of their youth still laugh and chatter on the seashore, but he who watches them gradually loses his right to love them, just as those he has loved lose the power to be loved. This melancholy is the melancholy of Proust. It was powerful enough in him to cause a violent rejection of all existence. But his passion for faces and for the light attached him at the same time to life. He never admitted that the happy days of his youth were lost forever. He undertook the task of re-creating them and of demonstrating, in the face of death, that the past could be regained at the end of time in the form of an imperishable present, both truer and richer than it was at the beginning. The psychological analysis of *Remembrance of Things Past* is nothing but a potent means to an end. The real greatness of Proust lies in having written *Time Regained*, which resembles the world of dispersion and which gives it a meaning on the very level of integration. His difficult victory, on the eve of his death, is to have been able to extract from the incessant flight of forms, by means of memory and intelligence alone, the tentative trembling symbols of human unity. The most definite challenge that a work of this kind can give to creation is to present itself as an entirety, as a closed and unified world. This defines an unrepentant work of art.

It has been said that the world of Proust was a world without a god. If that is true, it is not because God is never spoken of, but because the ambition of this world is to be absolute perfection and to give to eternity the aspect of man. *Time Regained*, at least in its aspirations, is eternity without God. Proust's work, in this regard, appears to be one of the most ambitious and most significant of man's enterprises against his mortal condition. He has demonstrated that the art of the novel can reconstruct creation itself, in the form that it is imposed on us and in the form in which we reject it. In one of its aspects, at least, this art consists in choosing the creature in preference to his creator. But still more profoundly, it is allied to the beauty of the world or of its inhabitants against the powers of death and oblivion. It is in this way that his rebellion is creative.

Rebellion and Style

By the treatment that the artist imposes on reality, he declares the intensity of his rejection. But what he retains of reality in the universe that he creates reveals the degree of consent that he gives to at least one part of reality—which he draws from the shadows of evolution to bring it to the light of creation. In the final analysis, if the rejection is total, reality is then completely banished and the result is a purely formal work. If, on the other hand, the artist chooses, for reasons often unconnected with art, to exalt crude reality, the result is then realism. In the first case the primitive creative impulse in which rebellion and consent, affirmation and negation are closely allied is adulterated to the advantage of rejection. It then represents formal escapism, of which our period has furnished so many examples and of which the nihilist origin is quite evident. In the second case the artist claims to give the world unity by withdrawing from it all privileged perspectives. In this sense, he confesses his need for unity, even a degraded form of unity. But he also renounces the first requirement of artistic creation. To deny the relative freedom of the creative mind more forcibly, he affirms the immediate totality of the world. The act of creation denies itself in both these kinds of work. Originally, it refused only one aspect of reality while simultaneously affirming another. Whether it comes to the point of rejecting all reality or of affirming nothing but reality, it denies itself each time either by absolute negation or by absolute affirmation. It can be seen that, on the plane of æsthetics, this analysis coincides with the analysis I have sketched on the historical plane.

But just as there is no nihilism that does not end by supposing a value, and no materialism that, being self-conceived, does not end by contradicting itself, so formal art and realist art are absurd concepts. No art can completely reject reality. The Gorgon is, doubtless, a purely imaginary creature; its face and the serpents that crown it are part of nature. Formalism can succeed in purging itself more and more of real content, but there is always a limit. Even pure geometry, where abstract painting sometimes ends, still derives its color and its conformity to perspective from the exterior world. The only real formalism is silence. Moreover, realism cannot dispense with a minimum of interpretation and arbitrariness. Even the very best photographs do not represent reality; they result from an act of selection and impose a limit on something that has none. The realist artist and the formal artist try to find unity where it does not exist, in reality in its crudest state, or in imaginative creation which wants to abolish all reality. On the contrary, unity in art appears at the limit of the transformation that the artist imposes on reality. It cannot dispense with either. This correction[7] which the artist imposes by his language and by a redistribution of elements derived from reality is called style and gives the re-created universe its unity and its boundaries. It attempts, in the work of every rebel, to impose its laws on the world, and succeeds in the case of a few geniuses. "Poets," said Shelley, "are the unacknowledged legislators of the world."

Literary art, by its origins, cannot fail to illustrate this vocation. It can neither totally consent to reality nor turn aside from it completely. The purely imaginary does not exist, and even if it did exist in an ideal novel which would be purely disincarnate, it would have no artistic significance, in that the primary necessity for a mind in search of unity is that the unity should be communicable. From another point of view, the unity of pure reasoning is a false unity, for it is not based on reality. The sentimental love story, the horror story, and the edifying novel deviate from art to the great or small extent that they disobey this law. Real literary creation, on the other hand, uses reality and only reality with all its warmth and its blood, its passion and its outcries. It simply adds something that transfigures reality.

[7] Delacroix notes—and this is a penetrating observation—that it is necessary to correct the "inflexible perspective which (in reality) falsifies the appearance of objects *by virtue of precision.*"

Likewise, what is commonly called the realistic novel tries to be the reproduction of reality in its immediate aspects. To reproduce the elements of reality without making any kind of selection would be, if such an undertaking could be imagined, nothing but a sterile repetition of creation. Realism should only be the means of expression of religious genius—Spanish art admirably illustrates this contention—or, at the other extreme, the artistic expressions of monkeys, which are quite satisfied with mere imitation. In fact, art is never realistic though sometimes it is tempted to be. To be really realistic a description would have to be endless. Where Stendhal describes in one phrase Lucien Leuwen's entrance into a room, the realistic artist ought, logically, to fill several volumes with descriptions of characters and settings, still without succeeding in exhausting every detail. Realism is indefinite enumeration. By this it reveals that its real ambition is conquest, not of the unity, but of the totality of the real world. Now we understand why it should be the official æsthetic of a totalitarian revolution. But the impossibility of such an æsthetic has already been demonstrated. Realistic novels select their material, despite themselves, from reality, because the choice and the conquest of reality are absolute conditions of thought and expression.[8] To write is already to choose. There is thus an arbitrary aspect to reality, just as there is an arbitrary aspect to the ideal, which makes a realistic novel an implicit problem novel. To reduce the unity of the world of fiction to the totality of reality can only be done by means of an *a priori* judgment which eliminates form, reality, and everything that conflicts with doctrine. Therefore so-called socialist realism is condemned by the very logic of its nihilism to accumulate the advantages of the edifying novel and propaganda literature.

Whether the event enslaves the creator or whether the creator claims to deny the event completely, creation is nevertheless reduced to the degraded forms of nihilist art. It is the same thing with creation as with civilization: it presumes uninterrupted tension between form and

[8] Delacroix demonstrated this again with profundity: "For realism not to be a word devoid of sense, all men must have the same minds and the same way of conceiving things."

matter, between evolution and the mind, and between history and values. If the equilibrium is destroyed, the result is dictatorship or anarchy, propaganda or formal insanity. In either case creation, which always coincides with rational freedom, is impossible. Whether it succumbs to the intoxication of abstraction and formal obscurantism, or whether it falls back on the whip of the crudest and most ingenious realism, modern art, in its semi-totality, is an art of tyrants and slaves, not of creators.

A work in which the content overflows the form, or in which the form drowns the content, only bespeaks an unconvinced and unconvincing unity. In this domain, as in others, any unity that is not a unity of style is a mutilation. Whatever may be the chosen point of view of an artist, one principle remains common to all creators: stylization, which supposes the simultaneous existence of reality and of the mind that gives reality its form. Through style, the creative effort reconstructs the world, and always with the same slight distortion that is the mark of both art and protest. Whether it is the enlargement of the microscope which Proust brings to bear on human experience or, on the contrary, the absurd insignificance with which the American novel endows its characters, reality is in some way artificial. The creative force, the fecundity of rebellion, are contained in this distortion which the style and tone of a work represent. Art is an impossible demand given expression and form. When the most agonizing protest finds its most resolute form of expression, rebellion satisfies its real aspirations and derives creative energy from this fidelity to itself. Despite the fact that this runs counter to the prejudices of the times, the greatest style in art is the expression of the most passionate rebellion. Just as genuine classicism is only romanticism subdued, genius is a rebellion that has created its own limits. That is why there is no genius, contrary to what we are taught today, in negation and pure despair.

This means, at the same time, that great style is not a mere formal virtue. It is a mere formal virtue when it is sought out for its own sake to the detriment of reality, but then it is not great style. It no longer invents, but imitates—like all academic works—while real creation is, in its own fashion, revolutionary. If stylization must necessarily be rather exaggerated, since it sums up the intervention of man and the desire for rectification which the artist brings to his reproduction of reality, it is nevertheless desirable that it should remain invisible so that the demand which gives birth to art should be expressed in its most extreme tension. Great style is invisible stylization, or rather stylization incarnate. "There is never any need," says Flaubert, "to be afraid of exaggeration in art." But he adds that the exaggeration should be "continuous and proportionate to itself." When stylization is exaggerated and obvious, the work becomes nothing but pure nostalgia; the unity it is trying to conquer has nothing to do with concrete unity. On the other hand, when reality is delivered over to unadorned fact or to insignificant stylization, then the concrete is presented without unity. Great art, style, and the true aspect of rebellion lie somewhere between these two heresies.

Creation and Revolution

In art, rebellion is consummated and perpetuated in the act of real creation, not in criticism or commentary. Revolution, in its turn, can only affirm itself in a civilization and not in terror or tyranny. The two questions that are posed by our times to a society caught in a dilemma— Is creation possible? Is the revolution possible?—are in reality only one question, which concerns the renaissance of civilization.

The revolution and art of the twentieth century are tributaries of the same nihilism and live in the same contradiction. They deny, however, all that they affirm even in their very actions, and both try to find an impossible solution through terror. The contemporary revolution believes that it is inaugurating a new world when it is really only the contradictory climax of the old one. Finally capitalist society and revolutionary society are one and the same thing to the extent that they submit themselves to the same means—industrial production—and to the same promise. But one makes its promise in the name of formal principles that it is quite incapable of incarnating and that are denied by the methods it employs. The other justifies its prophecy in the name of the only reality it recognizes, and ends by mutilating reality. The society based on production is only productive, not creative.

Contemporary art, because it is nihilistic, also flounders between formalism and realism. Realism, moreover, is just as much bourgeois, when it is "tough," as socialist when it becomes edifying. Formalism belongs just as much to the society of the past, when it takes the form of gratuitous abstraction, as to the society that claims to be the society of the future—when it becomes propaganda. Language destroyed by irrational negation becomes lost in verbal delirium; subject to determinist ideology, it is summed up in the slogan. Halfway between the two lies art. If the rebel must simultaneously reject the frenzy of annihilation and the acceptance of totality, the artist must simultaneously escape from the passion for formality and the totalitarian æsthetic of reality. The world today is one, in fact, but its unity is the unity of nihilism. Civilization is only possible if, by renouncing the nihilism of formal principles and nihilism without principles, the world rediscovers the road to a creative synthesis. In the same way, in art the time of perpetual commentary and factual reporting is at the point of death; it announces the advent of creative artists.

But art and society, creation and revolution, to prepare for this event, must rediscover the source of rebellion where refusal and acceptance, the unique and the universal, the individual and history balance each other in a condition of acute tension. Rebellion in itself is not an element of civilization. But it is a preliminary to all civilization. Rebellion alone, in the blind alley in which we live, allows us to hope for the future of which Nietzsche dreamed: "Instead of the judge and the oppressor, the creator." This formula certainly does not authorize the ridiculous illusion of a civilization controlled by artists. It only illuminates the drama of our times in which work, entirely subordinated to production, has ceased to be creative. Industrial society will open the way to a new civilization only by restoring to the worker the dignity of a creator; in other words, by making him apply his interest and his intelligence as much to the work itself as to what it produces. The type of civilization that is inevitable will not be able to separate, among classes as well as among individuals, the worker from the creator; any more than artistic creation dreams of separating form and substance, history and the mind. In this way it will bestow on everyone the dignity that rebellion affirms. It would be unjust, and moreover Utopian, for Shakespeare to direct the shoemakers' union. But it would be equally disastrous for the shoemakers' union to ignore Shakespeare. Shakespeare without the shoemaker serves as an excuse for tyranny. The shoemaker without Shakespeare is absorbed by tyranny when he does not contribute to its propagation. Every act of creation, by its mere existence, denies the world of master and slave. The appalling society of tyrants and slaves in which we survive will find its death and transfiguration only on the level of creation.

But the fact that creation is necessary does not perforce imply that it is possible. A creative period in art is determined by the order of a particular style applied to the disorder of a particular time. It gives form and formulas to contemporary passions. Thus it no longer suffices, for a creative artist, to imitate Mme de La Fayette in a period when our morose rulers have no more time for love. Today, when collective passions have stolen a march on individual passions, the ecstasy of love can always be controlled by art. But the ineluctable problem is also to control collective passions and the historical struggle. The scope of art, despite the regrets of the plagiarists, has been extended from psychology to the human condition. When the passions of the times put the fate of the whole world at stake, creation wishes to dominate the whole of destiny. But, at the same time, it maintains, in the face of totality, the affirmation of unity. In simple words, creation is then imperilled, first by itself, and then by the spirit of totality. To create, today, is to create dangerously.

In order to dominate collective passions they must, in fact, be lived through and experienced, at least relatively. At the same time that he experiences them, the artist is devoured by them. The result is that our period is rather the period of journalism than of the work of art. The exercise of these passions, finally, entails far greater chances of death than in the period of love and ambition, in that the only way of living collective passions is to be willing to die for them and by their hand. The greatest opportunity for authenticity is, today, the greatest defeat of art. If creation is impossible during wars and revolutions, then we shall have no creative artists, for war and revolution are our lot. The myth of unlimited production brings war in its train as inevitably as clouds announce a storm. Wars lay waste to the West and kill the flower of a generation. Hardly has it arisen from the ruins when the bourgeois system sees the revolutionary system advancing upon it. Genius has not even had time to be reborn; the war that threatens us will kill all those who perhaps might have been geniuses. If a creative classicism is, nevertheless, proved possible, we must recognize that, even though it is rendered illustrious by one name alone, it will be the work of an entire generation. The chances of defeat, in the century of destruction, can only be compensated for by the hazard of numbers; in other words, the chance that of ten authentic artists one, at least, will survive, take charge of the first utterances of his brother artists, and succeed in finding in his life both the time for passion and the time for creation. The artist, whether he likes it or not, can no longer be a solitary, except in the melancholy triumph he owes to all his fellow artists. Rebellious art also ends by revealing the "We are," and with it the way to a burning humility.

Meanwhile, the triumphant revolution, in the aberrations of its nihilism, menaces those who, in defiance of it, claim to maintain the existence of unity in totality. One of the implications of history today, and still more of the history of tomorrow, is the struggle between the artists and the new conquerors, between the witnesses to the creative revolution and the founders of the nihilist revolution. As to the outcome of the struggle, it is only possible to make inspired guesses. At least we know that it must henceforth be carried on to the bitter end. Modern conquerors can kill, but do not seem to be able to create. Artists know how to create but cannot really kill. Murderers are only very exceptionally found among artists. In the long run, therefore, art in our revolutionary societies must die. But then the revolution will have lived its allotted span. Each time that the revolution kills in a man the artist that he might have been, it attenuates itself a little more. If, finally, the conquerors succeed in molding the world according to their laws, it will not prove that quantity is king, but that this world is hell. In this hell, the place of art will coincide with that of vanquished rebellion, a blind and empty hope in the pit of despair. Ernst Dwinger in his *Siberian Diary* mentions a German lieutenant—for years a prisoner in a camp where cold and hunger were almost unbearable—who constructed himself a silent piano with wooden keys. In the most abject misery, perpetually surrounded by a ragged mob, he composed a strange music which was audible to him alone. And for us who have been thrown into hell, mysterious melodies and the torturing images of a vanished beauty will always bring us, in the midst of crime and folly, the echo of that harmonious insurrection which bears witness, throughout the centuries, to the greatness of humanity.

But hell can endure for only a limited period, and life will begin again one day. History may perhaps have an end; but our task is not to terminate it but to create it, in the image of what we henceforth know to be true. Art, at least, teaches us that man cannot be explained by history alone and that he also finds a reason for his existence in the order of nature. For him, the great god Pan is not dead. His most instinctive act of rebellion, while it affirms the value and the dignity common to all men, obstinately claims, so as to satisfy its hunger for unity, an integral part of the reality whose name is beauty. One can reject all history and yet accept the world of the sea and the stars. The rebels who wish to ignore nature and beauty are condemned to banish from history everything with which they want to construct the dignity of existence and of labor. Every great reformer tries to create in history what Shakespeare, Cervantes, Molière, and Tolstoy knew how to create: a world always ready to satisfy the hunger for freedom and dignity which every man carries in his heart. Beauty, no doubt, does not make revolutions. But a day will come when revolutions will have need of beauty. The procedure of beauty, which is to contest reality while endowing it with unity, is also the procedure of rebellion. Is it possible eternally to reject injustice without ceasing to acclaim the nature of man and the beauty of the world? Our answer is yes. This ethic, at once unsubmissive and loyal, is in any event the only one that lights the way to a truly realistic revolution. In upholding beauty, we prepare the way for the day of regeneration when civilization will give first place—far ahead of the formal principles and degraded values of history—to this living virtue on which is founded the common dignity of man and the world he lives in, and which we must now define in the face of a world that insults it.

Part Five

Thought at the Meridian

Rebellion and Murder

*

Far from this source of life, however, Europe and the revolution are being shaken to the core by a spectacular convulsion. During the last century, man cast off the fetters of religion. Hardly was he free, however, when he created new and utterly intolerable chains. Virtue dies but is born again, more exacting than ever. It preaches an ear-splitting sermon on charity to all comers and a kind of love for the future which makes a mockery of contemporary humanism. When it has reached this point of stability, it can only wreak havoc. A day arrives when it becomes bitter, immediately adopts police methods, and, for the salvation of mankind, assumes the ignoble aspect of an inquisition. At the climax of contemporary tragedy, we therefore become intimates of crime. The sources of life and of creation seem exhausted. Fear paralyzes a Europe peopled with phantoms and machines. Between two holocausts, scaffolds are installed in underground caverns where humanist executioners celebrate their new cult in silence. What cry would ever trouble them? The poets themselves, confronted with the murder of their fellow men, proudly declare that their hands are clean. The whole world absent-mindedly turns its back on these crimes; the victims have reached the extremity of their disgrace: they are a bore. In ancient times the blood of murder at least produced a religious horror and in this way sanctified the value of life. The real condemnation of the period we live in is, on the contrary, that it leads us to think that it is not blood·

thirsty enough. Blood is no longer visible; it does not bespatter the faces of our pharisees visibly enough. This is the extreme of nihilism; blind and savage murder becomes an oasis, and the imbecile criminal seems positively refreshing in comparison with our highly intelligent executioners.

Having believed for a long time that it could fight against God with all humanity as its ally, the European mind then perceived that it must also, if it did not want to die, fight against men. The rebels who, united against death, wanted to construct, on the foundation of the human species, a savage immortality are terrified at the prospect of being obliged to kill in their turn. Nevertheless, if they retreat they must accept death; if they advance they must accept murder. Rebellion, cut off from its origins and cynically travestied, oscillates, on all levels, between sacrifice and murder. The form of justice that it advocated and that it hoped was impartial has turned out to be summary. The kingdom of grace has been conquered, but the kingdom of justice is crumbling too. Europe is dying of this disappointing realization. Rebellion pleaded for the innocence of mankind, and now it has hardened its heart against its own culpability. Hardly does it start off in search of totality when it receives as its portion the most desperate sensations of solitude. It wanted to enter into communion with mankind and now it has no other hope but to assemble, one by one, throughout the years, the solitary men who fight their way toward unity.

Must we therefore renounce every kind of rebellion, whether we accept, with all its injustices, a society that outlives its usefulness, or whether we decide, cynically, to serve, against the interest of man, the inexorable advance of history? After all, if the logic of our reflection should lead to a cowardly conformism it would have to be accepted as certain families sometimes accept inevitable dishonor. If it must also justify all the varieties of attempts against man, and even his systematic destruction, it would be necessary to consent to this suicide. The desire for justice would finally realize its ambition: the disappearance of a world of tradesmen and police.

But are we still living in a rebellious world? Has not rebellion become, on the contrary, the excuse of a new variety of tyrant? Can the "We are" contained in the movement of rebellion, without shame and without subterfuge, be reconciled with murder? In assigning oppression a limit within which begins the dignity common to all men, rebellion defined a primary value. It put in the first rank of its frame of reference an obvious complicity among men, a common texture, the solidarity of chains, a communication between human being and human being which makes men both similar and united. In this way, it compelled the mind to take a first step in defiance of an absurd world. By this progress it rendered still more acute the problem that it must now solve in regard to murder. On the level of the absurd, in fact, murder would only give rise to logical contradictions; on the level of rebellion it is mental laceration. For it is now a question of deciding if it is possible to kill someone whose resemblance to ourselves we have at last recognized and whose identity we have just sanctified. When we have only just conquered solitude, must we then re-establish it definitively by legitimizing the act that isolates everything? To force solitude on a man who has just come to understand that he is not alone, is that not the definitive crime against man?

Logically, one should reply that murder and rebellion are contradictory. If a single master should, in fact, be killed, the rebel, in a certain way, is no longer justified in using the term *community of men* from which he derived his justification. If this world has no higher meaning, if man is only responsible to man, it suffices for a man to remove one single human being from the society of the living to automatically exclude himself from it. When Cain kills Abel, he flees to the desert. And if murderers are legion, then this legion lives in the desert and in that other kind of solitude called promiscuity.

From the moment that he strikes, the rebel cuts the world in two. He rebelled in the name of the identity of man with man and he sacrifices this identity by consecrating the difference in blood. His only existence, in the midst of suffering and oppression, was contained in this identity. The same movement, which intended to affirm him, thus brings an end to his existence. He can claim that some, or even almost all, are with him. But if one single human being is missing in the irreplaceable world of fraternity, then this world is immediately depopulated. If we are not, then I am not and this explains the infinite sadness of Kaliayev and the silence of Saint-Just. The rebels, who have decided to gain their ends through violence and murder, have in vain replaced, in order to preserve the hope of existing, "We are" by the "We shall be." When the murderer and the victim have disappeared, the community will provide its own justification without them. The exception having lasted its appointed time, the rule will once more become possible. On the level of history, as in individual life, murder is thus a desperate exception or it is nothing. The disturbance that it brings to the order of things offers no hope of a future; it is an exception and therefore it can be neither utilitarian nor systematic as the purely historical attitude would have it. It is the limit that can be reached but once, after which one must die. The rebel has only one way of reconciling himself with his act of murder if he allows himself to be led into performing it: to accept his own death and sacrifice. He kills and dies so that it shall be clear that murder is impossible. He demonstrates that, in reality, he prefers the "We are" to the "We shall be." The calm happiness of Kaliayev in his prison, the serenity of Saint-Just when he walks toward the scaffold, are explained in their turn. Beyond that farthest frontier, contradition and nihilism begin.

Nihilistic Murder

Irrational crime and rational crime, in fact, both equally betray the value brought to light by the movement of rebellion. Let us first consider the former. He who denies everything and assumes the authority to kill—Sade, the homicidal dandy, the pitiless Unique, Karamazov, the zealous supporters of the unleashed bandit—lay claim to nothing short of total freedom and the unlimited display of human pride. Nihilism confounds creator and created in the same blind fury. Suppressing every principle of hope, it rejects the idea of any limit, and in blind indignation, which no longer is even aware of its reasons, ends with the conclusion that it is a matter of indifference to kill when the victim is already condemned to death.

But its reasons—the mutual recognition of a common destiny and the communication of men between themselves—are always valid. Rebellion proclaimed them and undertook to serve them. In the same way it defined, in contradiction to nihilism, a rule of conduct that has no need to await the end of history to explain its actions and which is, nevertheless, not formal. Contrary to Jacobin morality, it made allowances for everything that escapes from rules and laws. It opened the way to a morality which, far from obeying abstract principles, discovers them only in the heat of battle and in the incessant movement of contradiction. Nothing justifies the assertion that these principles have existed externally; it is of no use to declare that they will one day exist. But they do exist, in the very period in which we exist. With us, and throughout all history, they deny servitude, falsehood, and terror.

There is, in fact, nothing in common between a master and a slave; it is impossible to speak and communicate with a person who has been reduced to servitude. Instead of the implicit and untrammeled dialogue through which we come to recognize our similarity and consecrate our destiny, servitude gives sway to the most terrible of silences. If injustice is bad for the rebel, it is not because it contradicts an eternal idea of justice, but because it perpetuates the silent hostility that separates the oppressor from the oppressed. It kills the small part of existence that can be realized on this earth through the mutual understanding of men. In the same way, since the man who lies shuts himself off from other men, falsehood is therefore proscribed and, on a slightly lower level, murder and violence, which impose definitive silence. The mutual understanding and communication discovered by rebellion can survive only in the free exchange of conversation. Every ambiguity, every misunderstanding, leads to death; clear language and simple words are the only salvation from this death.[1] The climax of every tragedy lies in the deafness of its heroes. Plato is right and not Moses and Nietzsche. Dialogue on the level of mankind is less costly

---

[1] It is worth noting that the language peculiar to totalitarian doctrines is always a scholastic or administrative language.

than the gospel preached by totalitarian regimes in the form of a monologue dictated from the top of a lonely mountain. On the stage as in reality, the monologue precedes death. Every rebel, solely by the movement that sets him in opposition to the oppressor, therefore pleads for life, undertakes to struggle against servitude, falsehood, and terror, and affirms, in a flash, that these three afflictions are the cause of silence between men, that they obscure them from one another and prevent them from rediscovering themselves in the only value that can save them from nihilism—the long complicity of men at grips with their destiny.

In a flash—but that is time enough to say, provisionally, that the most extreme form of freedom, the freedom to kill, is not compatible with the sense of rebellion. Rebellion is in no way the demand for total freedom. On the contrary, rebellion puts total freedom up for trial. It specifically attacks the unlimited power that authorizes a superior to violate the forbidden frontier. Far from demanding general independence, the rebel wants it to be recognized that freedom has its limits everywhere that a human being is to be found—the limit being precisely that human being's power to rebel. The most profound reason for rebellious intransigence is to be found here. The more aware rebellion is of demanding a just limit, the more inflexible it becomes. The rebel undoubtedly demands a certain degree of freedom for himself; but in no case, if he is consistent, does he demand the right to destroy the existence and the freedom of others. He humiliates no one. The freedom he claims, he claims for all; the freedom he refuses, he forbids everyone to enjoy. He is not only the slave against the master, but also man against the world of master and slave. Therefore, thanks to rebellion, there is something more in history than the relation between mastery and servitude. Unlimited power is not the only law. It is in the name of another value that the rebel affirms the impossibility of total freedom while he claims for himself the relative freedom necessary to recognize this impossibility. Every human freedom, at its very roots, is therefore relative. Absolute freedom, which is the freedom to kill, is the only one which does not claim, at the same time as itself, the things that limit and obliterate it. Thus it cuts itself off from its roots and —abstract and malevolent shade—wanders haphazardly until such time as it imagines that it has found substance in some ideology.

It is then possible to say that rebellion, when it develops into destruction, is illogical. Claiming the unity of the human condition, it is a force of life, not of death. Its most profound logic is not the logic of destruction; it is the logic of creation. Its movement, in order to remain authentic, must never abandon any of the terms of the contradiction that sustains it. It must be faithful to the *yes* that it contains as well as to the *no* that nihilistic interpretations isolate in rebellion. The logic of the rebel is to want to serve justice so as not to add to the injustice of the human condition, to insist on plain language so as not to increase the universal falsehood, and to wager, in spite of human misery, for happiness. Nihilistic passion, adding to falsehood and injustice, destroys in its fury its original demands and thus deprives rebellion of its most cogent reasons. It kills in the fond conviction that this world is dedicated to death. The consequence of rebellion, on the contrary, is to refuse to legitimize murder because rebellion, in principle, is a protest against death.

But if man were capable of introducing unity into the world entirely on his own, if he could establish the reign, by his own decree, of sincerity, innocence, and justice, he would be God Himself. Equally, if he could accomplish all this, there would be no more reasons for rebellion. If rebellion exists, it is because falsehood, injustice, and violence are part of the rebel's condition. He cannot, therefore, absolutely claim not to kill or lie, without renouncing his rebellion and accepting, once and for all, evil and murder. But no more can he agree to kill and lie, since the inverse reasoning which would justify murder and violence would also destroy the reasons for his insurrection. Thus the rebel can never find peace. He knows what is good and, despite himself, does evil. The value that supports him is never given to him once and for all; he must fight to uphold it, unceasingly. Again the existence he achieves collapses if rebellion does not support it. In any case, if he is not always able not to kill, either directly or indirectly, he can put his conviction and passion to work at diminishing the chances of murder around him. His only virtue will lie in never yielding to the impulse to allow himself to be engulfed in the shadows that surround him and in obstinately dragging the chains of evil, with which he is bound, toward the light of good. If he finally kills himself, he will accept death. Faithful to his origins, the rebel demonstrates by sacrifice that his real freedom is not freedom from murder but freedom from his own death. At the same time, he achieves honor in metaphysical terms. Thus Kaliayev climbs the gallows and visibly designates to all his fellow men the exact limit where man's honor begins and ends.

Historical Murder

Rebellion also deploys itself in history, which demands not only exemplary choices, but also efficacious attitudes. Rational murder runs the risk of finding itself justified by history. The contradiction of rebellion, then, is reflected in an apparently insoluble contradiction, of which the two counterparts in politics are on the one hand the opposition between violence and non-violence, and on the other hand the opposition between justice and freedom. Let us try to define them in the terms of their paradox.

The positive value contained in the initial movement of rebellion supposes the renunciation of violence committed on principle. It consequently entails the impossibility of stabilizing a revolution. Rebellion is, incessantly, prey to this contradiction. On the level of history it becomes even more insoluble. If I renounce the project of making human identity respected, I abdicate in favor of oppression, I renounce rebellion and fall back on an attitude of nihilistic consent. Then nihilism becomes conservative. If I insist that human identity should be recognized as existing, then I engage in an action which, to succeed, supposes a cynical attitude toward violence and denies this identity and rebellion itself. To extend the contradiction still farther, if the unity of the world cannot come from on high, man must construct it on his own level, in history. History without a value to transfigure it, is controlled by the law of expediency. Historical materialism, determinism, violence, negation of every form of freedom which does not coincide with expediency and the world of courage and of silence, are the highly legitimate consequences of a pure philosophy of history. In the world today, only a philosophy of eternity could justify non-violence. To absolute worship of history it would make the objection of the creation of history and of the historical situation it would ask whence it had sprung. Finally, it would put the responsibility for justice in God's hands, thus consecrating injustice. Equally, its answers, in their turn, would insist on faith. The objection will be raised of evil, and of the paradox of an all-powerful and malevolent, or benevolent and sterile, God. The choice will remain open between grace and history, God or the sword.

What, then, should be the attitude of the rebel? He cannot turn away from the world and from history without denying the very principle of his rebellion, nor can he choose eternal life without resigning himself, in one sense, to evil. If, for example, he is not a Christian, he should go to the bitter end. But to the bitter end means to choose history absolutely and with it murder, if murder is essential to history: to accept the justification of murder is again to deny his origins. If the rebel makes no choice, he chooses the silence and slavery of others. If, in a moment of despair, he declares that he opts both against God and against history, he is the witness of pure freedom; in other words, of nothing. In our period of history and in the impossible condition in which he finds himself, of being unable to affirm a superior motive that does not have its limits in evil, his apparent dilemma is silence or murder—in either case, a surrender.

And it is the same again with justice and freedom. These two demands are already to be found at the beginning of the movement of rebellion and are to be found again in the first impetus of revolution. The history of revolutions demonstrates, however, that they almost always conflict as though their mutual demands were irreconcilable. Absolute freedom is the right of the strongest to dominate. Therefore it prolongs the conflicts that profit by injustice. Absolute justice is achieved by the suppression of all contradiction: therefore it destroys freedom.[2] The revolution to achieve justice, through freedom, ends by aligning them against each other. Thus there exists in every revolution, once the class that dominated up to then has been liquidated, a stage in which it gives birth, itself, to a movement of rebellion which indicates its limits and announces its chances of failure. The revolution, first of all, proposes to satisfy the spirit of rebellion which has given rise to it; then it is compelled to deny it, the better to affirm itself. There is, it would seem, an ineradicable opposition between the movement of rebellion and the attainments of revolution.

But these contradictions only exist in the absolute. They suppose a world and a method of thought without meditation. There is, in fact, no conciliation possible between a god who is totally separated from history and a history purged of all transcendence. Their representatives on earth are, indeed, the yogi and the commissar. But the difference between these two types of men is not, as has been stated, the difference between ineffectual purity and expediency. The former chooses only the ineffectiveness of abstention and the second the ineffectiveness of destruction. Because both reject the conciliatory value that rebellion, on the contrary, reveals, they offer us only two kinds of impotence, both equally removed from reality, that of good and that of evil.

If, in fact, to ignore history comes to the same as denying reality, it is still alienating oneself from reality to consider history as a completely self-sufficient absolute. The revolution of the twentieth century believes that it can avoid nihilism and remain faithful to true rebellion, by replacing God by history. In reality, it fortifies the former and betrays the latter. History in its pure form furnishes no value by itself. Therefore one must live by the principles of immediate expediency and keep silent

---

[2] In his *Entretiens sur le bon usage de la liberté* (*Conversations on the Good Use of Freedom*), Jean Grenier lays the foundation for an argument that can be summed up thus: absolute freedom is the destruction of all value; absolute value suppresses all freedom. Likewise Palante: "If there is a single and universal truth, freedom has no reason for existing."

or tell lies. Systematic violence, or imposed silence, calculation or concerted falsehood become the inevitable rule.
Purely historical thought is therefore nihilistic: it wholeheartedly accepts the evil of history and in this way is
opposed to rebellion. It is useless for it to affirm, in com-
pensation, the absolute rationality of history, for historical
reason will never be fulfilled and will never have its full
meaning or value until the end of history. In the meanwhile, it is necessary to act, and to act without a moral rule
in order that the definitive rule should one day be realized.
Cynicism as a political attitude is only logical as a function
of absolutist thought; in other words, absolute nihilism on
the one hand, absolute rationalism on the other.³ As for
the consequences, there is no difference between the two
attitudes. From the moment that they are accepted, the
earth becomes a desert.

In reality, the purely historical absolute is not even
conceivable. Jaspers's thought, for example, in its essentials,
underlines the impossibility of man's grasping totality,
since he lives in the midst of this totality. History, as an
entirety, could exist only in the eyes of an observer outside
it and outside the world. History only exists, in the final
analysis, for God. Thus it is impossible to act according to
plans embracing the totality of universal history. Any historical enterprise can therefore only be a more or less
reasonable or justifiable adventure. It is primarily a risk.
In so far as it is a risk it cannot be used to justify any
excess or any ruthless and absolutist position.

If, on the other hand, rebellion could found a philosophy it would be a philosophy of limits, of calculated
ignorance, and of risk. He who does not know everything
cannot kill everything. The rebel, far from making an
absolute of history, rejects and disputes it, in the name of
a concept that he has of his own nature. He refuses his
condition, and his condition to a large extent is historical.
Injustice, the transcience of time, death—all are mani-

---

³ We see again, and this cannot be said too often, that
absolute rationalism is not rationalism. The difference between
the two is the same as the difference between cynicism and
realism. The first drives the second beyond the limits that give
it meaning and legitimacy. More brutal, it is finally less efficacious. It is violence opposed to force.

fest in history. In spurning them, history itself is spurned. Most certainly the rebel does not deny the history that surrounds him; it is in terms of this that he attempts to affirm himself. But confronted with it, he feels like the artist confronted with reality; he spurns it without escaping from it. He has never succeeded in creating an absolute history. Even though he can participate, by the force of events, in the crime of history, he cannot necessarily legitimate it. Rational crime not only cannot be admitted on the level of rebellion, but also signifies the death of rebellion. To make this evidence more convincing, rational crime exercises itself, in the first place, on rebels whose insurrection contests a history that is henceforth deified.

The mystification peculiar to the mind which claims to be revolutionary today sums up and increases bourgeois mystification. It contrives, by the promise of absolute justice, the acceptance of perpetual injustice, of unlimited compromise, and of indignity. Rebellion itself only aspires to the relative and can only promise an assured dignity coupled with relative justice. It supposes a limit at which the community of man is established. Its universe is the universe of relative values. Instead of saying, with Hegel and Marx, that all is necessary, it only repeats that all is possible and that, at a certain point on the farthest frontier, it is worth making the supreme sacrifice for the sake of the possible. Between God and history, the yogi and the commissar, it opens a difficult path where contradictions may exist and thrive. Let us consider the two contradictions given as an example in this way.

A revolutionary action which wishes to be coherent in terms of its origins should be embodied in an active consent to the relative. It would express fidelity to the human condition. Uncompromising as to its means, it would accept an approximation as far as its ends are concerned and, so that the approximation should become more and more accurately defined, it would allow absolute freedom of speech. Thus it would preserve the common existence that justifies its insurrection. In particular, it would preserve as an absolute law the permanent possibility of self-expression. This defines a particular line of conduct in regard to justice and freedom. There is no justice in society without natural or civil rights as its basis. There are no rights without expression of those rights. If the rights are expressed without hesitation it is more than probable that, sooner or later, the justice they postulate will come to the world. To conquer existence, we must start from the small amount of existence we find in ourselves and not deny it from the very beginning. To silence the law until justice is established is to silence it forever since it will have no more occasion to speak if justice reigns forever. Once more, we thus confide justice into the keeping of those who alone have the ability to make themselves heard—those in power. For centuries, justice and existence as dispensed by those in power have been considered a favor. To kill freedom in order to establish the reign of justice comes to the same as resuscitating the idea of grace without divine intercession and of restoring by a mystifying reaction the mystic body in its basest elements. Even when justice is not realized, freedom preserves the power to protest and guarantees human communication. Justice in a silent world, justice enslaved and mute, destroys mutual complicity and finally can no longer be justice. The revolution of the twentieth century has arbitrarily separated, for overambitious ends of conquest, two inseparable ideas. Absolute freedom mocks at justice. Absolute justice denies freedom. To be fruitful, the two ideas must find their limits in each other. No man considers that his condition is free if it is not at the same time just, nor just unless it is free. Freedom, precisely, cannot even be imagined without the power of saying clearly what is just and what is unjust, of claiming all existence in the name of a small part of existence which refuses to die. Finally there is a justice, though a very different kind of justice, in restoring freedom, which is the only imperishable value of history. Men are never really willing to die except for the sake of freedom: therefore they do not believe in dying completely.

The same reasoning can be applied to violence. Absolute non-violence is the negative basis of slavery and its acts of violence; systematic violence positively destroys the living community and the existence we receive from it. To be fruitful, these two ideas must establish final limits. In history, considered as an absolute, violence finds itself legitimized; as a relative risk, it is the cause of a rupture in communication. It must therefore preserve, for the rebel, its provisional character of effraction and must always be bound, if it cannot be avoided, to a personal responsibility and to an immediate risk. Systematic violence is part of the order of things; in a certain sense, this is consolatory. *Führerprinzip* or historical Reason, whatever order may establish it, it reigns over the universe of things, not the universe of men. Just as the rebel considers murder as the limit that he must, if he is so inclined, consecrate by his own death, so violence can only be an extreme limit which combats another form of violence, as, for example, in the case of an insurrection. If an excess of injustice renders the latter inevitable, the rebel rejects violence in advance, in the service of a doctrine or of a reason of State. Every historical crisis, for example, terminates in institutions. If we have no control over the crisis itself, which is pure hazard, we do have control over the institutions, since we can define them, choose the ones for which we will fight, and thus bend our efforts toward their establishment. Authentic arts of rebellion will only consent to take up arms for institutions that limit violence, not for those which codify it. A revolution is not worth dying for unless it assures the immediate suppression of the death penalty; not worth going to prison for unless it refuses in advance to pass sentence without fixed terms. If rebel violence employs itself in the establishment of these institutions, announcing its aims as often as it can, it is the only way in which it can be really provisional. When the end is absolute, historically speaking, and when it is believed certain of realization, it is possible to go so far as to sacrifice others. When it is not, only oneself can be sacrificed, in the hazards of a struggle for the common dignity of man. Does the end justify the means? That is possible. But what will justify the end? To that question, which historical thought leaves pending, rebellion replies: the means.

What does such an attitude signify in politics? And, first of all, is it efficacious? We must answer without hesitation that it is the only attitude that is efficacious today. There are two sorts of efficacity: that of typhoons and that of sap. Historical absolutism is not efficacious, it is efficient; it has seized and kept power. Once it is in possession of power, it destroys the only creative reality. Uncompromising and limited action, springing from rebellion, upholds this reality and only tries to extend it farther and farther. It is not said that this action cannot conquer. It is said that it runs the risk of not conquering and of dying. But either revolution will take this risk or it will confess that it is only the undertaking of a new set of masters, punishable by the same scorn. A revolution that is separated from honor betrays its origins that belong to the reign of honor. Its choice, in any case, is limited to material expediency and final annihilation, or to risks and hence to creation. The revolutionaries of the past went ahead as fast as they could and their optimism was complete. But today the revolutionary spirit has grown in knowledge and clear-sightedness; it has behind it a hundred and fifty years of experience. Moreover, the revolution has lost its illusions of being a public holiday. It is, entirely on its own, a prodigious and calculated enterprise, which embraces the entire universe. It knows, even though it does not always say so, that it will be world-wide or that it will not be at all. Its chances are balanced against the risk of a universal war, which, even in the event of victory, will only present it with an Empire of ruins. It can remain faithful to its nihilism, and incarnate in the charnel houses the ultimate reason of history. Then it will be necessary to renounce everything except the silent music that will again transfigure the terrestrial hell. But the revolutionary spirit in Europe can also, for the first and last time, reflect upon its principles, ask itself what the deviation is which leads it into terror and into war, and rediscover with the reasons for its rebellion, its faith in itself.

✳

The errors of contemporary revolution are first of all explained by the ignorance or systematic misconception of that limit which seems inseparable from human nature and which rebellion reveals. Nihilist thought, because it neglects this frontier, ends by precipitating itself into a uniformly accelerated movement. Nothing any longer checks it in its course and it reaches the point of justifying total destruction or unlimited conquest. We now know, at the end of this long inquiry into rebellion and nihilism, that rebellion with no other limits but historical expediency signifies unlimited slavery. To escape this fate, the revolutionary mind, if it wants to remain alive, must therefore return again to the sources of rebellion and draw its inspiration from the only system of thought which is faithful to its origins: thought that recognizes limits. If the limit discovered by rebellion transfigures everything, if every thought, every action that goes beyond a certain point negates itself, there is, in fact, a measure by which to judge events and men. In history, as in psychology, rebellion is an irregular pendulum, which swings in an erratic arc because it is looking for its most perfect and profound rhythm. But its irregularity is not total: it functions around a pivot. Rebellion, at the same time that it suggests a nature common to all men, brings to light the measure and the limit which are the very principle of this nature.

Every reflection today, whether nihilist or positivist, gives birth, sometimes without knowing it, to standards that science itself confirms. The quantum theory, relativity, the uncertainty of interrelationships, define a world that has no definable reality except on the scale of average greatness, which is our own. The ideologies which guide our world were born in the time of absolute scientific discoveries. Our real knowledge, on the other hand, only justifies a system of thought based on relative discoveries. "Intelligence," says Lazare Bickel, "is our faculty for not developing what we think to the very end, so that we can still believe in reality." Approximative thought is the only creator of reality.[1]

The very forces of matter, in their blind advance, impose their own limits. That is why it is useless to want to reverse the advance of technology. The age of the spinning-wheel is over and the dream of a civilization of artisans is vain. The machine is bad only in the way that it is now employed. Its benefits must be accepted even if its ravages are rejected. The truck, driven day and night, does not humiliate its driver, who knows it inside out and treats it with affection and efficiency. The real and inhuman excess lies in the division of labor. But by dint of this excess, a day comes when a machine capable of a hundred operations, operated by one man, creates one sole object. This man, on a different scale, will have partially rediscovered the power of creation which he possessed in the days of the artisan. The anonymous producer then more nearly approaches the creator. It is not certain, naturally, that industrial excess will immediately embark on this path. But it already demonstrates, by the way it functions, the necessity for moderation and gives rise to reflections on the proper way to organize this moderation. Either this value of limitation will be realized, or contemporary excesses will only find their principle and peace in universal destruction.

This law of moderation equally well extends to all the contradictions of rebellious thought. The real is not entirely rational, nor is the rational entirely real. As we have seen in regard to surrealism, the desire for unity not

---

[1] Science today betrays its origins and denies its own acquisitions in allowing itself to be put to the service of State terrorism and the desire for power. Its punishment and its degradation lie in only being able to produce, in an abstract world, the means of destruction and enslavement. But when the limit is reached, science will perhaps serve the individual rebellion. This terrible necessity will mark the decisive turning-point.

only demands that everything should be rational. It also wishes that the irrational should not be sacrificed. One cannot say that nothing has any meaning, because in doing so one affirms a value sanctified by an opinion; nor that everything has a meaning, because the word everything has no meaning for us. The irrational imposes limits on the rational, which, in its turn, gives it its moderation. Something has a meaning, finally, which we must obtain from meaninglessness. In the same way, it cannot be said that existence takes place only on the level of essence. Where could one perceive essence except on the level of existence and evolution? But nor can it be said that being is only existence. Something that is always in the process of development could not exist—there must be a beginning. Being can only prove itself in development, and development is nothing without being. The world is not in a condition of pure stability; nor is it only movement. It is both movement and stability. The historical dialectic, for example, is not in continuous pursuit of an unknown value. It revolves around the limit, which is its prime value. Heraclitus, the discoverer of the constant change of things, nevertheless set a limit to this perpetual process. This limit was symbolized by Nemesis, the goddess of moderation and the implacable enemy of the immoderate. A process of thought which wanted to take into account the contemporary contradictions of rebellion should seek its inspiration from this goddess.

As for the moral contradictions, they too begin to become soluble in the light of this conciliatory value. Virtue cannot separate itself from reality without becoming a principle of evil. Nor can it identify itself completely with reality without denying itself. The moral value brought to light by rebellion, finally, is no farther above life and history than history and life are above it. In actual truth, it assumes no reality in history until man gives his life for it or dedicates himself entirely to it. Jacobin and bourgeois civilization presumes that values are above history, and its formal virtues then lay the foundation of a repugnant form of mystification. The revolution of the twentieth century decrees that values are intermingled with the movement of history and that their historical foundations justify a new form of mystification. Moderation, confronted with this irregularity, teaches us that at least one part of realism is necessary to every ethic: pure and unadulterated virtue is homicidal. And one part of ethics is necessary to all realism: cynicism is homicidal. That is why humanitarian cant has no more basis than cynical provocation. Finally, man is not entirely to blame; it was not he who started history; nor is he entirely innocent, since he continues it. Those who go beyond this limit and affirm his total innocence end in the insanity of definitive culpability. Rebellion, on the contrary, sets us on the path of calculated culpability. Its sole but invincible hope is incarnated, in the final analysis, in innocent murderers.

At this limit, the "We are" paradoxically defines a new form of individualism. "We are" in terms of history, and history must reckon with this "We are," which must in its turn keep its place in history. I have need of others who have need of me and of each other. Every collective action, every form of society, supposes a discipline, and the individual, without this discipline, is only a stranger, bowed down under the weight of an inimical collectivity. But society and discipline lose their direction if they deny the "We are." I alone, in one sense, support the common dignity that I cannot allow either myself or others to debase. This individualism is in no sense pleasure; it is perpetual struggle, and, sometimes, unparalleled joy when it reaches the heights of proud compassion.

Thought at the Meridian

As for knowing if such an attitude can find political expression in the contemporary world, it is easy to evoke —and this is only an example—what is traditionally called revolutionary trade-unionism. Cannot it be said that even this trade-unionism is ineffectual? The answer is simple: it is this movement alone that, in one century, is responsible for the enormously improved condition of the workers from the sixteen-hour day to the forty-hour week. The ideological Empire has turned socialism back on its tracks and destroyed the greater part of the conquests of trade-unionism. It is because trade-unionism started from a concrete basis, the basis of professional employment (which is to the economic order what the commune is to the political order), the living cell on which the organism builds itself, while the Cæsarian revolution starts from doctrine and forcibly introduces reality into it. Trade-unionism, like the commune, is the negation, to the benefit of reality, of bureaucratic and abstract centralism.[2] The revolution of the twentieth century, on the contrary, claims to base itself on economics, but is primarily political and ideological. It cannot, by its very function, avoid terror and violence done to the real. Despite its pretensions, it begins in the absolute and attempts to mold reality. Rebellion, inversely, relies on reality to assist it in its perpetual struggle for truth. The former tries to realize itself from top to bottom, the latter from bottom to top. Far from being a form of romanticism, rebellion, on the contrary, takes the part of true realism. If it wants a revolution, it wants it on behalf of life, not in defiance of it. That is why it relies primarily on the most concrete realities—on occupation, on the village, where the living heart of things and of men is to be found. Politics, to satisfy the demands of rebellion, must submit to the eternal verities. Finally, when it causes history to advance and alleviates the sufferings of mankind, it does so without terror, if not without violence, and in the most dissimilar political conditions.[3]

But this example goes farther than it seems. On the very day when the Cæsarian revolution triumphed over the syndicalist and libertarian spirit, revolutionary thought lost, in itself, a counterpoise of which it cannot, without decaying, deprive itself. This counterpoise, this spirit which takes the measure of life, is the same that animates the long tradition that can be called solitary thought, in which, since the time of the Greeks, nature has always

[2] Tolain, the future Communard, wrote: "Human beings emancipate themselves only on the basis of natural groups."

[3] Scandinavian societies today, to give only one example, demonstrate how artificial and destructive are purely political opposites. The most fruitful form of trade-unionism is reconciled with constitutional monarchy and achieves an approximation of a just society. The first preoccupation of the historical and natural State has been, on the contrary, to crush forever the professional nucleus and communal autonomy.

been weighed against evolution. The history of the First International, when German Socialism ceaselessly fought against the libertarian thought of the French, the Spanish, and the Italians, is the history of the struggle of German ideology against the Mediterranean mind.[4] The commune against the State, concrete society against absolutist society, deliberate freedom against rational tyranny, finally altruistic individualism against the colonization of the masses, are, then, the contradictions that express once again the endless opposition of moderation to excess which has animated the history of the Occident since the time of the ancient world. The profound conflict of this century is perhaps not so much between the German ideologies of history and Christian political concepts, which in a certain way are accomplices, as between German dreams and Mediterranean traditions, between the violence of eternal adolescence and virile strength, between nostalgia, rendered more acute by knowledge and by books and courage reinforced and enlightened by the experience of life—in other words, between history and nature. But German ideology, in this sense, has come into an inheritance. It consummates twenty centuries of abortive struggle against nature, first in the name of a historic god and then of a deified history. Christianity, no doubt, was only able to conquer its catholicity by assimilating as much as it could of Greek thought. But when the Church dissipated its Mediterranean heritage, it placed the emphasis on history to the detriment of nature, caused the Gothic to triumph over the romance, and, destroying a limit in itself, has made increasing claims to temporal power and historical dynamism. When nature ceases to be an object of contemplation and admiration, it can then be nothing more than material for an action that aims at transforming it. These tendencies—and not the concepts of mediation, which would have comprised the real strength of Christianity—are triumphing in modern times, to the detriment of Christianity itself, by an inevitable turn of events. That God should, in fact, be expelled from this historical universe and German ideology

[4] See Marx's letter to Engels (July 20, 1870) hoping for the victory of Prussia over France: "The preponderance of the German proletariat over the French proletariat would be at the same time the preponderance of our theory over Proudhon's.

be born where action is no longer a process of perfection but pure conquest, is an expression of tyranny.

But historical absolutism, despite its triumphs, has never ceased to come into collision with an irrepressible demand of human nature, of which the Mediterranean, where intelligence is intimately related to the blinding light of the sun, guards the secret. Rebellious thought, that of the commune or of revolutionary trade-unionism, has not ceased to deny this demand in the presence of bourgeois nihilism as well as of Cæsarian socialism. Authoritarian thought, by means of three wars and thanks to the physical destruction of a revolutionary elite, has succeeded in submerging this libertarian tradition. But this barren victory is only provisional; the battle still continues. Europe has never been free of this struggle between darkness and light. It has only degraded itself by deserting the struggle and eclipsing day by night. The destruction of this equilibrium is today bearing its bitterest fruits. Deprived of our means of mediation, exiled from natural beauty, we are once again in the world of the Old Testament, crushed between a cruel Pharaoh and an implacable heaven.

In the common condition of misery, the eternal demand is heard again; nature once more takes up the fight against history. Naturally, it is not a question of despising anything, or of exalting one civilization at the expense of another, but of simply saying that it is a thought which the world today cannot do without for very much longer. There is, undoubtedly, in the Russian people something to inspire Europe with the potency of sacrifice, and in America a necessary power of construction. But the youth of the world always find themselves standing on the same shore. Thrown into the unworthy melting-pot of Europe, deprived of beauty and friendship, we Mediterraneans, the proudest of races, live always by the same light. In the depths of the European night, solar thought, the civilization facing two ways awaits its dawn. But it already illuminates the paths of real mastery.

Real mastery consists in refuting the prejudices of the time, initially the deepest and most malignant of them, which would reduce man, after his deliverance from excess, to a barren wisdom. It is very true that excess can be a form of sanctity when it is paid for by the madness of

Nietzsche. But is this intoxication of the soul which is exhibited on the scene of our culture always the madness of excess, the folly of attempting the impossible, of which the brand can never be removed from him who has, once at least, abandoned himself to it? Has Prometheus ever had this fanatical or accusing aspect? No, our civilization survives in the complacency of cowardly or malignant minds—a sacrifice to the vanity of aging adolescents. Lucifer also has died with God, and from his ashes has arisen a spiteful demon who does not even understand the object of his venture. In 1950, excess is always a comfort, and sometimes a career. Moderation, on the one hand, is nothing but pure tension. It smiles, no doubt, and our Convulsionists, dedicated to elaborate apocalypses, despise it. But its smile shines brightly at the climax of an interminable effort: it is in itself a supplementary source of strength. Why do these petty-minded Europeans who show us an avaricious face, if they no longer have the strength to smile, claim that their desperate convulsions are examples of superiority?

The real madness of excess dies or creates its own moderation. It does not cause the death of others in order to create an alibi for itself. In its most extreme manifestations, it finds its limit, on which, like Kaliayev, it sacrifices itself if necessary. Moderation is not the opposite of rebellion. Rebellion in itself is moderation, and it demands, defends, and re-creates it throughout history and its eternal disturbances. The very origin of this value guarantees us that it can only be partially destroyed. Moderation, born of rebellion, can only live by rebellion. It is a perpetual conflict, continually created and mastered by the intelligence. It does not triumph either in the impossible or in the abyss. It finds its equilibrium through them. Whatever we may do, excess will always keep its place in the heart of man, in the place where solitude is found. We all carry within us our places of exile, our crimes and our ravages. But our task is not to unleash them on the world; it is to fight them in ourselves and in others. Rebellion, the secular will not to surrender of which Barrès speaks, is still today at the basis of the struggle. Origin of form, source of real life, it keeps us always erect in the savage, formless movement of history.

Beyond Nihilism

*

There does exist for man, therefore, a way of acting and of thinking which is possible on the level of moderation to which he belongs. Every undertaking that is more ambitious than this proves to be contradictory. The absolute is not attained nor, above all, created through history. Politics is not religion, or if it is, then it is nothing but the Inquisition. How would society define an absolute? Perhaps everyone is looking for this absolute on behalf of all. But society and politics only have the responsibility of arranging everyone's affairs so that each will have the leisure and the freedom to pursue this common search. History can then no longer be presented as an object of worship. It is only an opportunity that must be rendered fruitful by a vigilant rebellion.

"Obsession with the harvest and indifference to history," writes René Char admirably, "are the two extremities of my bow." If the duration of history is not synonymous with the duration of the harvest, then history, in effect, is no more than a fleeting and cruel shadow in which man has no more part. He who dedicates himself to this history dedicates himself to nothing and, in his turn, is nothing. But he who dedicates himself to the duration of his life, to the house he builds, to the dignity of mankind, dedicates himself to the earth and reaps from it the harvest that sows its seed and sustains the world again and again. Finally, it is those who know how to rebel, at the appropriate moment, against history who really advance its interests. To rebel against it supposes an interminable tension and the agonized serenity of which René Char also speaks. But the true life is present in the heart of this dichotomy. Life is this dichotomy itself, the mind soaring over volcanoes of light, the madness of justice, the extenuating intransigence of moderation. The words that reverberate for us at the confines of this long adventure of rebellion are not formulas for optimism, for which we have no possible use in the extremities of our unhappiness, but words of courage and intelligence which, on the shores of the eternal seas, even have the qualities of virtue.

No possible form of wisdom today can claim to give more. Rebellion indefatigably confronts evil, from which it can only derive a new impetus. Man can master in himself everything that should be mastered. He should rectify in creation everything that can be rectified. And after he has done so, children will still die unjustly even in a perfect society. Even by his greatest effort man can only propose to diminish arithmetically the sufferings of the world. But the injustice and the suffering of the world will remain and, no matter how limited they are, they will not cease to be an outrage. Dimitri Karamazov's cry of "Why?" will continue to resound; art and rebellion will die only with the last man.

There is an evil, undoubtedly, which men accumulate in their frantic desire for unity. But yet another evil lies at the roots of this inordinate movement. Confronted with this evil, confronted with death, man from the very depths of his soul cries out for justice. Historical Christianity has only replied to this protest against evil by the annunciation of the kingdom and then of eternal life, which demands faith. But suffering exhausts hope and faith and then is left alone and unexplained. The toiling masses, worn out with suffering and death, are masses without God. Our place is henceforth at their side, far from teachers, old or new. Historical Christianity postpones to a point beyond the span of history the cure of evil and murder, which are nevertheless experienced within the span of history. Contemporary materialism also believes that it can answer all questions. But, as a slave to history, it increases the domain of historic murder and at the same time leaves it without any justification, except in the future—which again demands faith. In both cases one must wait, and meanwhile the innocent continue to die. For twenty centuries the sum total of evil has not diminished in the world. No paradise, whether divine or revolutionary, has been realized. An injustice remains inextricably bound to all suffering, even the most deserved in the eyes of men. The long silence of Prometheus before the powers that overwhelmed him still cries out in protest. But Prometheus, meanwhile, has seen men rail and turn against him. Crushed between human evil and destiny, between terror and the arbitrary, all that remains to him is his power to rebel in order to save from murder him who can still be saved, without surrendering to the arrogance of blasphemy.

Then we understand that rebellion cannot exist without a strange form of love. Those who find no rest in God or in history are condemned to live for those who, like themselves, cannot live: in fact, for the humiliated. The most pure form of the movement of rebellion is thus crowned with the heart-rending cry of Karamazov: if all are not saved, what good is the salvation of one only? Thus Catholic prisoners, in the prison cells of Spain, refuse communion today because the priests of the regime have made it obligatory in certain prisons. These lonely witnesses to the crucifixion of innocence also refuse salvation if it must be paid for by injustice and oppression. This insane generosity is the generosity of rebellion, which unhesitatingly gives the strength of its love and without a moment's delay refuses injustice. Its merit lies in making no calculations, distributing everything it possesses to life and to living men. It is thus that it is prodigal in its gifts to men to come. Real generosity toward the future lies in giving all to the present.

Rebellion proves in this way that it is the very movement of life and that it cannot be denied without renouncing life. Its purest outburst, on each occasion, gives birth to existence. Thus it is love and fecundity or it is nothing at all. Revolution without honor, calculated revolution which, in preferring an abstract concept of man to a man of flesh and blood, denies existence as many times as is necessary, puts resentment in the place of love. Immediately rebellion, forgetful of its generous origins, allows itself to be contaminated by resentment; it denies life, dashes toward destruction, and raises up the grimacing cohorts of petty rebels, embryo slaves all of them, who end by offering themselves for sale, today, in all the marketplaces of Europe, to no matter what form of servitude. It is no longer either revolution or rebellion but rancor, malice, and tyranny. Then, when revolution in the name of power and of history becomes a murderous and immoderate mechanism, a new rebellion is consecrated in the name of moderation and of life. We are at that extremity now. At the end of this tunnel of darkness, however, there is inevitably a light, which we already divine and for which we only have to fight to ensure its coming. All of us, among the ruins, are preparing a renaissance beyond the limits of nihilism. But few of us know it.

Already, in fact, rebellion, without claiming to solve everything, can at least confront its problems. From this moment high noon is borne away on the fast-moving stream of history. Around the devouring flames, shadows writhe in mortal combat for an instant of time and then as suddenly disappear, and the blind, fingering their eyelids, cry out that this is history. The men of Europe, abandoned to the shadows, have turned their backs upon the fixed and radiant point of the present. They forget the present for the future, the fate of humanity for the delusion of power, the misery of the slums for the mirage of the eternal city, ordinary justice for an empty promised land. They despair of personal freedom and dream of a strange freedom of the species; reject solitary death and give the name of immortality to a vast collective agony. They no longer believe in the things that exist in the world and in living man; the secret of Europe is that it no longer loves life. Its blind men entertain the puerile belief that to love one single day of life amounts to justifying whole centuries of oppression. That is why they wanted to efface joy from the world and to postpone it until a much later date. Impatience with limits, the rejection of their double life, despair at being a man, have finally driven them to inhuman excesses. Denying the real grandeur of life, they have had to stake all on their own excellence. For want of something better to do, they deified themselves and their misfortunes began; these gods have had their eyes put out. Kaliayev, and his brothers throughout the entire world, refuse, on the contrary, to be deified in that they refuse the unlimited power to inflict death. They choose, and give us as an example the only original rule of life today: to learn to live and to die, and, in order to be a man, to refuse to be a god.

At this meridian of thought, the rebel thus rejects divinity in order to share in the struggles and destiny of all men. We shall choose Ithaca, the faithful land, frugal and audacious thought, lucid action, and the generosity of the man who understands. In the light, the earth remains our first and our last love. Our brothers are breathing under the same sky as we; justice is a living thing. Now is born that strange joy which helps one live and die, and which we shall never again postpone to a later time. On the sorrowing earth it is the unresting thorn, the bitter brew, the harsh wind off the sea, the old and the new dawn. With this joy, through long struggle, we shall remake the soul of our time, and a Europe which will exclude nothing. Not even that phantom Nietzsche, who for twelve years after his downfall was continually invoked by the West as the blasted image of its loftiest knowledge and its nihilism; nor the prophet of justice without mercy who lies, by mistake, in the unbelievers' plot at Highgate Cemetery; nor the deified mummy of the man of action in his glass coffin; nor any part of what the intelligence and energy of Europe have ceaselessly furnished to the pride of a contemptible period. All may indeed live again, side by side with the martyrs of 1905, but on condition that it is understood that they correct one another, and that a limit, under the sun, shall curb them all. Each tells the other that he is not God; this is the end of romanticism. At this moment, when each of us must fit an arrow to his bow and enter the lists anew, to reconquer, within history and in spite of it, that which he owns already, the thin yield of his fields, the brief love of this earth, at this moment when at last a man is born, it is time to forsake our age and its adolescent furies. The bow bends; the wood complains. At the moment of supreme tension, there will leap into flight an unswerving arrow, a shaft that is inflexible and free.

ALBERT CAMUS, one of France's leading writers, was born in Algiers in 1913. After winning a degree in philosophy, he worked at various jobs, ending up in journalism. In the thirties, he ran a theatrical company, and during the war was active in the French Resistance, editing an important underground paper, Combat. He is the author of two novels, The Stranger (1946), also available as a Vintage Book, and The Plague (1948), in addition to plays and philosophical essays. Among the latter is The Rebel.